INFUSING TECHNOLOGY INTO THE K-12 CLASSROOM

REVISED EDITION

INFUSING TECHNOLOGY INTO THE K-12 CLASSROOM

REVISED EDITION

Jackie Deluna

CAMBRIA
PRESS

YOUNGSTOWN, NEW YORK

This book has been registered with the Library of Congress.
Deluna, Jackie
      Infusing Technology into the K-12 Classroom: Revised Edition /
      Jackie Deluna
      p.   cm.
      Includes bibliographical references

      ISBN-10: 1-934043-40-0

      ISBN-13: 978-1-934043-40-0

TABLE OF CONTENTS

INTRODUCTION

The Need for Technology in Today's Education World

To prepare students for success in the information age, technology must become a tool that every student can use effectively. Technology infusion in K-12 education requires students to actively use technology, not just view technology-based content created by their teachers. The goal of this book is for teachers to apply the use of technology in a seamless manner so that it supports and extends curriculum objectives and engages students in meaningful learning. By infusing the information from this book, students and educators will:

- Enhance student achievement by integrating technology skills into the core curriculum: Reading and Language Arts, Math, Science and Social Studies
- Promote student technology literacy by addressing the ISTE National Educational Technology Standards (NETS) for students
- Enable teachers to adapt instruction based on student assessment results
- Allow educators to save time by integrating technology with what they are already teaching
- Provide the flexibility to be easily managed in a variety of classroom settings: one or multiple computers
- Motivate teachers to teach with technology

Teachers should strive to make technology a part of everyday life in the classroom, while using it to enrich learning activities. They should not use technology just to use it. They should find ways to use it so that it enhances instruction and improves student learning. The focus of technology integration activities should not be on the technology that is used, but on the student activities that are conducted using technology.

The Issues at Hand

Technology infusion does not happen by accident. Teachers must learn how to incorporate student use of technology into meaningful activities in their lesson plans. There is a learning curve to becoming proficient in technology infusion, but once the skills are learned and activities are identified and developed, teachers find that technology can actually reduce preparation time.

For many teachers, a lack of personal experience with technology presents an additional challenge. In order to incorporate technology-based activities and projects into their curriculum, teachers must first find the time to learn to use the tools and understand the terminology necessary for participation in projects or activities. If used properly, however, technology can be a tool for teachers as well as for students. Incorporating technology more fully into their daily routines helps teachers new to technology gain experience in using it and hence, become more "tech infused".

Over the course of the past few years, studies have shown that the vast investments in technology have been largely ineffective. There have been little, if any, demonstrated effect on student learning based on the way it has been used. The problem lies not with tools, but with how the tools are being used. When used appropriately as a tool of discovery, new technologies can profoundly transform learning. Unfortunately, this has not happened.

The use of technology is still unconventional for education. Even after years of use, there has been very little discussion about the real role of new technology in learning, as well as deep levels of misunderstanding about the role technology should play in education and its potential to transform the learning cycle. Unless the use of technology in the classroom is directly related to measurable student learning, it is not effective.

The issues at hand are not technology, but teaching and learning. Teachers face the challenges of preparing students to live, learn, and work successfully in today's knowledge-based digital society. This requires high-performance learning of academic content using 21st century skills and tools. To accomplish this, teachers must answer several critical questions:

- What value do educational technologies bring to my classroom?
- How can the effectiveness of instructional technology be determined?
- How can students be engaged as active participants in the self-assessment process?
- How can objective data be gathered and applied?
- How should progress be measured?
- How can data be aggregated to inform plans for continuous improvement?
- What kind of professional development is necessary to ensure my results?

The following chapters cover a range of topics from why technology infusion is important to how we can assess its effectiveness. The chapters also provide clear lesson plan examples with comprehensive information on the lesson description, prerequisite knowledge, preparation time, methods and tips, resources and finally, grading and evaluation processes. School administrators and staff developers can use this book as a platform for infusing their schools with technology. This purpose of this book is to help guide teachers through the process of infusing technology into classroom learning

CHAPTER 1

LEARNING WITH
TECHNOLOGY INFUSION

In this chapter, we will discuss and explore:

- *Technology infusion for the classroom*

- *The issues at hand for using technology.*

- *The necessity for technology for teachers*

- *Why learning with technology is essential for students*

Definition of Infusion

1: to be permeated with something (as a principle or quality) that alters usually for the better <*infuse* the team with confidence>

2: to instill < teach and impress by frequent repetitions or admonitions to impart gradually <*instilling* a love of learning in children> ~ *Merriam Webster*

By the definitions above, "technology infusion" means to permeate quality with technology so that it alters for the better, and to instill by frequent repetitions. Infusing technology into the curriculum is a priority, if not a mandate, in most schools today. Most educational technology experts agree, however, that technology should be infused, not as a separate subject or as a once-in-a-while project, but as a tool to promote and extend student learning on a daily basis. The challenge, of course, is in finding ways to use technology, help students use it and not take time away from core subjects.

Public education is lagging behind the technological changes taking place outside education. Many educators are unable and unwilling to accept that technology can positively change instructional delivery. Even when it is used, there is a primary focus on getting and installing the technology instead of using it to reinvent learning. Many schools are stuck at the immature stage of implementation. Regardless of whether they use technology or not in their lessons, a teacher who focuses on the end product will have students use technology as little more than a glorified typewriter to produce a nice, neat, final copy. In contrast, an English teacher who teaches the writing process will use different tools to enhance student understanding of the planning, drafting, revision, proofing stages of the writing cycle to produce better writers.

Why Technology?

Technology cannot and will not replace real teachers, but the reality is, outside public education, new technologies are already replacing some of the traditional things that teachers have always done. Inevitably, new technologies are already transforming traditional educational thinking and practices.

Technology will only become an even more integral part of life in the educational community. Today, we are operating under a completely different set of rules that have turned many of our assumptions about learning upside down. What does it really mean to be literate in an age of computers, networks, electronic mail, multimedia communications and Internet publishing? What are the new basics that all students need to have in an electronic age?

Regardless of whether the task is writing a short story, exploring information resources, examining a diverse culture, tracking a chemistry experiment, testing a mathematical concept, developing new instructional materials, or tracking grades, technology plays an increasingly important role in the teaching and learning process. Technology infusion into the curriculum is essential for preparing students for the 21st Century!

In more and more schools today, technology is becoming recognized as an instructional tool, not as a subject of instruction. Still, many educators, less familiar and less comfortable with technology than their students, struggle to seamlessly integrate a growing list of technology tools into their regular curriculum.

Using technology in the classroom is becoming easier for teachers because students are coming to class with more skills. Whether a teacher requires it or not, most students use technology for their projects. The technology tool used most often for student projects is the Internet.

Technology is much more than computers in the classroom. In a learning environment where technology is truly infused and not taught as a separate class, students and teachers use technology tools to enhance all areas of the teaching and the learning process. With computers, students can access, organize, and analyze a vast world of rich resources. They are able to do anything from downloading original source documents from the Library of Congress (http://www.loc.gov/index.html) to taking a virtual tour of a museum. Students on different campuses can collaborate on projects, sharing and accommodating their diverse perspectives. They can participate in original research projects that put them in touch with actual researchers in the field, and they can receive electronic mentoring from noted experts around the world. Technology gives students powerful tools for communicating what they have learned, and can also motivate them to learn more.

The infusion of technology into the classroom is most effective when infused into the curriculum. When analyzing student achievement from technology infusion, the key is to set clear, measurable educational objectives. Teachers need to be engaged in more student-centered practice using a number of long term projects, authentic assessment, and small group work to improve performance. **A teacher should act as a facilitator of education instead of a presenter of information. Students take more ownership of their learning when they can see a product of their learning.**

Optimal Learning

For all parties to accept and embrace the notion of infusing technology into the classroom, the issues below should be first addressed:

- *Why should new technologies be used in schools?*
  By understanding the reasons and benefits behind an activity/ concept, people are more likely to accept it. This question is not typically addressed by many. Others continue to struggle to answer the question. If this question is not resolved first, it results in a ready, fire, aim approach to the use of technology which results in underutilized equipment and a perception by many that money is being wasted.

- *How should it be implemented?*
  Now that we have all on board the technology infusion bandwagon, how exactly do we carry this out? Should it be taught in computer classes or should it systematically introduced to all students in all subjects throughout school? If this is not addressed, people will comfortably avoid dealing with this and continue to teach the way they have always taught. What is the proper role of technology in learning? Should it replace teachers? Should it change the role of the teacher in classroom? Should it change what students study?

Examples of optimal uses of technology are:

- The technology supports student's performance of a learning task
- The technology use is infused into learning as a core part of the classroom curriculum
- Technology is treated as a tool to help accomplish a complex task, rather than a subject of study for its own sake

Traditional uses of technology should not be construed as "bad" practice, but simply as activities that are not likely to transform a classroom or school. You can view case studies of traditional uses of technology at http://www.ed.gov/pubs/EdReformStudies/EdTech/traditionaluses.html.

The kinds of complex, meaningful projects that optimize classroom technology infusion require extended periods of time for their implementation. They almost always call on skills and knowledge from different disciplines (e.g., mathematics to analyze survey responses, meteorology to consider natural disasters that might strike a city).

Optimal infusion is naturally conducive to small group work, with different students performing different functions as in a sports or workplace team, and with the teacher acting as a coach and facilitator for multiple groups. In these ways, such projects exert pressure to break down traditional school schedules of short blocks of time, artificial barriers between what are viewed as separate subject areas, and the boundaries between the classroom and the outside world.

At the same time, such optimal uses of technology have advantages over more instructive uses simply because they are so flexible. Many tutorial or exploratory technology applications are not adopted by schools and teachers because the content they convey does not match the objectives of the particular teacher, district, or state. Thus, the technology application is used only with a few students as "enrichment" or is never adopted at all. In contrast, technology applications that can be used as a tool or a communications vehicle (e.g., word processing and spreadsheet software, drawing programs, internet) can support any curriculum and can be fully assimilated into a teacher's ongoing core practice.

Learning with Technology

The most important points about technology infusion into the classroom are that:

- Technology is transforming society. Schools do not have the choice of not incorporating technology. Rather, the question is how well will they use it to enhance learning?
- Technology's major purpose must be to improve learning and not to create a new content area
- Technology offers great opportunities to reform and improve education
- Technology planning is a process involving planning committee members who work to establish technology implementation directions and priorities
- Technology does not replace the good teacher, but instead enhances his or her abilities and creativity
- Technology has great potential for making education far more meaningful and productive for students, but only if they are allowed to become active learners involved in real tasks

While technology by itself is not the answer to making systemic changes, it can be used to support meaningful engaged learning experiences in the classroom. For more information on meaning engaged learning, visit http://www.ncrel.org/sdrs/engaged.htm. Those involved in technology planning and implementation efforts need to be well informed about innovative approaches to using technology to facilitate various approaches to learning. For information on approaches to learning, go to http://www.ncrel.org/tandl/build2.htm.

CHAPTER 2

ASSESSMENT & STANDARDS

In this chapter, we will discuss and explore:

- *How today's classroom reflects a very different assessment*
- *Examples of multiple methods of assessment*
- *Case Study: Leaning about rainforests (Elementary Level)*
- *Case Study: Turning a new novel into a movie (High School)*
- *Case Study: Building maps using technology*
- *Online Testing*
- *Rubric Examples*

Assessing Student Learning

In the past, standards were taught through activities, learning was assessed with tests and exams, and teaching was geared to standardized tests. With today's shift, standards are used to help design the project, assessment is planned ahead of time and embedded throughout, and tests are just one of many types of assessment. Performance tasks, rubrics, checklists, and tests are used as assessment tools. These multiple forms of assessment, implemented throughout learning, account for learning as a process, instead of a single event. Through ongoing assessment, teachers can feel confident that they have reached their objectives and that students understand the content.

Twenty years ago, a typical classroom may have encompassed one of three assessment scenarios, students taking a written exam, students making oral presentations, or the teacher administering a quiz with oral questions, while students responded on paper. The teacher would teach the content, assess the students using one of these strategies, record the grade, and move on to the next unit of study.

Today's classroom reflects a very different assessment scenario. Tests and quizzes are still present but are not the sole method of assessing student learning. Instead, different types of assessment take place at multiple points in a unit of study: teachers and students give and receive feedback in the form of peer and teacher conferencing, checklists and rubrics help students understand expectations and manage learning progress, self evaluations support meta-cognition and reflections on learning, and rubrics define quality for products that are assessed by peers and the teacher.

The primary purpose of classroom assessment today is to improve learning and the method of instruction. Assessment is not a solitary event, but rather a continual process throughout a project. Embedded and ongoing assessment is at the heart of project-based learning and provides a way for students to show what they know in many ways. Assessment becomes a tool for improvement rather than a test of intelligence or accumulation of facts. With assessment embedded throughout a unit of instruction, teachers learn more about their students' needs and can adjust instruction to improve student achievement.

In a traditional classroom setting, there are limited assessment tools like test taking and oral speeches. These methods are quick and easy, but they provide relatively limited information about a student's progress and effectiveness of instruction within a unit of instruction. With ongoing and broader types of assessment, other goals of assessment can be met, such as to:

- Gauge students' prior knowledge
- Clearly define and communicate learning targets to students
- Provide diagnostic feedback to teacher and student
- Assess and improve teaching effectiveness
- Identify students' strengths and weaknesses
- Improve students' awareness of learning progress
- Engage students in self-assessment and communication of learning progress

Good projects are designed with the end in mind. This means starting with the goals, determining what students need to know, and then defining how to assess understanding. All of this is considered before activities are developed. This "backwards" approach to instructional design helps a project stay focused on learning targets. Assessment for project-based units should be planned to:

- Use a variety of assessment methods
- Embed assessment throughout the learning cycle
- Assess the important objectives of the unit
- Engage students in assessment processes

A project-based learning environment provides the structure for students to demonstrate learning in performance tasks. Performance tasks like story writing, science lab experiments, and debates are assessed progressively, throughout the learning experience, and then evaluated upon completion to assess the end product and process as well.

These tasks complement traditional tests and quizzes. Instead of recalling information, students must apply new knowledge in a meaningful way by using a process. Tasks engage students to think in new and different ways. They ask students to use knowledge to convince others that they really understand material that quizzes and short answer tests only *suggest* they understand (Wiggins, 1998). Performance tasks give concrete evidence of learning and help reach assessment goals by:

- Offering the teacher a broader view of students' understanding
- Placing the student in the center of the learning process
- Giving students a choice in selecting how they will express their under standing
- Addressing the requirements and explicit scoring systems up front
- Assessing specific objectives

Planning Assessment

An assessment plan ensures a project stays focused on intended learning goals and should be developed along with project activities and tasks. Because project tasks allow for broader expression of individual learning, assessment strategies need to be open enough to accommodate a range of student work, yet focused on expected results.

An assessment plan outlines methods and tools that define clear expectations and standards for quality in products and performances. It also defines project monitoring checkpoints and methods to both inform the teacher and keep students on track. The plan should involve students in reviewing and managing their learning progress during the project. A plan will answer key questions:

- How will you know your students have met the learning goals?
- By what criteria will students be assessed?
- What methods of assessment will you use throughout the project in order to inform you and your students about their learning progress?
- What reporting and monitoring methods will you use to encourage student self-management and progress during independent and group work?

Sample Assessment Timeline

The following diagram shows how assessment can be embedded throughout a unit. There are endless combinations of assessment methods and plans that can be woven into a unit plan.

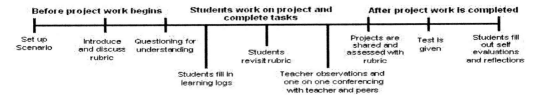

Multiple Methods of Assessment

There are many assessment methods and tools; each provides information to both the teacher and students. Similar assessment methods and tools may be used for different purposes depending on how they are structured and what is done with the results. The tables below outline a variety of assessment methods, purposes, and tools in three categories: 1) Methods to Check for Understanding or to Encourage Metacognition, 2) Methods to Demonstrate Understanding and Skill and 3) Product and Performance Tests.

Methods to Check for Understanding or to Encourage Metacognition

Assessment Method	Purpose	When Used	Tool
Written Journals or Notebook	Extended written reflections on progress or entries in reaction to prompts. In addition to reflections, prompts can elicit specific thinking skills at key points in the project, for example, "How has what you investigated or learned, changed or confirmed your viewpoint on this issue?"	Journals are written throughout the project or at key points. They are checked periodically or at the end of the project.	Prompts for entries, Journal review plan
Video and Photo Journals	Students develop visual documentation of progress in a project in a structured way. The "entries" are meant to capture reactions and reflections or can be used for demonstration of skill development.	These journals are kept throughout the project, but may be integrated into final products or performances.	Outline of photo sequence and topic (shot list), Schedule for video scenes
Structured Interviews and Observations	Teachers or outside experts schedule formal oral interviews with individuals or teams related to development of understanding. Interview questions (protocol) ask students to explain and give reasons for their current understanding. Structured observations are similar but used with skill, process, and performance assessment.	Structured interviews are often done at the end of a project.	Interview or observation protocol (a script)
Written and Oral Tests and Quizzes	Tests and quizzes offer direct evidence of knowledge acquisition and comprehension.	Tests and quizzes are often used at key points within the project and at the end of the project.	Test and quiz questions

Methods to Demonstrate Understanding and Skill

Assessment Method	Purpose	When Used	Tool
Products	Things that students create and build that show learning. (Examples in table below.)	Depends on product and length of project; often completed at end of project.	Rubrics that define quality with several criteria
Performances	Demonstrations, productions, and events that students design and conduct to show learning. (Examples in table below.)	Depends on product and length of project; often presented at end of project.	Rubrics that define quality with several criteria

Products and Performance Tasks

Products	Reports	Historical research, scientific research, journal article for publication, policy recommendations
	Designs	Product design, home design, building or school design blueprints, transportation alternatives
	Constructions	Models, machines, exhibits, dioramas
	Essays	Letters-to-the editor, guest column for local newspaper or community publication, book and movie reviews, story writing
	Artistic expressions	Pottery, sculpture, poetry, fine art, posters, cartoon, mural, collage, painting, song writing, movie script
	Print media	Nature trail guide, self-guided walk through community history, public service announcement, history scrapbook, photo timeline, investigative documentary, commercial, training manual, animation/cartoon
	Multimedia	Informational kiosk, video, photo journal, slideshow, digital book
Performances	Presentations	Persuasive proposal, inspiring speech, debate, informative lecture, research analysis and conclusions, newscast
	Skill demonstrations	Science laboratory processes, constructions, specific sports skills, teaching or mentoring younger students
	Artistic/creative performances	Interpretive dance, play, skit, character study, docu-drama, readers' theater, radio plays
	Simulations	Mock trial, reenactment of historical event, role play

The days of using only tests and quizzes to evaluate student knowledge are long gone. This type of traditional classroom assessment can be subjective and limits the ability for students to learn from their mistakes and improve upon them. Project-based learning demands a more progressive means of assessment where students can view learning as a process and use problem-solving skills to meet or exceed project expectations.

Rubrics have been implemented into today's classroom to give students and teachers a better understanding of what is being evaluated, what criteria grades are based upon, and what clear and compelling product standards are addressed. The focus of a rubric is to monitor and adjust progress, rather than just to assess the end result. Though the use of rubrics is a good thing, they are not always used in the right way. The definition we will use to define a rubric is best stated by Heidi Goodrich (1997), a rubrics expert. Simply put, a rubric is a "scoring tool that lists the criteria for a piece of work or what counts."

Rubrics can be thought of as a scoring scale that shows levels of quality with a set of descriptors for each level of performance. A holistic rubric is used to obtain an overall impression of the quality of a performance (Wiggins & McTighe, 2004). They are most effectively used as a final evaluation that provides a single score for the complete performance or product. An analytical rubric involves the use of separate criteria in scoring work, typically involving separate rubrics for each key criterion (Wiggins & McTighe, 2004). They are most effectively used when diagnosing individual student progress and needs. They are developed to evaluate very specific content or processes and provide the student feedback about the performance or product.

Rubrics can be teacher generated, but are even more effective when generated with student input. Students tend to be even more critical of their own work than teachers, and they can create more challenging rubrics than teachers create on their own. This practice also gives the students an opportunity to own their learning and the outcome because standards and expectations are committed to from the beginning. At the very least, rubrics must be shared and discussed with students.

One self-managing tool that is excellent to use in conjunction with a rubric is a checklist. Checklists are self-managing tools that can be created from the content of the rubric. Checklists specify steps or conditions that must be present in a performance or product, and students then check off the presence or absence of the traits listed. The checklist puts students in charge of their progress by giving them a tool to prioritize tasks and manage their time efficiently. This in turn places students in the center of the learning process, which is a guiding characteristic of a project-based learning environment. In a project-based learning unit, there may be many tasks to complete in order to reach the final product. A checklist can assist the teacher and student through the project requirements outlined on the rubric.

It is apparent that the primary reason to use rubrics and checklists is to increase the quality of work. They define clear expectations and force students to be responsible for the work they create. With the use of rubrics, students are able to articulate what they have learned and know exactly what they need to do to be successful. Rubrics are tools for clear communication with students, teachers, and parents. This communication allows everyone involved to understand the expectations and ensures student learning and success.

Take for example, an elementary school teacher who is beginning a unit on rainforests. As part of the study of ecosystems in the third grade, students are expected to know examples of diverse life forms in different environments. To address this standard, the teacher designs a project, keeping assessment in mind from the beginning. Using books and online resources, students research a particular animal from the rainforest. They collect information explaining the animal's place in the food chain, its survival adaptations, its place in the rainforest layers, and any other interesting facts. They create rainforest animal puppets and a dialogue that includes the information they researched. Students present a puppet show to share what they learned. After the performance, their puppets are displayed on a classroom bulletin board depicting a rainforest ecosystem.

To begin, the teacher and the students generate a rubric to outline project requirements and expectations. The teacher explains the project requirements and then asks the students prompting questions such as: *What should a project that meets expectations look like? How will the project show what you know?* These questions direct students to think about expectations and outcomes. Once a description of a project that meets expectations is outlined, the students and the teacher modify the language to describe projects that would be below expectations and ones that are above expectations. The responses are compiled by the teacher, and a copy of the rubric is given to each student to refer to throughout the project. The teacher reinforces expectations by modeling exemplary work with student examples. At this point, students have an opportunity to ask questions and the teacher has a chance to check for understanding before they begin.

With the rubric in place, students are aware of project expectations and objectives, and are given responsibility for their quality of work. As they work on tasks to complete the project, they are guided by the use of their rubrics. The rubric assures the teacher that students are aware of what they need to do. At the same time, the teacher is concerned that there are many tasks for them to complete, and that these young students may need help prioritizing and managing their time. To assist in this challenge, the teacher has students organize their time with checklists and timelines, and keeps them accountable by meeting with a few students each day for short check-up conferences. In addition, at the end of every day, as they complete project time, students fill out short self-evaluations that prompt them to reflect on their work for the day. This process not only keeps students in check, but also recognizes their daily efforts.

By embedding assessment checkpoints throughout the unit, the teacher can make informed decisions. At pivotal points, student learning of the intended objectives and engagement in higher-level thinking can be assessed. If the teacher does not feel that these processes are taking place, then there is an opportunity to address these issues at the most crucial times.

When the performance task is completed, students have an opportunity to share what they have learned. The unit culminates with a test, covering objectives and specific areas of learning. The students' final product is then assessed with the class created rubric. Progress has been evaluated along the way with timelines, checklists, and anecdotal notes from conferences. Using this structure of ongoing assessment, both teacher and student can feel confident that they have reached their objectives.

A high school English teacher is beginning a new novel. To meet the language arts objective, students must determine each character's traits by what the characters say about themselves in narration and dialogue. Using this standard, the teacher creates a project that integrates technology and introduces it to his students. Students are first presented with the scenario that this book is soon to become a movie. They are being asked by top movie producers to create a "movie" soundtrack based on what they know about what the characters say and do in the book. The students are required to choose the character traits that best represent each character and specific examples that support these traits. These ideas are assembled into a multimedia presentation and shared with other class members for feedback. Students then choose three songs that represent these characters and build evidence based upon their reading to support the use of these songs.

The teacher creates a rubric to assess student learning and shares it with the class after the scenario is presented. Each student in the class receives a copy of the rubric, and the teacher explains the scoring system, expectations, and requirements for each level on the rubric. The rubric is accompanied by a checklist of project requirements. Exemplary student work samples are also shared and discussed with the class. The students ask clarifying questions, and the teacher asks specific questions about the project to check for understanding. Once students are aware of project expectations, they begin the work.

Along the way, students prioritize tasks with a timeline and are expected to get peer feedback at pivotal points. There are also specific teacher check points to ensure students are on the right track and allow for teacher feedback and recommendations. The students use these conference times to improve upon their work, and the teacher uses them to guide teaching throughout the reading of the novel.

After several conferences with students, the teacher realizes that some crucial elements are not being addressed. After making some anecdotal records, he brainstorms a few mini-lessons to teach over the next few periods that will help students understand the importance of citing concrete examples to support their opinions. Through teacher modeling, examples and practice exercises, many of the students are able to revise their work to reflect this new learning and make appropriate changes to meet expectations and deepen their understanding.

Once projects are complete, the multimedia presentations and the soundtracks are graded using the rubric, and an essay is assigned to give students another opportunity to demonstrate what they know. By focusing on the objectives, giving students clear and compelling standards to help them create their projects, and allowing opportunities to improve upon their work, the teacher has created a classroom environment where instruction can be adjusted and students can demonstrate what they know.

Another way technology can be used for assessment is through the use of concept maps built with programs like Inspiration. Before a unit is taught, students can be asked to build a map of the prior understanding of the topic. On completing the unit, the students would then create final concept maps which would show how much they had learned, and how well-integrated their knowledge of the subject had become. While concept maps can be created with paper and pencil, the computer-based maps can form the basis for everything from essays to web pages and multimedia projects. Completed projects can then be posted on the web for evaluation by peers both in and outside the classroom.

The effective application of technology to the assessment of student learning means, first having a clear idea of what is being assessed, and how best to measure mastery of these concepts.

Standards of Assessment and School's Accountability

Standards of assessment and schools' accountability for each student now mean new challenges for everyone. However, research has shown that your best strategy to achieve adequate yearly progress (AYP) is by employing technology. By integrating technology into your school's assessment and accountability systems, you can:

- streamline testing and reporting processes,
- centralize student information systems,
- keep track of diverse student data,
- monitor student progress years into the future,
- take advantage of online curriculum, and
- align your coursework with state standards

Integrating technology can seem like a frightening task to the K-12 educator. But what if there was a way to bring computers into the curriculum while saving time and engaging the learner? Online assessment can provide the regular classroom teacher with a painless and productive tool for testing with technology.

Are you looking for a simple way to integrate technology while motivating your students and decreasing the time you spend grading? Why not put your next test on the Internet? Online assessment, the use of Web-based quizzes and activities for classroom testing has become an effective teaching tool in today's K-12 classroom. Numerous Web sites provide ready-made tests and also offer teachers the capability to custom design their own tests with ease. Even tech-leery teachers find that putting tests online takes no more time than typing them into a word-processing program.

With online testing, students access the Internet, go to the site, and take the test. The testing site grades the tests and returns the results. Teachers can view their students' scores, as well as the time it took each student to complete the test, on a password- protected Web page or via e-mail. Students also can obtain their results immediately (if the teacher selects that option).

Any concept that can be tested objectively can be tested online using multiple-choice, true-false, fill-in-the blank, and short answer questions. A few sites even allow students to type essays, which are later e-mailed to the teacher for grading. With both free and paid sites available, almost any teacher with Internet access on even a single computer can take advantage of the benefits of online assessment.

The Pros and the Cons

The pros of online testing include:

- *Increased student engagement in the curriculum.* When students see their test results immediately, they are more likely to be interested in the outcome than when they have to wait days for a grade. Let that adrenalin rush of test taking work for you!

- *A flexible test environment.* Students can take a test from anywhere that provides access to the Internet. Students have taken tests while on vacation in the Caribbean or home sick with mononucleosis.

- *Practice with technology-based test formats.* Many standardized tests, such as the Graduate Record Examination (GRE), can now be taken on a computer. The skills necessary for taking tests digitally (whether using software or the Internet) are different from those required for pen-and-paper tests. Many computerized tests, for example, do not allow students to return to a question after submitting an answer. The first guess, therefore, must be the best guess. Using online assessment introduces students to these emerging test strategies.

- *A painless way to integrate technology.* Often, administrators, school districts, and tech staffs encourage the use of technology in the classroom but do not give teachers the time or resources they need to implement technology plans. Testing online is an easy way to begin using technology on a regular basis—without using extra time or resources.

- *A time-saver.* Online testing saves teachers grading time. More importantly, online testing saves instructional time; students can complete online tests in less time than it takes to complete pen-and-paper tests. The extra time can be used for higher-order thinking projects that apply the material on the tests!

The cons of online testing include:

- *Student confidentiality violations.* Check your school's policy on transmitting student information via the Internet. Even if your school approves online testing, you might want to assign pseudonyms, so only you know individual students' scores.

- *A lack of primary sites.* Even if the actual questions are age-appropriate, directions on many online assessment sites can be beyond the reading levels of Pre-K-1 students. Screen each site to ensure that students can navigate the test with ease.

- *Rigid scoring.* Online testing sites are not able to intuitively read creative spelling the way a teacher can. Unless perfectly spelled answers are a test requirement, opt for true-false or multiple-choice formats, rather than fill-in-the-blanks or short answer tests.

Testing Tips

The following tips will help you get the most out of online testing programs:

- *Randomize your questions.* Most sites offer the option of randomizing tests; students see the questions in different orders. Such randomization can help discourage cheating. An even better option is to input more questions than you will use and have the test site randomly pull only a portion of each type of question for each test. That way, each student gets a slightly different test.

- *Restrict or close a test.* By restricting public access to a test until after students have taken it, you prevent students from previewing the test. You can also prevent students from prematurely accessing a test by calling it a slightly unusual name (The Walrus Osmosis Quiz, for example). If students do not know the name of the test, they cannot find it ahead of time!

- *Monitor testing.* Sometimes, students do not feel as though they are taking a test when they are using the computer; they tend to chat or look around more than they would if they were taking a pen-and-paper test. Be sure to reinforce proper test-taking behaviors.

- *Rotate in a one-computer classroom.* If you have only one classroom computer with Internet access, begin a project with the whole class. Then, as students work on the project, rotate them onto the computer individually for a quick objective assessment.

- *Be flexible.* Testing online will be new for most students. If scores are low for the whole class, or if some students struggle even though you suspect they know the material, re-teach and retest.

- *Have a back up plan.* Sites are busy. Servers go down. Power goes out. Life happens. Be prepared to punt!

According to Using Electronic Assessment to Measure Student Performance, an issue brief from the NGA (National Governors Association) Center for Best Practices, "The benefits of electronic assessment are clear. By using this technology to measure student performance, state policymakers technology can help customize learning and assessment. Finally, the use of electronic can improve the return of test results to teachers so they inform instruction. In addition, the assessment may allow educators to integrate assessment with instruction to produce powerful learning tools."

Recommended Online Testing Sites

- Discovery School's QuizCenter (http://school.discovery.com/quizcenter/quizcenter.html)
  This free and easy-to-use site can be slow loading due to high traffic.

- QuizStar (http://quizstar.4teachers.org/)
  Free and simple to use, this site does warn against use for formal testing. You might want to use it for reviews only.

- Quia (http://www.quia.com/)
  The granddaddy of all online testing sites offers loads of extras and the longest track record. The cost is low yearly fee for one teacher, with discounts for multiple teachers at a single school.

- QuizLab (http://www.quizlab.com/)
  A yearly individual QuizLab Pro account can be purchased for teachers or group accounts.

Rubric Samples

Participant Holistic Rubric

4	3	2	1
· Offers enough solid analysis, without prompting, to move the conversation forward · Demonstrates a deep knowledge of the text and the question · Comes to the seminar prepared, with notes and a marked or annotated text · Shows active listening · Offers clarification and/or follow-up that extends the conversation · Makes comments that refer to specific parts of the text	· Offers solid analysis without prompting · Demonstrates a good knowledge of the text and the question · Comes to the seminar prepared, with notes and a marked or annotated text · Shows active listening, offers clarification and/or follow-up · Relies on the text to drive his or her comments	· Offers some analysis, but needs prompting from the seminar leader · Demonstrates a general knowledge of the text and question · Is less prepared, with few notes and no marked or annotated text · Actively listens, but does not offer clarification and/or follow-up to others' comments · Relies more on his or her opinion, and less on the text to drive his or her comments	· Offers little commentary · Comes to the seminar ill-prepared with little understanding of the text and question · Does not listen to others, offers no commentary to further the discussion

Analytic Rubric

Content Standards	4	3	2	1
· Understand Process of Plant Growth · Understand the features and processes of plant growth	· Accurately identifies and explains in detail all necessary conditions for plant growth · Describes the complete life cycle of plants · Makes several informed inferences about the role of plants in the environment	· Identifies and explains the necessary conditions for plant growth · Describes the life cycle of plants · Makes informed inferences about the role of plants in the environment	· Explains the necessary conditions for plant growth with some errors · Describes the life cycle of plants but leaves out some important information · Makes some informed inferences and some incorrect ones about the role of plants in the environment	· Explains the necessary conditions for plant growth with many errors · Describes the life cycle of plants inaccurately, leaving out important information · Makes incorrect inferences about the role of plants in the environment
· Design and Conduct an Experiment · Hypothesize, plan, and carry out experiments · Organize evidence of change over time	· Develops a testable hypothesis · Plans an experiment that can prove or disprove the hypothesis · Successfully carries out an experiment that controls all variables · Always observes, measures, and records change over time with accuracy	· Develops a hypothesis · Plans an experiment that tests the hypothesis · Carries out an experiment that controls some variables · Usually observes, measures, and records change over time with accuracy	· Develops a hypothesis with some assistance · Plans an experiment that tests the hypothesis with some assistance · Carries out an experiment that controls variables with some assistance · Observes, measures, and records change over time with some errors	· Develops a hypothesis with a great deal of assistance · Plans an experiment that tests the hypothesis with a great deal of assistance · Carries out an experiment that controls variables with a great deal of assistance · Observes, measures, and records change over time with lots of errors

• Analyze Results and Draw Conclusions • Analyze and report conclusions of experiment • Compare prior knowledge to the results of a scientific investigation • Develop models (illustrations and charts) to explain how objects, events, and/or processes work	• Successfully draws several conclusions based on evidence • Communicates ideas clearly and concisely • Considers additional variables when comparing findings with others to determine the best conditions for growing plants • Compares previous knowledge about plants to the results of the experiment and describes new learning in detail • Develops detailed models (illustrations and charts) with correct labeling to explain how plants grow	• Draws some conclusions based on evidence • Communicates ideas clearly • Compares findings with those of others to determine the best conditions for growing plants • Compares previous knowledge about plants to the results of the experiment and describes new learning • Develops models (illustrations and charts) with correct labeling to explain how plants grow	• Draws some conclusions that are not based on evidence • Communicates ideas but may be unclear • Compares findings with those of others but has difficulty determining the best conditions for growing plants • Compares previous knowledge about plants to the results of the experiment, but the comparison is confusing or inaccurate • Develops models (illustrations and charts) with labeling to explain how plants grow, but some elements are missing or incorrect	• Does not draw conclusions • Does not communicate ideas clearly • Does not compare findings or cannot determine the best conditions for growing plants • Does not compare previous knowledge about plants to the results of the experiment • Develops models (illustrations and charts) with labeling to explain how plants grow, but most elements are missing or incorrect
• Manage Project • Complete all components of the project • Choose effective processes that lead to the successful completion of a project • Work cooperatively with others in a group	• Independently and successfully completes all parts of the project • Chooses helpful processes: uses timelines, asks for feedback, develops and follows a plan, monitors and adjusts as needed • Works cooperatively and provides leadership in a group	• Independently completes all parts of the project • Chooses some helpful processes: uses timelines, asks for feedback, develops and follows a plan, monitors and adjusts as needed • Works cooperatively in a group	• Completes all of the parts of the project with assistance or independently completes some of the project • Chooses some helpful processes with assistance: uses timelines, asks for feedback, develops and follows a plan, monitors and adjusts as needed • Works cooperatively in a group some of the time	• Completes some of the parts of the project with assistance • Does not choose helpful processes • Fails to work cooperatively in a group

Multimedia Presentation Checklist

Our Names: _____

Written Content

☐ We used a storyboard to organize our thoughts.
☐ We have a title slide that clearly states our topic.
☐ We included the names of everyone in our group.
☐ Information is correct.
☐ Sources are cited.
☐ We have listened to suggestions from the teacher or a friend.
☐ We addressed the Essential and Unit Questions.

Layout and Design

☐ The words on our slides are easy to read.
☐ Graphics enhance our presentation and are easy to see.
☐ We have animation effects that enhance the presentation.
☐ The presentation contains all the necessary transitions for the
    viewer to navigate through the presentation.
    All transitions work properly.
☐ Pictures have a caption.
☐ There is enough time to read and see everything on the slides.

Mechanics

☐ There are no mistakes in mechanics.
☐ Words are spelled correctly.

Resources

☐ We used books, magazines, or the computer to find information.
☐ We looked at maps and drawings to find information.
☐ We made a list of things we planned to use in the project.

Technology

☐ We each took turns navigating on the computer (using the mouse, typing,
    inserting graphics and photos, etc.)
☐ We were able to do research on the Internet using the online encyclopedia and
    visiting recommended Web sites.
☐ We have all practiced presenting our project using eye contact and an
    expressive voice.
☐ We remembered to save our work to the desktop folder.

CHAPTER 3

WHY WE NEED TO TAP PRIOR KNOWLEDGE AND HOW TO DO IT

In this chapter we will discuss and explore:

- *The importance of tapping prior knowledge*
- *Using writing activities such as quick writes, journals and learning logs to prompt students to write and reflect about new content*
- *Using organizational charts such as K-W-L for recall*
- *Different strategies for discussion groups*
- *The Socratic Questioning Technique*
- *Examples and resources of thinking maps and different graphic organizers*

Instructional strategies that engage students and involve them in the learning process are at the heart of what great teachers do. Research shows that certain strategies help students achieve success and learn at higher levels.

Imagine a classroom where . . .

- A second grader says, "I was really scared when I came to this new school for the first time. I bet that is how the immigrants felt when they came to America."
- A sixth grader asks, "How many peer conferences should we hold for our ecosystem report? I've already finished my K-W-L chart and am ready to get some ideas before I get started."
- An eighth grader announces, "Can we meet with our groups for part of the period today? I'm having trouble changing fractions to percents, and I think they can help me figure it out."

- An eleventh grader suggests, "I think I've got my biome newsletter for the Community Night all ready to go. I want to add two more graphics, and then I'll be ready to share my work!"

In a classroom where a variety of instructional strategies are present every day, students are deeply engaged, challenged, and learn at high levels. The teachers in these classrooms see the benefits of using these strategies to put their students in charge of their own learning.

About Tapping Prior Knowledge

For a student, new content can be overwhelming. There are new vocabulary words, ideas, and concepts that others seem to understand easily or have experienced before. Teachers can help their students make the transition from the unfamiliar by tapping students' prior knowledge. Research shows that we can jump-start learning by accessing pre-existing attitudes, experiences, and knowledge and bridge the gap between what is being taught and what is already known.

Teachers can also use prior knowledge to make instruction more meaningful. Many researchers (Peshkin, 1992; Protheroe & Barsdate, 1992; and Lee, 1992) emphasize the importance of incorporating a student's cultural background into the curriculum. As the world changes, students must learn to understand and appreciate the experiences and contributions of people from different backgrounds. A culturally-responsive education links curriculum, instruction, and assessment to the students' experiences, language, and culture, in other words, to their prior knowledge.

Additionally, this instructional strategy defines a proper starting place for instruction and the sequence of instructional activities. As stated by educational psychologist David Ausubel, "The most important single factor influencing learning is what the learner already knows".

Exercises to access prior knowledge can be used at any grade level, with any content area, and with any subject. Prior knowledge is the proper entry point for instruction because it builds on what is already known, supports comprehension, and makes sense of new learning (Kujawa and Huske, 1995). Tapping students' prior knowledge is an effective way to start a new unit or lesson and an even better way to get students involved right from the start. Referring back to this knowledge throughout a unit of study will keep students engaged in their learning and keep the material relevant.

From simply asking questions aloud to formally using a journal to document students' prior knowledge, there are a wide range of activities teachers can use. The following examples can be used across the curriculum and at any grade level.

Written activities prompt students to write and reflect about what they already know about new content. These include quick writes, journals, and learning logs.

Written activities to tap prior knowledge

1. Quick writes

Quick writes are usually done at the beginning of the lesson or unit to get students to think about the new content or respond to a prompt. The writing is not graded and allows students the freedom to express their ideas and make personal connections to the new content being addressed. Occasionally, teachers will challenge students to write or brainstorm their ideas within a time limit. Once they are completed, these quick writes stimulate class discussion.

Example Prompt: Take five minutes to write about what friendship means to you. Use examples and brainstorm characteristics of a good friend.

Example Response: Friendship means a lot to me. I have many friends. We like to play together and tell each other our secrets. My friend, Melanie, spends the night at my house. She is kind, caring, and funny. That is what I like about her. Friends should never be mean and if they are, they should apologize and say they're sorry. Friends are important people. Everyone should have one.

2. Journals

Another way to prompt students and activate prior knowledge is journal writing. Like a quick write, but longer and not necessarily timed, journal writing allows students to respond to a prompt or write what they already know about a topic.

These journal responses may be collected and reviewed to give feedback to the student. The journal may cover several topics over the course of a semester or quarter. The entries could be shared with partners or small groups to spark discussion. If graded, journals should not be graded for content but rather for effort, completeness, and thoroughness.

Journaling can be used across the curriculum and is not just a language arts activity. Journaling can be just as effective in a mathematics classroom as it is in an English classroom. Allowing students to organize their thinking, respond to new content, and make personal connections without the threat of grades, is very important in tapping students' prior knowledge.

Example Journal Prompt: How do you feel about voting? Give examples and support your opinion.

Example Journal Entry: I believe in voting. I believe that democracy is a privilege even if your vote is one voice in a million. It is hard to see how one vote will make a difference when a simple majority wins. But that is why it is important to vote, your vote may make the difference. Recently, a governor in Washington State was elected by a difference of 200 or so votes in a race where several millions voted.

3. Learning Logs

Learning logs are an excellent way to get students to record thought processes, ideas, and questions throughout a unit of study. Learning logs are similar to quick writes and journals but focus on documenting a learning experience. Students describe what they investigated, accomplished, or learned in an activity or class exercise. Logs are appropriate across the curriculum and at all grade levels. Questions, prompts, or free writes can be incorporated into the learning logs. They can be used by teachers as informal ways to check for student understanding. Many times, the teacher uses the learning logs as a way to have a written discussion by responding to the student's entries and posing more thought-provoking questions. For younger students, words and pictures can be a way to record ideas and thoughts. These can be written documents that students maintain throughout a project.

Example Learning Log

Question: What do you know about plants?

Student entry: January 14

> I know a lot about plants. We have plants at my house. I know you have to water them or they will die. I know they have to be planted in dirt so they can grow. I know there are lots of types of plants. I know there are ferns. That is the type of plant my mom has. I know plants grow outside and they are pretty.

Teacher entry: January 15

> It sounds like you know a lot about plants. It is very important to water plants and make sure they do not die. I think it is great that you know what a fern is. That is the type of plant I have at my house too. How has your plant been doing?

> The journal entries can carry on until the teacher has a full understanding of the student's knowledge.

Bring New Strategies to Your Classroom

Graphic organizers help students to think about, visualize, and arrange their knowledge. In a traditional classroom setting, most teachers rely on talking, reading, and writing for representing and communicating concepts. Studies show that when students create nonlinguistic representations of their knowledge there is increased activity in the brain (Gerlic & Jausovec, 1999). Whether creating a concept map, a flow chart, or a simple storyboard, students must draw upon analysis skills to clarify relationships, organize their thoughts, and formulate plans or process steps. The process of creating the representations helps students retain information and extends students' ability to convey and exchange their thinking in collaborative group work.

Using graphic organizers, such as the application Inspiration, is a universal strategy that is equally appropriate across all grade levels and subject areas. It can be introduced at the beginning of a unit of study and referred to throughout, and used as a means of assessment. There are many uses for graphic organizers.

- A high school English teacher uses a chain-of-events graphic organizer while students are reading a novel. This organizer helps them to document events as they read, reflect upon prior reading, make predictions, and prepare for discussions. The completed work is used as an assessment.

- An elementary school teacher has students create a T-chart to compare and contrast the differences and similarities of two Indian tribes. This T-chart is then used to help students with a multimedia presentation.

- In middle school, a science teacher has students build a causal map to show the causes and effects of tectonic plate movement in a study of earthquakes. Discussions of each student's maps lead students to deeper analysis of their findings.

Types of Graphic Organizers

1. Concept Maps

Concept maps are an effective way to organize, cluster, and brainstorm ideas. Causal maps are used to illustrate cause-and-effect relationships.

2. Cluster Maps

These maps are a useful way to help students cluster and brainstorm ideas and information or show relationships. They can be used as a starting point before beginning a larger project or as a pre-writing activity to be checked by a peer or teacher. This visual representation helps all students to see their ideas on paper and then use these ideas to write essays, reports, or create multimedia presentations. From simple clusters to more complex ones, students at all levels and in all subject areas can use clustering strategies to generate ideas. See an example of a cluster map at the end of this chapter.

3. Sequencing Activities

These activities help students to sequence information and organize their thoughts in a logical way. These include chain of events, timelines, and storyboard planners.

4. Chain-of-Events

The use of a chain-of-events graphic organizer is a valuable way to:

- Organize steps in a procedure
- Trace plot development in a story or novel

- Document actions of a character
- Record the important stages of an event

5. Timelines

Like a chain-of-events organizer, timelines help students place events and people in chronological order. Throughout a lesson or unit, students can add to the timeline, use it as a reference and a benchmark to make sense of dates and events and to see patterns in history. By sequencing important events, students can make connections to past and current content. Individual and class timelines can be effective ways to represent events and time periods.

6. Storyboard Planners

Storyboard planners are helpful ways to construct ideas and organize information before creating a product. Students can create storyboards, using multimedia technology or paper and pencil. These storyboards can be used as pre-writing or brainstorming activity before students create a final product. The storyboards can be checked by a peer or teacher to make sure the student is on-track and provide feedback before getting to work. See examples of sequencing, timelines, and storyboard planners at the end of this chapter.

7. Classification Charts

T-charts and Venn diagrams are charts that help students organize information visually for comparing, contrasting, or finding similarities and differences. With classification charts, students organize information visually to compare related ideas.

8. Venn Diagrams

Venn Diagrams are used across the curriculum and with any grade level to compare information. A Venn diagram is made up of two or more overlapping circles. The similarities between topics are listed in the intersection of the two circles. The differences are listed in the remaining sections. From simple two circle Venn Diagrams to four-circle Venn Diagrams, students construct visual representations of their learning. Students use the diagrams to organize information as an aid for developing multimedia presentations, reports, essays, or oral presentations. Teachers can use Venn Diagrams as a way to assess student learning or as a quick, informal means to check for student understanding.

9. T-Charts

Another type of classification chart is a T-chart. With T-charts, students can clarify concepts or ideas by comparing and contrasting them visually by listing and examining two facets of a topic. They can, for example, list pros and cons, advantages and disadvantages, facts and opinions, strengths and weaknesses, or problems and solutions. Like the Venn diagram, the T-chart can be used to organize learning for a report, presentation, or essay. See Classification Chart. See examples at the end of this chapter.

10. Know-Wonder-Learn Charts (K-W-L)

An instructional technique used to activate students prior knowledge, set goals, and record new knowledge gleaned from a unit of study. A Know-Wonder-Learn (K-W-L) chart is one of the most commonly used graphic organizers to tap students' prior knowledge. This simple chart activates students' prior knowledge by asking them what they already know about a particular subject. This allows the students to make personal connections before the content is deeply explored. The students brainstorm their ideas on the Know section of the chart. Then the students independently or collaboratively brainstorm questions they have about the content in the Want to Learn section. Once students begin to answer these questions during a project, they record this information on the Learn section of the chart. By using this chart, students are constructing meaning from what they have been learning, comparing their new knowledge to what they already know, and are able to clarify their ideas. This also helps keep students focused and interested in the content. This is a great tool to keep track of what they are learning. Ultimately, the chart could be used as a document for an assessment portfolio to show what the student has learned.

A K-W-L chart can be used across the curriculum at any grade level. It can be used to start a new unit of study and referred to throughout the unit. It is usually not a graded document but rather a place for students to write down their ideas and questions without the fear of being judged or graded. This chart also helps with student organization and can be a starting point for peer-to-peer or whole class discussion. See an example of a K-W-L Chart at the end of this chapter.

11. Organized Lists

Making a list is a pretty simple task, but when a student is required to order and prioritize the list, higher-level skills of analysis and evaluation are put to use. With the use of ordered lists, students visually construct information on paper or with a computer. These lists promote collaboration and discussion among students while they compare their lists and reasoning in a visual diagram. The Visual Ranking Tool helps students analyze and evaluate criteria for the decisions they make in forming a list. By ranking lists, students must identify and refine criteria as they assign rank to a list. While using this graphic organizer, students can manipulate and order information and visually represent content being learned. These lists can be used to spark debates, create proposals, or to understand the quality of a character in a story. Making organized lists that rank items in an order that makes sense to the student is one way to use helps students organize what they know as way of tapping prior knowledge. The Visual Ranking Tool (http://www97.intel.com/en/ThinkingTools/VisualRanking):

- Is an online thinking tool for ordering and prioritizing items in a list
- Helps students analyze and evaluate criteria for their decisions

- Compares reasoning visually to promote collaboration and discussion

With the use of this tool, students can use prior knowledge at the beginning of a unit or lesson to rank items and then see how their new knowledge expands their viewpoint over the course of study.

Example Visual Ranking List:

Working in pairs, students are given a list of animals and asked which one most resembles a human. They use Visual Ranking to put the animals into order, ranking them on their human-like qualities. Another thinking activity that has proven effective at all grade levels and across all curricular areas is the use of predictions. At the beginning of a unit or during the middle of a unit, having students make predictions about what they are going to learn based on their prior knowledge is an effective strategy. Students are given an opportunity to make "educated guesses" without the threat of being wrong. Because they can check the accuracy of their prediction, students are more focused and engaged in the content and have a "stake" in the knowledge. Usually, if their prediction is incorrect, they are armed with new knowledge to correct their thinking and learn from their previous understanding. The use of predictions also sparks students' higher-level thinking by tapping into their evaluative, comparative, and analysis skills.

Example Prompt Prediction: Based upon what you know about frogs and frog habitat, what do you predict might happen to a frog if it is taken out of its natural habitat and placed into an artificial one? Why do you think this might happen?

Example Student Prediction: I predict that the frog will eventually die. I predict this because it will have difficulty adapting to a new environment. It may have the same things like water, rocks, and food but it won't be the same as its home in the wild. The main thing that will be missing is the space and the other frogs. Plus, the water in the natural habitat has a balance of the right type of bacteria in the water and it is hard to keep the artificial water the exact same as it would be in the wild. If the aquarium is indoors it might also be hard to keep the temperature just right for the frog. I think my prediction will be right, and I will be sad if it is.

Learn About Discussions

Teacher-to-student and whole-class discussions are great ways to activate students' prior knowledge by allowing them opportunities to orally share their ideas and discuss their opinions. The art of discussion is an important piece in the learning process. A common mistake many teachers make is to present a question or idea and expect most of their students to respond and discuss. It can be frustrating and a waste of time for both the teacher and students to listen to a select few students have a discussion. To conduct successful discussions, teachers need to:

- be armed with the right types of questions and ready to respond to various answers
- be able to use "teachable moments " to spark student interest and keep the discussion lively
- use the discussion as a jumping off point for new content
- pose questions that directly relate to students and their prior knowledge
- allow the students to lead the discussion with teacher facilitation and probing
- accept all appropriate answers as correct and encourage additional responses by others
- permit "think time" and use think-pair-share strategies to think about answers before having students respond

1. Whole Class Discussion

Using whole class discussions to tap prior knowledge can benefit all students who are participating and listening by connecting what they already know to what they are going to learn. The discussion, if engaging, can get students excited about the new content and how it relates to them. Teachers can also use the discussions as a way to direct and redirect teaching based on student response and interest.

2. Student-Teacher Discussions

Individual student-to-teacher discussions are another way to tap students' prior knowledge on a smaller scale. Setting aside time to discuss needs and interests helps students make personal connections to content. While students are working, sitting down and discussing work one-on-one is an excellent way to make individual opinions and knowledge noticed and recognized. These discussions can be quick and informal, but they let the student know what they have to say is important. It also gives the teacher an insight into the student's thoughts and shows how to direct further teaching of the topic.

Cooperative Learning Strategies

Learn about different cooperative learning strategies and see how to embed them throughout the instructional cycle. Two heads learn better than one. This variation on the classic saying is very true for students in a classroom. Cooperative group work is an important part of an effective classroom. However, there is much more to group learning than just having students "work together." The primary goal of group work is to get students actively involved in their learning where there is an accepted common goal. This grouping allows students to work together to maximize their own and each other's learning.

"In a cooperative learning situation, interaction is characterized by positive goal interdependence with individual accountability." (Johnson & Johnson, 1998) One frustration many teachers, students, and parents have with cooperative groups is that many times the high-achieving students do most of the work. In order for cooperative grouping to be effective and make good use of classroom time, group work must have clear role responsibilities, goals, and individual accountability.

In a classroom setting, cooperative groups give students opportunities to learn from and teach one another under "real" world conditions. "By the 1990's, teamwork became the most frequently valued managerial competence in studies of organizations around the world" (Goleman, 1998). We can prepare our students to enter the working world by giving them these valued opportunities to work together to create products and solve problems.

By organizing a classroom around cooperative group work, the ultimate goal is to get students actively involved in their learning. Grouping students in pairs or small groups increases their chances of involvement. Students feel less pressure when asked to complete a task with a peer than they do completing it independently. Cooperative learning should be used strategically. "Research has established that the cooperative structure outperforms competitive and individualistic structures academically and socially, regardless of content or grade level" (Kagan 1997). Students often view school as a competitive enterprise where they try to outdo their classmates. Research shows that students are more positive about school, subject area, and teachers when they are provided structure to work cooperatively (Johnson & Johnson).

With time and patience, any teacher at any grade level can incorporate cooperative learning into instruction. The keys to success are maintaining high expectations, keeping students individually and collectively accountable, and creating a classroom environment where cooperation is encouraged.

1. Analogies

The use of analogies as a tapping prior knowledge thinking activity is a quick and easy strategy to use with students. Analogies help to arm students with comparative skills and language to compare what they are learning to what they already know. This strategy gives the student a point of reference and an opportunity to make sense of new content. Analogies are effective thinking strategies for all grade levels and content areas and can help spark discussions. *Example Analogy* Prompt: Now that we have begun to study the eye, can you look at the diagram of a camera and think about how an eye is like a camera? *Example Analogy:* Both a camera and an eye have a lens that lets in the light. The pupil of an eye gets bigger and smaller like the aperture of a camera. We have learned that the eye sees things upside down, and so does a camera.

2. Reciprocal Teaching Strategy

Reciprocal teaching (Palincsar, 1984) is a cooperative grouping strategy that calls on students to become "the teacher" and work as a group to bring meaning to text.

Teachers and students engage in dialogue regarding segments of text. The dialogue is structured by using four strategies:

- Summarizing
- Question generating
- Clarifying
- Predicting

It is important that each of the above strategies has been taught and practiced before reciprocal teaching takes place. The stages of reciprocal teaching are easy to set up.

The teacher hands out a passage of text to each student in the group. Each student reads the passage and writes summarizing, clarifying, or predicting questions related to what they have read. The "teacher" of the group, asks one of the questions. The "teacher" is the lead group member who starts off the questioning. One group member responds, using the text to support their answer. The student, who answers the question, then asks a question and the process repeats. See an example at the end of this chapter.

3. The Jigsaw Strategy

The jigsaw cooperative-learning technique promotes better learning, improves student motivation, and allows greater amounts of content to be studied and shared by students in a group. The jigsaw technique was first developed by Elliot Aronson and his college students. The technique allows for:

- An efficient way to learn content
- Development of listening, engagement, and empathy skills
- A way for students to work independently
- Interaction among all students

Students are divided into small groups of five or six. Each group's task is to learn about one aspect of a subject area and become "experts" on the subject. In this "expert" group, students do research together and collaboratively create a report or presentation. Each student is also individually responsible since they will teach others about the content. Once students have become "experts" they are reassigned a new group. Each new group is formed with "experts" from the original groups. The task for each "expert" is to teach the others in their group about the content they have studied. Once all "experts" have presented, each group member has learned five or six new aspects of the subject area and is ready to take an exam, write an essay, or group with another "expert" to create a multimedia presentation.

4. The Think-Pair-Share Strategy

Think-Pair-Share is a cooperative discussion strategy where students talk about the content and discuss ideas before sharing with a whole group. It introduces the elements of "think time" and peer interaction, which are two important features of cooperative learning. Think-Pair-Share's purpose is to help students process information, develop communication skills, and refine their thinking.

With this strategy the teacher:
- Poses an open-ended question or problem
- Gives students a minute or two to think about their answer, pairs students to discuss the answer and share ideas
- Gives opportunities for students to share their response with a small group or the whole class

Because students have time to think about their answer, then share with a peer and get a different perspective, they may be more willing and less apprehensive about sharing with a larger group. It also gives them time to change their response if needed and relieves the fear of giving the "wrong" answer.

5. Brainstorm Groups

The use of cooperative brainstorming is an effective and valuable strategy that calls upon teams of students to brainstorm thoughts and build upon one another's flow of ideas in a safe environment. With creative groupings, students have opportunities to work together and learn important content at the same time. Dr. Spencer Kagan, an expert on cooperative grouping structures has created a myriad of cooperative grouping structures to use with students of all ages. The main goal of these structures is to promote:
- Participation in structured interactions
- Equal participation
- Student interaction
- Effective communication
- Cooperative learning as part of any lesson

Through many years of research and training, Dr. Spencer Kagan has refined and developed over 160 structures. All of these give teachers a well planned way to group students and teach them important content in engaging ways.

6. Providing Feedback to Students

Feedback enhances student achievement by highlighting progress rather than deficiency. With progress feedback, a student is given opportunities for checking in with the teacher and multiple opportunities to ask questions. Students answer the following questions during progress feedback:

- Am I on the right track?
- What improvements can I make?
- What am I doing well?
- How am I doing overall?

With progress feedback a student will be able to successfully self-monitor, have higher aspirations for further achievement, greater self-satisfaction, and higher performance overall. By taking the time to sit down with a student and offer constructive criticism, give necessary help, offer suggestions, and provide positive feedback, teachers can positively impact student learning. Marzano, Pickering and Pollock (2001) cite providing feedback as one of the nine effective classroom strategies in their book, *Classroom Strategies that Work: Researched-Based Strategies for Increasing Student Achievement*. Effective feedback should:

- Be "corrective" in nature. Feedback should provide students with an explanation of what they are doing correctly and what they are doing that is not correct.

- Be timely. Immediate feedback is necessary in order for it to be the most effective.

- Be specific to a criterion. Feedback should reference a specific level of skill or knowledge and not be norm-referenced.

- Allow students to provide their own feedback. Students should be able to effectively monitor their own progress through self-evaluation based on the feedback given by the teacher.

Feedback can be informal or formal. With informal feedback, teachers can "drop by" students' desks and comment on their work. With this type of feedback, students receive instantaneous suggestions and can make immediate changes. With formal feedback, students attend a conference with the teacher where teachers check progress toward goals, discuss progress, and work with students to set new goals. Conferences help develop self-direction and protect students from the fear of failure. When students are given feedback along the way, they are able to learn from their mistakes, make the necessary changes and achieve at higher levels. "The best feedback appears to involve an explanation as to what is accurate and what is inaccurate in terms of student responses. In addition, asking students to keep working on a task until they succeed appears to enhance achievement." (Marzano, p. 96) There are two types of teacher feedback. They are:

a) Informal Teacher Feedback

Check-ups and check-ins are used to see how students are progressing, answer questions, or help with ideas.

b) Formal Teacher Feedback

With the use of conferences, teachers can provide suggestions and comments along with individualized goal setting.

7. Peer Feedback

Students value each other's opinions and ideas. In most cases, they enjoy working with one another. If given the opportunity, students can give and receive important and valuable ideas from a peer. When set up correctly, structured peer to-peer conferences give students time to get suggestions, ideas, and compliments on their work. When conferences are productive, students are aware of what to look for and have specific criteria to follow as they work with their peers. Evaluation guides or checklists can be handy tools to keep students on task and remind them to offer positive feedback as well as suggestions and ideas. With practice and modeling, teachers can implement this strategy into the classroom at any time for a variety of purposes. Teacher and peer feedback can take place at any grade level and with any subject area. Embedding informal and formal feedback into the classroom is an effective and worthwhile strategy. Learn about ways to implement this strategy into the classroom. Peer-to-Peer feedback is another form of student feedback. With the use of structured peer conferences, students give and receive feedback on their current work.

8. Recognition

Can you remember a time when a peer, teacher, or coach recognized the work you did as being valuable and important? How did that make you feel? The power of recognition has an overwhelmingly positive effect on students but unfortunately, does not happen as often as it should. Once a project has been completed, are students recognized for a job well done? How are they given an opportunity to share their work with others, receive recognition for their effort, and showcase the finished product? Educational reformer, Dr. Phillip Schlechty best defines affirmation of performances as, "Persons who are significant in the lives of the student, including parents, siblings, peers, public audiences, and younger students, are positioned to observe, participate in, and benefit from student performances, as well as the products of those performances, and to affirm the significance and importance of the activity to be undertaken" (2002). Giving students an opportunity to have their work affirmed and recognized by others makes learning authentic and worthwhile. Some students may engage in the work from the start because they know their work will be affirmed by important people at the end. Recognition in this sense should not be confused with praise or other kinds of extrinsic rewards. Although, praising students for the work they are doing is important, recognition is far deeper than that. Schlechty states that to "affirm or recognize student work is not to approve or disapprove; it is to declare that what happened matters and is important. Affirmation suggests significance and thus attaches importance to the event or action" (1997). Teachers hope that students take their projects home, share with their parents, and possibly save them in a portfolio. But the reality may be that students' work never makes it home, and all the hard work and effort the students put forth is never shared or recognized. By making the work visible to others, the students get that opportunity to hear "Job well done."

Recognition of student work can take place in many different ways across all grade levels and subject areas. Providing students simple opportunities to display work in the hallways of the school or on a bulletin board in the classroom showcases exemplary work to peers and school faculty and staff. Holding Parent and Community Nights, inviting experts into the classroom to see the work students have completed, and sharing work with younger and older buddy classes are all significant ways in which students can be recognized for their hard work and effort. Not only do students share the work products but the important learning that took place as well.

Questioning

Questioning is at the heart of good teaching. Choosing the right types of questions to ask students is necessary to spark thought-provoking answers and engage students in productive discussions. The instructional strategy of questioning is about asking probing and challenging questions that call for higher cognitive thinking skills such as analysis, synthesis, and evaluation. By asking challenging questions, we call upon students to explore ideas and apply new knowledge to other situations.

Using different types of questioning allows students to think in different and unique ways. At the core of a project-based learning classroom are enduring Essential Questions and higher-level Curriculum-Framing Questions. These questions are posed at the beginning of a unit of study, and students continue to explore and revisit these questions throughout.

Questions that require students to defend or explain their positions are open-ended questions. Closed questions are limiting and allow for one or two students to answer either correctly or incorrectly. Open-ended questions are probing and encourage students to think about several ideas. There is not just one correct answer. By posing open-ended questions to a group of students, the amount of ideas and answers are limitless. Open-ended questions:

- Tell students what is valued and what is important
- Elicit a range of responses
- Involve teacher and student communication
- Stir discussion and debate in the classroom

Effective questioning involves both teacher and student. It is important for the teacher to give "wait time" before asking for responses. Wait time is defined as the amount of time that lapses between a teacher-initiated question and the next verbal answer given by a student. This allows students the opportunity to reflect and think before they speak. Allowing many student ideas, rather than just a couple, is imperative as well. All who want to share should have an opportunity to do so. If time does not allow, these students should have a place to go such as a journal, a learning log, or a whiteboard, to record ideas that can be discussed at a later time.

Questions for Different Kinds of Thinking

Different kinds of questions generate different kinds of thinking. These definitions and examples describe three kinds: elaborating, hypothetical, and clarification questions.

Questioning Technique	Definition	Examples
Elaborating Questions	These questions help to extend and broaden the importance of the meaning. Students can elaborate on the question making it more personal to them.	• What are the implied or suggested meanings? • What does this mean to you? • How could you take the meaning farther? • What could the next step be?
Hypothetical Questions	These questions help to explore possibilities and test theories. These are the "what would happen if..." questions, allowing students to use their imaginations based on the facts they have learned.	• What if the earth had no sun? • What if the polar ice caps melted? • What if Charlotte in Charlotte's Web had lived? • What are the possible pros and cons?
Clarification Questions	These questions help to define words and concepts and clarify meaning.	• How did the character get to this point? • How did they gather the data? Was it a reliable process? • What is the sequence of ideas and how do they relate to one another?

The Socratic Questioning Technique

The Socratic approach to questioning is based on the practice of disciplined, thoughtful dialogue. Socrates, the early Greek philosopher/teacher, believed that disciplined practice of thoughtful questioning enabled the student to examine ideas logically and to determine the validity of those ideas. In this technique, the teacher professes ignorance of the topic in order to engage in dialogue with the students. With this "acting dumb" method, the student develops the fullest possible knowledge about the topic.

The Socratic Questioning technique is an effective way to explore ideas in depth. It can be used at all levels and is a helpful tool for all teachers. It can be used at different points within a unit or project. By using Socratic Questioning, teachers promote independent thinking in their students and give them ownership of what they are learning. Higher-level thinking skills are present while students think, discuss debate, evaluate, and analyze content through their own thinking and the thinking of those around them.

These types of questions may take some practice on both the teacher and students' part since it may be a whole new approach.

Tips for Using Socratic Questioning:

- Plan significant questions that provide meaning and direction to the dialogue
- Use wait time: Allow at least thirty seconds for students to respond
- Follow up on students' responses
- Ask probing questions
- Periodically summarize in writing key points that have been discussed
- Draw as many students as possible into the discussion
- Let students discover knowledge on their own through the probing questions the teacher poses

Types of Socratic Questions and Examples of techniques can be found at the end of this chapter.

Teacher Modeling

How do students know what is expected of them? Through explicit teacher modeling, the teacher provides students with a clear example of a skill or strategy. The teacher provides a structure to guide students by:

- Describing the skill or strategy
- Clearly describing features of the strategy or steps in performing the skill
- Breaking the skill into learnable parts
- Describing/modeling using a variety of techniques
- Engaging students in learning through showing enthusiasm, keeping a steady pace, asking good questions, and checking for student understanding

The teacher makes sure to clearly describe the concept, and then models the desired outcome by using visual, auditory, tactile, and/or kinesthetic instructional techniques while thinking aloud. The teacher can provide examples and non-examples to show students the expectations and stop frequently to get student input or ask questions. This technique of modeling provides high levels of student-teacher interaction.

Explicit teacher modeling should happen at every grade level and with every subject area. In order for the modeling to be successful, teachers need to plan the modeling experience carefully. The following steps are important for good modeling:

1. Make sure students have the appropriate background knowledge and prerequisite skills to perform the task.
2. Break down the skill into small learnable segments.
3. Make sure the context of the skill is grade appropriate.
4. Provide visual, auditory, kinesthetic, and tactile ways to illustrate important pieces of the concept/skill.
5. Think aloud as you show each step.
6. Make the important connections between steps.
7. Check for student understanding along the way and re-model the steps that might be causing confusion.
8. Make sure the timing is at a pace where students can follow along but not become bored and lose focus.
9. Model the concept/skills as many times needed to make sure all students are ready to do it on their own.
10. Allow many opportunities for students to ask questions and get clarification.

The time it takes to model a concept or skill is dependent on the size of the task students are being required to do. Modeling some skills may take just a few minutes while other, more complex skills, may take extended teaching time. It is important that the teacher know ahead of time what she wants students to know as a result of the modeling, so when students are set out to work on their own they know expectations and requirements. Specifying the desired behaviors before modeling them also makes assessment more constructive and accurate.

Classroom Management of Resources and Technology Access

Technology can play a big part in project-based units. The use of technology enhances the learning experience and allows students make connections to the outside world. It gives students a place to find resources and to create work products. Efficient management of available technology during projects takes planning and organization.

The One-Computer Classroom

One of the biggest challenges many teachers face is the lack of computers. Even with only one computer in the classroom, there are many ways to use technology effectively to improve student learning.

- Pair students up and set up a daily computer use schedule.
- Try to find time to have open blocks of time for individual student use.
- Use a timer to keep students to their time limits.
- Make sure computer time is used for creating products and doing research. All other pre-planning work should be done ahead of time (storyboards are a good way to do this).
- Use teacher-created templates for students to fill in to save time.
- Display posters using computer terms and commands.
- Make sure computer etiquette and guidelines have been modeled.

In a one-computer classroom, students can conduct research in smaller chunks of time, create work products piece by piece, and send and receive email to outside experts. Time is probably the biggest issue with a one-computer classroom, but through creative scheduling, computer use can happen. For example, allowing students to work on the computer when they have finished with other subject work is a resourceful solution. Another solution is to group students and give them a day of the week for their computer day.

On the designated days, particular groups of students have access to the computer. They can work independently or in pairs depending on the work that needs to be completed. If a computer is open and not being used by a member of the assigned group, anyone can use it until it is needed.

Learning Stations

Learning stations provide teachers and students a structured way to rotate through a small number of computers during class time. With access to three or four computers, students get more time and extended opportunities to work with technology to create projects. Stations should be connected to one another in a way that makes sense for the students to rotate through in a timely fashion. These stations can be set up so the content they are learning and work they are producing relates to each other. For example:

- Station One: Storyboard planning
- Station Two: Peer reviewing and feedback
- Station Three: Revising and drafting
- Station Four: Computer use to create work products
- Station Five: Computer use: researching, working with experts on the computer, publishing

The amount of time devoted to learning stations depends on how much time is available and the amount of work that will be expected of the students. The important piece in using learning stations effectively is making sure students are aware of what to do at each station through teacher modeling and monitoring. They should be held accountable for their work with checklists and/or teacher conferencing and have a place to store their works in progress for the next day.

Computer Labs

Computer labs are another way to get students using technology. With the use of computer labs, students are given chunks of time during the week to use computers. With these labs, students must come prepared with the work they need to complete using the computer. Because time is always limited, students need to be able to work independently and efficiently. Depending on how many computers there are, students can work on the computers independently or in pairs. Non-computer learning stations can take place in the classroom beforehand, and the computer station can be saved for the visit to the lab.

RESOURCES AND EXAMPLES

EXAMPLE K-W-L CHART

Name_____

| K-W-L Chart |
| For |
| The Cheetah |
| _____ |
| *(Your animal)* |

Write about what you **know** about your African animal. Then write questions about what you **want** to know. When we have finished the unit, you can write about what you've **learned**.

What I Know:	What I Want to Know:	What I Learned:
Example A cheetah eats antelope.	Example How does a cheetah kill the antelope? Where do antelope live? How many antelope will a cheetah eat in one week? Do antelope ever escape from the cheetah?	Example Cheetahs will run at 70 mph to catch the antelope. They find the antelope grazing on the African savannah. The cheetahs have to suffocate the antelope because they have small jaws and can't kill in one bite.

EXAMPLE OF RECIPROCAL TEACHING:

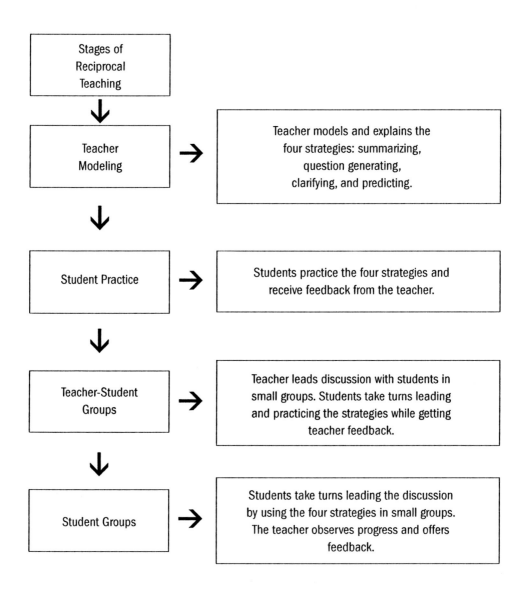

EXAMPLE CLUSTER MAP:

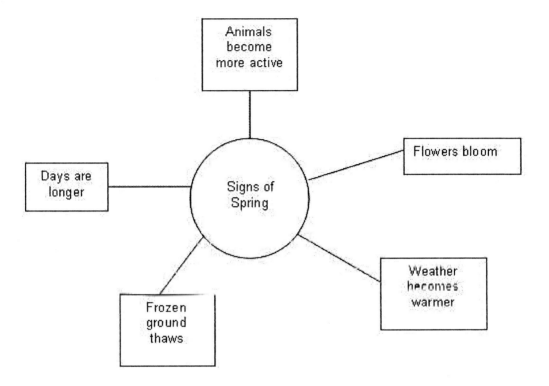

SEQUENCING EXAMPLE

Example of a Chain-of-Events Organizer
Chain-of-Events for *Where the Wild Things Are*

> **First Event:**
>
> Max is being bad and is sent ot bed without eating anything. His room becomes a forest.
>
> *Students could illustrate the event here.*

⬇

> **Second Event:**
>
> Max sails on his boat to the land of the wild things. They call him the king of all wild things. they have a parade and jump around.
>
> *Students could illustrate the event here.*

⬇

> **Third Event:**
>
> Max gets sad and lonely and misses his home. He sails back to his room and finds his dinner waiting for him.
>
> *Students could illustrate the event here.*

EXAMPLE OF A TIMELINE ORGANIZER

Civil War Timeline

This is a sample timeline a student might create.

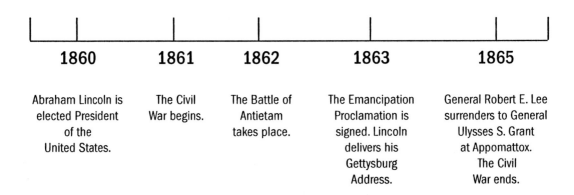

1860	1861	1862	1863	1865
Abraham Lincoln is elected President of the United States.	The Civil War begins.	The Battle of Antietam takes place.	The Emancipation Proclamation is signed. Lincoln delivers his Gettysburg Address.	General Robert E. Lee surrenders to General Ulysses S. Grant at Appomattox. The Civil War ends.

WEB SITE STORYBOARD EXAMPLE

This is a sample storyboard a student might use.
This storyboard is from the Unit Plan, African Adventure Safari.

Work with your group to decide what will go on each page.

Web Site Storyboard

Names_____
_____

Introduction

Tell about your animals.

Habitat

Describe the habitat, where your animals live in the habitat, and what other plants and animals will be found there.

Food Web

Combine information from your individual food webs and show the producer, consumer, decomposer, and sun relationships in the food web.

Survival Strategies

Describe how your animals get along in their habitat. What adaptations do they have to make them perfect for their niche? What would happen if there were too many or too few of any one animal?

Compare

Compare your animal to other animals or to humans (size, speed, longevity, sensory acuity, food consumption, care of young, etc.)

Conservation

Find out about the health of your animals in their habitat. Compare populations over time. Compare risks over time. Give suggestions for how people can help.

VENN DIAGRAM EXAMPLE

Cinderella Venn diagram

This sample Venn diagram is from the Unit Plan, Where in the World is Cinderella?

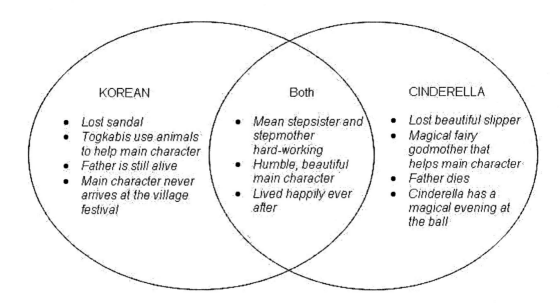

KOREAN

- Lost sandal
- Togkabis use animals to help main character
- Father is still alive
- Main character never arrives at the village festival

Both

- Mean stepsister and stepmother hard-working
- Humble, beautiful main character
- Lived happily ever after

CINDERELLA

- Lost beautiful slipper
- Magical fairy godmother that helps main character
- Father dies
- Cinderella has a magical evening at the ball

T-CHART EXAMPLE

Destination America: Our Hope, Our Future

Compare Ellis Island immigrants to Angel Island immigrants using the T-Chart below.

	Ellis Island	Angel Island
Where are the immigrants from?	Mostly European countries (Italy, Poland, Ireland, England)	Mostly from Asian countries (China, Japan, Korea, India, Philippines)
Where is the island located?	East coast – across the Atlantic Ocean in New York Harbor	West coast -- across the Pacific Ocean in San Francisco Bay
Reasons immigrants came to America:	Religious and political persecution, crop famine, loss of jobs, overpopulation, free expression, personal opportunity and government incentives in America	Poverty, limited job opportunities in homeland, war, high taxes, the hope to have a better life in America
Nickname:	Gateway to America	Guardian of the Western Gate
When was island open for immigrants?	Opened for immigrants between 1892 to 1924	Immigrants and emigrants between 1910 and 1940
Why were the islands built?	To regulate immigration into America – a stopping point to America	Designed to control the flow of Chinese immigrants with the passage of the Chinese Exclusion Act of 1882. Process and detain Chinese and other Asian immigrants.
How many people passed through the gates?	Over 22 million immigrants passed through the doors to American through Ellis Island	Estimated 1 million people entered and left the country. 175,000 Chinese 150,000 Japanese
What did the immigrants have to do when they got there?	Medical examinations and full physicals for everyone by 1917. If a problem was curable, they were sent to the island hospital. If not, they were sent back home.	Humiliating and barbaric medical examinations performed. Interrogation sessions took place.
What were the conditions like?	The Statue of Liberty greeted the immigrants and welcomed them to America. The conditions were crowded.	Harsh prison-like conditions while awaiting the demanding hearing process to prove their status as legal immigrants
How long did they stay?	Process took 3-5 hour with the interviews. Some stayed for months waiting for family members or other reasons.	Some stayed over night, while others stayed for months. Chinese immigrants stayed an average of 2-3 weeks. While waiting for their immigration status, many of the immigrants etched poems of depression and fear on the walls of the barracks.
How were they granted permission to stay?	Prove they could be in America legally. Prove their country of origin, where they expected to live and work in America. Anyone with a criminal record or suspected of being an indentured servant was rejected. By 1921 a literacy test had to be passed and a passport or visa had to be shown. Had to have at least 20 dollars to be allowed to enter America. Their money was exchanged on the island.	Prove their identity by matching details of their lives with the answers of their relative in the United States. Often had to wait months while their case was being investigated.

SOCRATIC QUESTIONS AND EXAMPLES

The Socratic Questioning technique involves different type of questions. Some examples of these are:

Socratic Question Type	Example
Clarification questions	· What do you mean by...? · Could you put that another way? · What do you think is the main issue? · Could you give us an example? · Could you expand upon that point further?
Questions about an initial question or issue	· Why is this question important? · Is this question easy or difficult to answer? · Why do you think that? · What assumptions can we make based on this question? · Does this question lead to other important issues and questions?
Assumption questions	· Why would someone make this assumption? · What is _____ assuming here? · What could we assume instead? · You seem to be assuming_____. · Do I understand you correctly?
Reason and evidence questions	· What would be an example? · Why do you think this is true? · What other information do we need? · Could you explain your reason to us? · By what reasoning did you come to that conclusion? · Is there reason to doubt that evidence? · What led you to that belief?
Origin or source questions	· Is this your idea or did you hear if from some place else? · Have you always felt this way? · Has your opinion been influenced by something or someone? · Where did you get that idea? · What caused you to feel that way?
Implication and consequence questions	· What effect would that have? · Could that really happen or probably happen? · What is an alternative? · What are you implying by that? · If that happened, what else would happen as a result? Why?
Viewpoint questions	· How would other groups of people respond this question? Why? · How could you answer the objection that _____would make? · What might someone who believed _____ think? · What is an alternative? · How are _____ and _____'s ideas alike? Different?

SOCRATIC QUESTIONING EXAMPLE

This questioning dialogue would take place after the unit had been introduced and was well underway.

Teacher:	What is happening to our global climate?
John:	It is getting warmer.
Teacher:	How do you know it is getting warmer? What evidence do you have to support your answer?
John:	It is in the news all of the time. They are always saying that it is not as cold as it used to be. We have all of these record heat days.
Teacher:	Has anyone else heard of this kind of news?
Denise:	Yeah. I have read about it the newspaper. They call it global warming, I think.
Teacher:	Are you saying that you learned about global warming from newscasters? Are you assuming they know that global warming is occurring?
Jill:	I heard it too. It is terrible. The ice caps in the Arctic are melting. The animals are losing their homes. I think the newscasters hear it from the scientists that are studying the issue.
Teacher:	If that is the case and the scientists are telling the newscasters, how do the scientists know?
Chris:	They have instruments to measure climate. They conduct research that measures the Earth's temperature.
Teacher:	How long do you think scientists have been doing this?
Grant:	Probably 100 years.
Candace:	Maybe a little more than that.
Teacher:	Actually, it is been studied for about 140 years. Since about 1860.
Heidi:	We were close.
Teacher:	Yes. How did you know that?
Grant:	I just figured that seems like when instruments were available and scientists had the means to measure climate like that.
Teacher:	So, looking at the last 100 year's climate on this graph, what can we say about the earth's climate?
Raja:	The 20th century has become much warmer than previous centuries.
Teacher:	Can we hypothesize why?
Raja:	One word: pollution.
Teacher:	What are you assuming when you say that pollution is the cause for the temperatures to rise?
Jill:	Carbon dioxide from cars causes pollution and chemicals from factories.
Frank:	Hair spray causes dangerous chemicals to get into the atmosphere.
Teacher:	Okay. Let's take a minute to review what we've discussed so far.

CHAPTER 4

INFUSING TECHNOLOGY INTO PROJECT BASED LEARNING

In this chapter we will discuss and explore:

- *Student centered learning*
- *Projects focused on learning objectives that are aligned with standards*
- *Projects driven by curriculum-framed questions*
- *Ongoing and multiple types of assessment*
- *How students can demonstrate knowledge through a product or performance*
- *How technology supports and enhances student learning*
- *Thinking skills are integral to project work*
- *Varying Instructional strategies and supporting multiple learning styles*

"Better learning will not come from finding better ways for the teacher to instruct but from giving the learner better opportunities to construct." – Seymour Papert, Professor Emeritus, MIT Media Lab

Student Centered Projects

Why pull my hair out through by using projects in my classroom? Two answers to this commonly asked question:

1. Project-based units engage students in meaningful work and promote higher-order thinking.
2. Socratic questioning and ongoing assessment keep project work focused on important learning goals.

Project-based learning is a student-centered, instructional model. It develops content area knowledge and skills through an extended task that promotes student inquiry and authentic demonstrations of learning in products and performances. Project-based curriculum is driven by important Curriculum-Framing Questions that tie content standards and higher-order thinking to real-world contexts.

Project-based units include varied instructional strategies to engage all students regardless of their learning style. Often students collaborate with outside experts and community members to answer questions and gain deeper meaning of the content. Technology is used to support learning. Throughout project work multiple types of assessment are embedded to ensure that students produce high quality work.

There are many kinds of projects implemented in classrooms. Effective projects balance the level of student control with teacher-planned structure that guides and focuses student work. The characteristics below help define effective project-based units.

1) Students are at the center of the learning process.

Well-designed, project-based units engage students in open-ended, authentic tasks. Compelling project tasks empower students to make decisions and apply their interests and passions to culminating products and performances. Students learn through inquiry and have some control over decisions about how they complete project tasks. The teacher takes on the role of a facilitator or coach. Students often work in collaborative groups, assuming roles that make best use of their individual talents.

2) Projects focus on important learning objectives that are aligned with standards.

Good projects are developed around core curricular concepts that address national or local standards. The project has clear objectives that align with standards and focus on what students should know as a result of their learning. With a focus on objectives, the teacher defines appropriate demonstrations of learning in an assessment plan and organizes learning activities and instruction. Project work culminates in student products and performance tasks such as persuasive presentations and informational newsletters that demonstrate understanding of content standards and learning objectives.

3) Projects are driven by Curriculum-Framing Questions.

Questions keep projects focused on important learning. Students are introduced to a project with questions that pose big and enduring ideas that cross many disciplines. They are challenged to dig deeper with subject-specific content questions that focus on standards and objectives. There are three types of Curriculum-Framing Questions: Essential, Unit, and Content Questions. *Essential Questions* are broad and open-ended questions that address big ideas and enduring concepts. They often cross disciplines and help students see how subjects are related. *Unit Questions* are tied directly to the project and support investigation into the Essential Question. Unit Questions help demonstrate how well students understand the core concepts of the project. *Content Questions* are more fact-based and align to identified standards and objectives.

4) Projects involve on-going and multiple types of assessment.

Clear expectations are defined at the beginning of a project and are revisited with multiple checks for understanding using varied assessment methods. Students have models and guidelines for high quality work and know what is expected of them from the beginning of the project. Opportunities for reflection, feedback, and adjustment are embedded in the project.

5) The project has real-world connections.

Projects are relevant to students' lives and may involve community or outside experts who provide a context for learning. Students may present their learning to an authentic audience, connect with community resources, tap into experts in the field of study, or communicate through technology.

6) Students demonstrate knowledge through a product or performance.

Projects typically culminate with students demonstrating their learning through presentations, written documents, constructed displays, proposals, or even simulated events such as a mock trial. These final products allow for student expression and ownership of learning.

7) Technology supports and enhances student learning.

Students have access to different types of technology, which are used to support the development of thinking skills, content expertise, and creation of final products. With the help of technology, students have more control over final results and an opportunity to personalize products. Students can reach beyond the walls of the classroom by collaborating with distant classes through email and self-made Web sites, or presenting their learning through multimedia.

8) Thinking skills are integral to project work.

Project work supports the development of both meta-cognitive and cognitive thinking skills such as collaboration, self-monitoring, analysis of data, and evaluation of information. Throughout the project, Curriculum-Framing Questions challenge students to think and make connections to concepts that matter in the real world.

9) Instructional strategies are varied and support multiple learning styles.

Instructional strategies create a richer learning environment and promote higher-order thinking. A range of instructional strategies ensures that the curricular material is accessible to all students and provides opportunities for every student to succeed. Instruction may include the use of different cooperative grouping strategies, graphic organizers, and teacher and peer feedback.

Project-based learning is one instructional technology approach in a teacher's repertoire. While it is effective with giving students important 21st-century skills and connecting ideas across subject areas, it is not the only approach for teaching all skills and knowledge. Teachers who move to project-based instruction face challenges as they shift from traditional practices.

As teachers and students work together on projects and integrate technology, their roles change. Project work in the classroom requires a shift in the role of the teacher. Teachers who are accustomed to lecturing and relying on textbooks or pre-created materials may have trouble shifting to a more student-centered classroom which entails giving up control and allowing students to work in multiple directions on different activities at the same time. While planning project work requires more time upfront on the part of the teacher, once a project is underway, the teacher has less preparation to do on a daily basis and acts as a coach or facilitator throughout the project. Teachers find this exciting and a way to connect with students' individual styles and creativity.

Project work also calls for a shift in the role of the student. Students may not be used to being placed in an active role in the classroom. In projects, they are called upon to make many decisions, to work collaboratively, to take initiative, to make public presentations, and in many cases, to construct their own knowledge. Although this may be challenging for students at first, most students find project work more meaningful, relevant to their lives, and engaging. Thus, they are generally more motivated, perform better on projects, and retain new learning.

Although technology is not essential to project work, it can enhance the learning experience and allow students the opportunity to make connections to the outside world, find resources, and create products. Some teachers may not be comfortable with newer technologies or may feel that a one-computer classroom is a barrier to using computers as part of project work. These challenges can be overcome. Many teachers may need to accept that they are not the experts of everything and that their students may know more, especially when it comes to technology. Learning the technical skills side-by-side with students or having students act as technical mentors are some ways to overcome this barrier. Relationships both inside and outside the classroom expand and grow with project work.

In the past, community may be integrated into the curriculum in the form of a field trip or a guest speaker. During projects, community is often the focus. Projects may include partnerships with local groups such as universities, foundations, or community experts. Students contribute to their communities in service-learning projects and serve as environmentalists, data specialists, social workers, or scientists to gain different perspectives of what is happening in their community. Products and tasks become authentic when experts are invited into the classroom to question, speak, assess student projects, and work in collaboration with students.

In many projects, these connections with experts are essential to assist students in completing quality work and promoting the learning process. Many educators may see this as more work, but connections are surprisingly easy to create and once made; take on a life of their own. The relationships built are invaluable to fostering authentic engagement and lifelong learning.

Working in a group is a life skill and an essential part of a project-based learning environment. Students work in cooperative groups to brainstorm, discuss, give feedback, complete tasks, or share resources. Although, this shift to group work may raise the concern of individual accountability, this challenge can be addressed in many ways. By providing students with specific, individualized tasks within the group and incorporating peer evaluations or individualized checklists, students are held responsible for their work and their contributions to the group. Project work involves viewing traditional practices and methods from a new perspective.

Some teachers may find the organized chaos of classroom projects disconcerting. A project-based classroom is a student-centered classroom, where collaboration, conversation, and movement are necessities. Desks may be organized in pods for collaboration and big tables provide space for project work. Resources and supplies are accessible to students and the classroom tone is established for risk-taking. The environment is one where students feel comfortable to share opinions and ideas, and are encouraged to think for themselves and at higher levels. Clear expectations and organization are essential, but teachers will find that advance planning will lead to engaged and productive students.

Project-based learning takes time, and this is often a major concern of many teachers shifting to this type of curriculum planning. A well-designed, project-based unit should first determine what knowledge is worth spending time to uncover? (Wiggins, 2001).The answer to this question is key to effective time management. By focusing on big ideas that have enduring value beyond the classroom, students become actively engaged and own more of the decisions and direction of their work and ultimately think and produce at higher levels. In order to turn more control over to students yet maintain standards and academic rigor, projects must be planned to the smallest detail. Students must have very clear direction that defines expectations, responsibilities, processes, and timelines. Essentially, what takes longer to prepare, pays off in learning outcomes.

Socratic Questioning

Asking intriguing, open-ended questions is an effective way to encourage students to think deeply and to provide them with a meaningful context for learning. When students are given questions that they are truly interested in finding the answers to, they engage. When questions help them see the connections between the subject matter and their own lives, learning has meaning. We can help our students become more motivated and self-directed by asking the right questions. But what are the right questions?

Curriculum-Framing Questions provide a structure for organizing questioning throughout projects and promote thinking at all levels. They give projects a balance between content understanding and exploration of intriguing and enduring ideas that make learning relevant to students. Curriculum-Framing Questions guide a unit of study, and include Essential, Unit, and Content Questions.

Essential and Unit Questions provide the rationale for learning. They help students to recognize the "why" and "how" and encourage inquiry, discussion, and research. They involve students in personalizing their learning and developing insights into a topic. Good Essential and Unit Questions engage students in critical thinking, promote curiosity, and develop a questioning approach to the curriculum. In order to answer such questions, students must examine topics in depth and construct their own meaning and answers from the information they have gathered.

Content Questions help students to identify the "who", "what", "where", and "when", and support the Essential and Unit Questions by providing a focus for understanding the details. They help students to focus on the factual information that must be learned in order to meet many of the content standards and learning objectives.

Curriculum-Framing Questions build upon each other. Content Questions support Unit Questions and both support Essential Questions. Essential Questions are often the most intriguing and posed first. The questions below from a civics unit show the relationship between each.

Essential Question

- *Why do we need others?*

Unit Questions

- *Which of our community helpers is the most important?*
- *Which community helper would you most like to be?*

Content Questions

- *Who are some community helpers?*
- *What do community helpers do?*

Essential Questions:

- *Introduce big, enduring ideas that cross all subjects. They provide a bridge between many units, subject areas, or even a year's worth of study.*
- *Have many answers. Answers to these questions are not found in a book. They are often life's big questions. For example: Am I my brother's keeper?*
- *Capture students' attention and require higher-order thinking; they challenge students to dissect their thinking, apply their values, and interpret their experiences.*

Unit Questions:

- *Are open-ended and invite exploration of ideas that are specific to a topic, subject, or unit of study. Teams of teachers from different subjects can use their own unique Unit Questions to support one common, unifying Essential Question across the team.*
- *Pose problems or serve as discussion starters that support the Essential Question. For example: How can we help prevent and relieve famine?*
- *Encourage exploration, provoke and sustain interest, and allow for unique responses and creative approaches. They force students to interpret the facts themselves.*

Content Questions:

- *Typically have clear-cut answers or specific "right" answers and are categorized as "closed" questions.*
- *Align with content standards and learning objectives and support the Essential and Unit Questions.*
- *Test students' ability to recall fact based information. They usually require students to address who, what, where, and when. For example: What is famine?*
- *Require knowledge and comprehension skills to answer.*

When Essential and Unit Questions are integrated in project activities, students are challenged to develop and apply new understanding. According to the Maryland State Department of Education publication, Better Thinking and Learning (1991), teachers who ask higher-order questions promote active participation in the learning process. Because the answers to such questions cannot be looked up in a book, students must apply higher-order thinking skills such as comparison, prediction, and interpretation. With interesting, open-ended questions, students shift from passive to active learning, engage in what they are doing, and construct understanding about concepts and ideas.

For example, in a project on insects, students take on the role of an insect living in their own backyard. Their task is to convince a family member, who is deathly afraid of bugs, just how important insects are to the ecosystem and that there is absolutely no reason to fear them. As they tackle this task, students must consider and answer the following Curriculum-Framing Questions:

Essential Question

- *How can something so small be capable of so much?*

Unit Questions

- *Why shouldn't we be afraid of bugs?*
- *If an insect could talk, what would it say to you?*

Content Questions

- *What makes an insect an insect?*
- *How do insects grow and change?*
- *In what ways are insects helpful and harmful?*

These Curriculum-Framing Questions are compelling, allowing for unique responses and creative approaches. While the content is not unique to an insect unit (insect anatomy, habitat, and life cycle changes), the open-ended questioning urges students to interpret the facts from their own vantage point and draw their own conclusions, promoting a deeper level of engagement and higher levels of thinking.

Developing good Essential and Unit Questions takes practice. Jay McTighe and Grant Wiggins, co-authors of *Understanding by Design* (1998), suggest that in order to develop student understanding and engage and focus student inquiry, teachers should build their units around the questions that gave rise to the content knowledge. This means a look at the big ideas, the broad themes, and the overarching concepts that get at the heart of the subject.

A good place to start is by looking at your standards and thinking about general themes in the subject. Then begin formulating questions that require students to make a decision or plan a course of action related to those big ideas.

Example

Action	Example
Look at content standards	Social Studies standard for fourth grade: Entrepreneurs are people who take the risks of organizing productive resources to make goods and services. Profit is an important incentive that leads entrepreneurs to accept the risks of business failure.
Identify the general subject theme(s) related to the standard(s)	Taking risks
Brainstorm questions related to the theme that require a decision or plan of action	Decision: Are risks worth taking? Why should we take risks? Plan of Action: How can we reduce risk?

Make sure each question will take time to fully understand and answer. Do not worry about the mechanics and language in the beginning or whether the question is Essential or Unit; concern yourself more with whether it requires higher-order thinking skills. Remember, that truly good Essential and Unit Questions, motivate students, promote inquiry, target higher-order thinking, and get to the heart of what it is that you want your students to learn and remember.

Once you have developed your questions, put them to the test. Use the following list to assess whether or not each question is open-ended and will incite students to really think.

- Can the question serve as a discussion starter or problem poser?
- Will the question generate curiosity, invite an exploration of ideas, and hold student interest?
- Does the question pose a reasonable challenge and does it require students to construct their own meaning and support it with information they have gathered?
- Would different people answer the question differently and does it allow for creative approaches and unique responses?
- Does the question require students to answer how and why?
- Does the question help to uncover the subject's controversies?
- Does the question in some way connect to students' lives?
- Does the question require students to dissect their thinking?

Once you have evaluated your questions, modify and adjust them as necessary. Remember to word them using language that will appeal to your students. Let your questions evolve over time and when appropriate, let your students develop the questions themselves.

Finally, give your Essential and Unit Questions a try. When you do, you are likely to discover that your lessons have purpose and depth that you had never planned on and authentic learning that you did not know could exist. If you can draw your students into an interactive form of learning stimulated by effective questioning practices, you are likely to foster life-long learners.

Incorporating Essential and Unit Questions into the curriculum is an effective way to promote student inquiry and target higher-order thinking, but it takes more than a few good questions to truly transform a classroom and engage all students in learning.

Research and development specialists, Jackie Walsh and Beth Sattes (2005), authors of *Quality Questioning: Research-Based Practice to Engage Every Learner*, claim that knowing how to formulate quality questions is only the first step in the process of transforming classrooms. They argue that if educators wish to engage all students in answering the questions, they must also teach new questioning behaviors to students and adopt classroom norms that support them.

To begin the process of transforming your classroom, establish a risk-free setting where students feel comfortable asking and answering questions. Make sure that everyone understands that no question is a bad question, and always allow plenty of time for students to formulate, process, and answer the questions.

Next, assign projects that require students to answer the "big questions" and back them up with evidence. Present students with scenarios or problems where they must derive the solutions themselves. In the beginning, students that are unfamiliar with open-ended questioning, most likely will need guidance as well as assurance that there may be many right answers. Provide students with appropriate scaffolds that will ensure success and frequently monitor their work. Remind students to provide rationale for their opinions and to formulate hypotheses, based on facts.

Make time for questions. Use probing techniques to urge students to clarify their ideas and explain their reasoning. Then, challenge them with even more complex questions. Help students to understand that in order to answer the big questions, they may need to address the smaller questions first.

Once students are accustomed to exploring and answering open-ended questions supported by evidence, take a step back and assume the role of facilitator. Teach students how to generate their own questions and encourage them to elaborate and build on each other's ideas.

Finally, as you begin to assess student work, consider the effectiveness of your own questioning practices. If students are unable to adequately answer the Essential and Unit Questions and support their answers with evidence, is it because you need to modify the questions? Do you need to utilize more effective probing techniques to urge students to clarify their ideas and explain their reasoning? Or do you need to provide more scaffolds to ensure objectives are met? If all students are not engaged in the learning, do you need to reinforce classroom practices so that all students feel free to share their ideas or state their opinions? If student work does not demonstrate higher-order thinking and include unique responses or creative approaches, do you need to modify your project requirements or assessment tools to target these skills? Or do you need to provide more practice and guidance in how to address open-ended questions?

Transforming your classroom into a place where all students are engaged and interested in asking and answering the big questions will require time and work, and monitoring and adjusting, but the rewards of students engaged in thinking and learning is worth the effort.

Project-based units require extra planning and preparation. To teach something well and ensure that students are engaged in learning, teachers need to plan and prepare effectively. If the goal is for students is to achieve at high levels, then proper planning and preparation are expected, no matter what type of teaching is going on. Project-based learning is no exception.

In order to be successful, projects need to be designed with the end in mind. Without closely focused learning goals, the purpose of the project can become unclear and expectations for student learning outcomes can be mis-communicated. When designing projects, it is important to ensure that the activities planned will help your students meet the intended learning objectives. By reviewing curriculum goals, objectives, and standards, teachers make choices for establishing curricular priorities. At a very basic level, project planning involves the following steps:

1. Determine specific learning goals by using content standards and the desired higher-order thinking skills
2. Develop Curriculum-Framing Questions
3. Make an assessment plan
4. Design activities

This simple four-step process is deceiving. Project planning is not linear; it always involves circling back to previous steps to ensure alignment. The use of Curriculum-Framing Questions and a project approach should all work together to support the learning goals and targeted standards of the unit. Throughout the unit, there should be multiple opportunities for assessment and monitoring to measure your students' progress.

When people hear the phrase, "project-based learning", different concepts and definitions may come to mind. These may include some of the common misconceptions below.

Projects involve all kinds of "hands-on" or "minds-on" tasks of varying complexity and length. Tasks can be as detailed and involved as a service-learning project on pollution or as simple as an in-class debate. A project will be focused as long as it is well-planned, aligned to important standards and learning targets, and clearly states student expectations.

Project-based learning is an instructional method in a repertoire of methods. It is not appropriate for the teaching of all skills and knowledge. It incorporates and accounts for varied teaching strategies and learning styles, and is a way to build on current instruction to enrich learning experiences and make more efficient use of time. The focus of an educator has not changed. The goal remains to teach students what they need to know and need to be able to do. Project-based learning simply provides a new approach to reaching this goal.

For some teachers, the shift to project-based learning may not encompass many challenges, but for others the idea may be overwhelming. If you are new to projects, it is best to start small and build upon what works well. Starting small means incorporating one or two instructional methods at a time, while building up to the complete design and implementation of a project-based unit. Starting small can mean incorporating:

- Community experts
- A project scenario
- A student generated rubric
- Cooperative grouping strategies

Little by little, the benefits of project-based learning will be uncovered and the shift to more projects will develop over time, and lead to bigger ideas and better designs.

CHAPTER 5

PREPARING TO TEACH WITH TECHNOLOGY

In this chapter we will discuss and explore:

- *Eight reported items teachers use for more student-centered instruction practices with technology*
- *In order for teachers to teach their skill, they must first know how to use their skill*
- *The two most valuable tools for teachers: Microsoft Word and internet search engines*
- *Teacher resources and websites to get them started*
- *Case Study: Creating a Gallery of Student Work*
- *Case Study: Creating a Power Point Presentation for Teachers with Tips and Tricks*
- *Case Study: Creating a Web Page with Microsoft Word*

So you may be thinking, "I do not need a computer to teach math." Of course you do not, but the computer can add an element of excitement and interest that paper and pencil might not have, especially for the "modest achievers" who sit in our classrooms and challenge us to motivate them. Technology offers our reluctant learners an additional opportunity for success that they might not otherwise experience in their daily lessons. Technology provides our students with yet another strategy for success. It can add excitement and creativity to lessons that might otherwise be routine.

It is probably no surprise that students are outpacing teachers in their familiarity with and use of technology — after all, today's students are part of a generation for whom technology use is almost as common as breathing. However, the difference in perceptions between students and teachers about technology in the classroom is somewhat surprising, and can lead to very different classroom realities. It is my belief that this divergence is preliminary evidence of a trend that may prove to be a core issue for schools in the future.

Listed are eight different items in which teachers reported on their inclinations to use technology for more student-centered instruction practices. These include:

- cooperative learning
- the use of higher-level thinking skills
- interactions with the world outside of school
- interdisciplinary activities
- activities that students find engaging
- providing extra help
- coaching rather than lecturing, and
- achievement measures based on products, progress and effort

While the increase in teachers' competencies and perceptions of their work is good news for schools, the widening gap between the perceptions of what teachers and students believe is or is not happening in the classroom is a startling red flag.

The lightning bolt of realization is, while teachers feel they are making dramatic leaps in their ability to harness the power of technology to create stimulating, engaging and challenging learning experiences for students, the students themselves have seen few changes in classroom instruction. Moreover, students are hungry for more opportunities to use technology in challenging and meaningful ways in the learning environment. Educators must begin to address the growing demand among students for technologically-charged learning experiences. We also must address the widening gap in perceptions between students and teachers about how well technology is being incorporated into the classroom and into learning experiences outside school walls.

In order for teachers to teach their skill they must first know how to use their skill. There are many websites, organizations, and colleges offering classes for teachers to learn to use and integrate technology into their classroom, but the one tried and truly tested way to learn is through experience. You must make it an everyday practice which will form a life long habit. The two most valuable tools for teachers to learn to use fluently are word processing applications such as Microsoft Word and internet search engines. If a teacher can learn how to fully utilize these two items, they will have the two most important tools for the classroom.

TEACHER RESOURCES

- http://www.4teachers.org/
  This site helps teachers locate and create ready-to-use Web lessons, quizzes, rubrics and classroom calendars. There are also tools for student use. Discover valuable professional development resources addressing issues such as equity, ELL, technology planning, and at-risk or special-needs students

- http://teach-nology.com/
  The Art and Science of Teaching with Technology® represents a vision that embraces the future of teaching in a world driven by technology. They offer a range of services that are designed to assist and support educational agencies in their attempt to develop the knowledge, competencies, or skills that teachers need to effectively incorporate technology in teaching.

- http://www.online.tusc.k12.al.us/tutorials/search/searching.htm
  This tutorial presents an overview of searching for information on the Internet. It covers search engine basics, the searching process (steps, guidelines, credibility of information, types of web sites, and potential problems), types of search engines (major search engines, meta search engines, all-in-one search pages, specialty search engines, and shopping bots), and advanced searching tips and techniques.

TITLE:	Creating a Gallery of Student Work
SUBJECT:	Teacher Technology Skills Improvement
UNIT:	Web Design/Front Page
OBJECTIVES:	Learners will create a gallery of student work in FrontPage using tables and images.

PRE-REQUISITE KNOWLEDGE:

1. Basic familiarity with FrontPage
2. Keyboarding skills
3. Basic Internet skills

MATERIALS NEEDED:

1. FrontPage software
2. A computer with access to the Internet
3. Printer for printing step-by-step directions as needed

PROCESS:

View the skill videos listed on the next page. Follow the step-by-step directions to create a gallery of student work. Upon completion of the video, continue working in Class Server to complete this lesson.

Create Sub-Pages

Approximate length of project: 4 Hours

Outcome: Create an electronic gallery of student work using FrontPage which includes images and tables.

CLASSROOM IDEAS:

Teacher Professional Portfolio / Growth Plan

Collect work samples from students in your class. Choose work samples from the beginning, middle and end of the school year. Reflect on individual student growth as a learner.

Student Work Portfolio

Students will select exceptional work pieces from throughout the term, or school year. Portfolios can be subject specific or cross subject areas. Works can include text, images, sound files and video. Students will annotate their work samples with reflection.

For Practice

- Build a student gallery.
- Select student work samples.

If student work samples are not electronic, use a scanner to digitize the selections.

- Create a main page (save the page as "index.htm").
- Use a table to organize sub page links (see Insert tables' skill video).
- Build your supporting pages which include student work.
- Insert images (see Insert Images skill video).
- Link your pages using hyperlinks.
- Save your pages using an intuitive naming convention.
  (index.htm for the main page and course codes for the sub pages for example)

Example:

Mrs. Deluna's Class Web Site	Gallery of Student Work				
	English 9A	English 10A	English 11A	Business Writing 12	Writing 12
Home Page	Poetry Samples	Book Reports	Classics	Resume Writing	Short Stories Examples
Event Calendar	Ode to Grade 9	Term 1	Romanticism	Examples	
Unit Plan	Reflections on Shakespeare	Term 2	Greek Tragedy	Business Plan Writing	Poetry Examples
Student Resources		Term 3	Shakespeare	Examples	Plays Examples
Homework	Creative Writing	Creative Writing	Odes	Job Descriptions	Scripts Examples
Gallery of Student Work	My Summer	Daily Samples	Plays	Examples	Letters Examples
Class Newsletter	Future Aspirations	Journals	Scripts	Job Advertisement	Electronic Examples
Site Map	Life as a teenager	Play Writing		Examples	
Last Updated February 2006	Anti-Smoking	Script Writing			
		Poetry Samples			

TIPS: When creating a web site, it is extremely important to stay organized. Keep all of your documents for your web site in a single folder to avoid confusion. Remember to be consistent with font (type, size and color) backgrounds, navigation and layout. Once your page is saved you can see what it would look like by going to the File menu and selecting Web Page Preview

ASSESSMENT: Answer the following questions. Read the questions over once, and then if needed, watch the suggested videos again.

1. To insert an image you downloaded from the internet.
    a. Under Insert > Picture > clipart

    b.   Under Format > Picture > Insert

    c.   Under File > Insert > Picture

    d.   Under Insert > Picture > From File

2.   Which of the following is not an image format?

    a.   JPG

    b.   PNG

    c.   ZIP

    d.   GIF

3.   If you do not want a border for your table,

    a.   Select "no border" under Format > Borders

    b.   Enter 0 in the Border Size box

    c.   Select no color under Border > Color

4.   When referring to tables, "padding" is:

    a.   The width of the border

    b.   The space between the text and cell border

    c.   The space outside of the box between the table and surrounding text

5.   To add a table to your web page,

    a.   Select Image > Insert

    b.   Select Format > Table

    c.   Select Table > Insert > Table

6.   An efficient way to convert a Word document into HTML is by:

    a.   Saving the Word document as HTML under File

    b.   Copying and the pasting the text into FrontPage

    c.   You can't covert a Word document into HTML

RESOURCES: *Web Resources on Inserting and Editing Images in FrontPage*

- Images (FP Tutorial)
  http://www.actden.com/fp2000/java/3.htm

- More Images (advanced)
  http://www.actden.com/fp2000/java/4.htm

- Inserting and Resizing Graphics (FP)
  http://www.siec.k12.in.us/~west/online/website/step8.htm

- Editing Graphics with FrontPage Editor
  http://www.siec.k12.in.us/~west/online/website/step9.htm

- Inserting Images with FrontPage
  http://www.learningspace.org/tech/FrontPage/images.htm
- Creating Tables with FrontPage
  http://www.learningspace.org/tech/FrontPage/table.htm
- Tables
  http://www.actden.com/fp2000/java/6.htm
- Adding Tables to your Web Pages
  http://www.siec.k12.in.us/~west/online/website/step13.htm
- *Converting Word Docs to HTML* - Expand with Word 2000
  http://www.actden.com/fp2000/java/8_4.htm
- Tutorials, Tips and Tricks - Front Page
  http://www.rshweb.com/FPtips/fp98c.html
- Microsoft Manual on Front Page - "Getting your bearings"
  http://www.microsoft.com/education/downloads/Tutorials/IOC/FrontPage2k/bearings.doc
- Microsoft document - "Adding Content to a Web Site"
  http://www.microsoft.com/education/downloads/Tutorials/IOC/FrontPage2k/content.doc
- Design Resources (Free Clipart)
  http://members.tripod.com/~nbrick33/freeresources.htm

TITLE:	Creating a PowerPoint Presentation
SUBJECT:	Teacher Technology Skills Improvement
UNIT:	Power Point
OBJECTIVES:	Learners will explore the basics of creating a multimedia presentation using PowerPoint.

PRE-REQUISITE KNOWLEDGE:

1. Basic familiarity with PowerPoint
2. Keyboarding skills
3. Ability to navigate the Internet

MATERIALS NEEDED:

1. PowerPoint software
2. A computer with access to the Internet
3. Printer for printing step-by-step directions as needed

PROCESS: View the skill videos listed on the next page. Follow the step-by-step directions to create a simple PowerPoint multimedia presentation. Upon watching the video/s, complete this lesson.

RESOURCES:

Web Resources on PowerPoint

- PowerPoint - Creating Classroom Presentations
  http://www.education-world.com/a_tech/tech013.shtml
- PowerPoint in the Classroom *(amazing resources and information)*
  http://www.actden.com/pp/index.htm
- Tutorials in Print
  http://www.actden.com/pp/print.htm
- PowerPoint Tutorial
  http://www2.umist.ac.uk/isd/lwt/apt/ppclass/index.shtml
  (Tons of information including more advanced elements)
- Technology for Teachers: PowerPoint
  http://www.orst.edu/instruction/ed596/ppoint/pphome.htm

*Always make a plan or **storyboard** for your slide show*
You can find templates on these websites

- http://www.tulsaschools.org/teacher_resources/strybrd.htm
- http://www.mcli.dist.maricopa.edu/authoring/studio/guidebook/sb.html

Great PDF storyboard template available here

- http://www.uni.edu/profdev/powerpoint/three/storyboardtemplate.pdf

HANDS-ON

Classroom Ideas:

Build an academic electronic portfolio using PowerPoint.

For Practice...

- **Step 1** - Create a Storyboard
- **Step 2** - Create an electronic academic portfolio using PowerPoint
- **Step 1**
  Select a storyboard template from *Resources*, or use one of your own.
  Your presentation should include the following slides:
- title slide
- content of the portfolio, a list of categories (academic subjects for example)
- a slide for each category selected
- Complete your storyboard (include at least 5 slides).
- Make as many notes as possible on the storyboard regarding what content you want to see on each slide.

Step 2

Open a new PowerPoint presentation.

Choose a **slide design**.

Slide 1 - Select Title slide as the **layout** for your first slide. Add a title (and subtitle if you wish).

Slide 2 - Add another slide. (Use the "New Slide" button on the top menu bar or go under Insert, to New Slide) Choose a "Title and Text" slide layout.

Brainstorm categories for the portfolio (see example below). You may wish to organize your portfolio using academic subjects areas or by project or unit within a subject.

Add images. You could add your school logo or related clip art.
Add an image by selecting Insert from the top menu bar and selecting – Insert Picture – From File. Locate the picture you wish to add and select Insert.

Slide 3 -Add another slide. Choose "Title and Text" layout. Choose a topic area from the previous slide and list academic / performance examples. Include an image.

Repeat this step for each category listed on the second slide (contents). Each category will have a slide listing the work samples available to view in the portfolio.

Make at least 5 slides. Save the file.

Give the file an intuitive file name such as StewartPortfolio.ppt

EXAMPLE: Remember to be consistent with font (type, size and color) backgrounds, layout. You may wish to include digital images, scanned art work or assignments you are proud of. As you finish various projects through out the year add your work to your portfolio.

ASSESSMENT:

1. Using PowerPoint, you can add which of the following multimedia elements to your presentation?
   a) Sound
   b) Video
   c) Images
   d) All of the above

2. In PowerPoint, a transition is:
   a) Altering the file format of a presentation
   b) Adding images to a presentation
   c) Adding small images to slides
   d) The motion or movement added between slides

3. You can change the style, type, color and size of font by:
   a) Selecting Format > Font
   b) Selecting the font formatting options on the formatting tool bar
   c) All of the above

4. To add a new slide to your presentation you can:
   a) Select the *New Slide* button
   b) Under *Insert* select *New Slide*
   c) CTRL + M
   d) All of the above

5. The extension for your PowerPoint presentation file will be:
   a) .ptp
   b) .ppt
   c) .ttp

TITLE:	Adding Hyperlinks and Navigation
SUBJECT:	Teacher Technology Skills Improvement
UNIT:	Power Point
OBJECTIVES:	Learners will add hyperlinks and actions buttons to a PowerPoint presentation.

PRE-REQUISITE KNOWLEDGE:

1. Basic familiarity with PowerPoint
2. Keyboarding skills
3. Ability to navigate the Internet

MATERIALS NEEDED:

1. PowerPoint software
2. A computer with access to the Internet
3. Printer for printing step-by-step directions as needed

RESOURCES:

- PowerPoint - Creating Classroom Presentations
  http://www.education-world.com/a_tech/tech013.shtml
- PowerPoint in the Classroom *(amazing resources and information)*
  http://www.actden.com/pp/index.htm
- Tutorials in Print
  http://www.actden.com/pp/print.htm
- PowerPoint Tutorial
  http://www2.umist.ac.uk/isd/lwt/apt/ppclass/index.shtml
  (Tons of information including more advanced elements)
- Technology for Teachers: PowerPoint
  http://www.orst.edu/instruction/ed596/ppoint/pphome.htm

HANDS-ON

Classroom Ideas:

Add to your PowerPoint presentations by including hyperlinks and actions buttons. Hyperlinks may link to slides within your presentation or to files or website. The hyperlink itself can be text or an object such as a picture, graph, shape, or WordArt. Your hyperlinks become active when you view the presentation, not when you are creating it.

Action buttons are used when you want to include buttons with commonly understood symbols for going to the next, previous, first, and last slides. PowerPoint action buttons may also be used to play movies or sounds.

Your "to do list" for this lesson...

1. Add hyperlinks to your content / index page of the portfolio. These links will jump to the corresponding slides within the presentation.
   a.   Select the text or object that you wish to hyperlink from
   b.   Click "Insert Hyperlink"
   c.   Under "Link To" Click "Existing File or Webpage
   d.   Click on the or type in the address (destination)
   e.   Click "OK"

2. Add action buttons to further help with navigation.
   a.   Under Slide Show, select *Action button.*
   b.   Pick an appropriate object to represent the button (choices are provided).
   c.   Once selected, your cursor will change from an arrow to a + symbol.
   d.   Draw a square with your mouse where you want the button to be located. A window will appear where you can define the color and specific action of the button.
   e.   Each page should have a home button, back and forward buttons.
        Your contents page will link to corresponding slides using hyperlinks.

ASSESSMENT:
   1.   In your own words, describe what a hyperlink is used for when using PowerPoint (as used in this lesson).
   2.   What are action buttons?
   3.   What are the benefits of using action buttons and hyperlinks in a PowerPoint presentation?

TITLE: Creating a Web Page Using a MS Word Document
SUBJECT: All subjects
UNIT: Power Point
OBJECTIVES: Learners will convert a MS Word document into a web page.

PRE-REQUISITE KNOWLEDGE:

1. Basic familiarity with MS Office including navigation of toolbars, menus and dialog boxes.
2. Keyboarding skills

MATERIALS NEEDED:

1. Floppy Disk
2. MS Word document.
3. Printer for printing step-by-step directions as needed.

HAND OUTS:

Classroom Ideas:

Anything you can do in Word can be converted to a Web Page. The options are limitless. Some possible ideas for your class room are:

Electronic Notes. Students work in teams to research a particular topic. Each student within the group is given a sub-topic. The student types his/her notes in MS Word. Each document is saved as web page for teammates to view

How-to Manual. Students create a how-to manual for a classroom process or for working with a piece of equipment. Save as a web page for others to view.

Classroom or School Newspaper. Students create a newspaper in MS Word. Save as a web page for others to view.

Research paper. Student completes a research paper in MS Word. Save as a web page for others to view.

FOR PRACTICE:

Just to get a little hands on practice, create a permission form like the one below. When you're done, you can post this page on the Web using a Web hosting service like Geocities (www.geocities.com a free web hosting service) so that parents can print it directly from the Web... even if their child forgot to bring the form home.

1. Open Word and use the regular text tools to create a document like the one shown below:

West Morris Central High School
FIELD TRIP PERMISSION FORM

Your child's class will be attending a field trip to: The Bronx Zoo in NYC

Date:	Monday April 8, 2002
Depart time:	8:00 am
Return time:	8:00 pm
Location:	Bus departs from the school parking lot at 8. Parents must be at the school parking lot at 8 for pickup.
Cost:	$14 to cover transportation
Notes:	Students will need lunch money or a bag lunch.

Please return this permission slip by: _____

I give permission for my child,_____ , in room, _____

to attend the field trip to on_____   _____

from_____ to_____

Enclosed is $ _____ to cover the cost of the trip. (Exact cash or check made payable to the school.)

In case of an emergency, I give permission for my child to receive medical treatment. In case of such an emergency, please contact:

Name: _____ Phone:_____

Guardian signature:_____ Date: _____

2. Go to the File menu and select Save as Web Page. If you do not see the Save as Web Page option (and you are using Office 2000), your menu may look like the one shown here. Office 2000 has adaptive menus. The menu only shows the options that you have recently used. If you do not see the option you seek, click on the double down arrows located at the bottom of the menu and the menu will expand to show you all of the options.

3. Save your web page. You will notice that your document will have an .htm file extension instead of the normal PowerPoint .ppt extension.

IMPORTANT: When creating a Web Site, it is extremely important to stay organized. Keep all of your documents for your Web Site in a single folder to avoid confusion. Once your page is saved you can see what it would look like by going to the File menu and selecting **Web Page Preview.**

RESOURCES:

Helpful Resources:
Internet-based Project Links
PBS Teacher Source
Web quest Home Page
Kathy Schrock's guide for Educators

ASSESSMENT:

1. When saving your document, you will be prompted to enter a page title. What is a page title?
   a. The name of the document. When you attempt to locate this document again, you will need to look for the page title.
   b. The text that will appear in the title bar of the Web Page.

2. To create a New Folder within Explorer, select the "A" drive and click:
   a. FILE->NEW->FOLDER
   b. FILE->NEW->FILE
   c. START->NEW FILE
   d. START->PROGRAMS->NEW FOLDER

3. To open documents located on a floppy drive, click:
   a. FILE->OPEN and select "31/2 Floppy (A:)"
   b. FILE->OPEN and select "My Documents"
   c. FILE->OPEN AS WEB PAGE and select "My Webpage"
   d. FILE->OPEN and select "Compact Disk (D:)"

4. To save a document as a web page, click:
   a. FILE->SAVE
   b. FILE->SAVE AS WEB PAGE
   c. FILE->CONVERT AS WEB PAGE->SAVE
   d. FILE->INSERT HTML->SAVE

A Word document that you have saved as a Web Page will have the following file extension:
   1. doc
   2. pdf
   3. htm or html
   4. ppt

TITLE:	Improving Your Power Points by Adding Movies
SUBJECT:	Teacher Technology Skills Improvement
UNIT:	Power Point
OBJECTIVES:	Learners will add a movie to their portfolio created in PowerPoint.

PRE-REQUISITE KNOWLEDGE:

- PowerPoint
- Keyboarding Skills
- Ability to Navigate the Internet

MATERIALS NEEDED:

- Computer with access to the Internet
- Microsoft PowerPoint Software
- Movie Clip
- Printer for Printing Step by Step directions as needed

PROCESS

1. View the "Adding Movies" skill video located on the next page.
2. Follow the step-by-step directions in the "Hands-On" section to add a movie to your portfolio.
3. Upon watching the video/s, complete this lesson.

Adding a Movie to Your Presentation
Approximate length of project: 2 hours
Outcome: Portfolio with movie embedded

RESOURCES:

- http://office.microsoft.com/assistance/2000/pptmovies.aspx
  Assistance for Adding Movies to PowerPoint Presentation
- http://search.office.microsoft.com/assistance/producttask.aspx?p=PowerPoint
  General Help Using PowerPoint

HAND OUTS:

Have students create an academic portfolio using PowerPoint and include a movie clip (i.e. demonstrating a science experiment, reciting their poem, interviewing a parent or guardian, explaining a math problem, acting in a drama skit, saying a speech, debating or participating in extracurricular activities).

For practice
Complete the following tasks (A, B, C, and D):

A. Follow these steps **to insert a movie into your PowerPoint presentation:**

    1. Display the slide to which you want to add a movie.

    2. Click *Insert menu*, select *Movies and Sounds*.

    3. Click *Movie from File*, locate the folder that contains the file you want, and then double-click the file.

    4. When a message is displayed, does one of the following:

        a. to play the movie automatically when you go to the slide, click Yes **OR**

        b. To play the movie only when you click it, click no.

B. To set the **automatic rewind** after a movie plays (this will make your movie automatically return to the first frame and stops after playing once):

    1. On the slide, click the *movie*, right-click your mouse, and click *Edit Movie Object.*

    2. Then, Select the *Rewind* movie when done playing check box.

C. **To review your movie:**

    1. Select the normal view

    2. Display the slide

    3. Click *Slide Show* in the lower-left corner of the Microsoft PowerPoint window.

D. **To set your movie to loop** (the movie plays until you advance to the next slide):

    1. on the slide, right-click the *movie.*

    2. On the shortcut menu, click *Edit Movie Object.*

    3. Select the *Loop* until stopped check box.

ASSESSMENT:

Complete the following questions:

    1. Define "Movies". Give two examples of file formats and file extensions.

    2. You have inserted a movie into your PowerPoint presentation.

Describe how you would set the movie to rewind?

    3. The process for adding an animated GIF is the same as embedding a movie.
       TRUE OR FALSE?

    4. Microsoft PowerPoint does not maintain the proportions (locks the aspect ratio) of the movie as you drag.
       TRUE OR FALSE?

CHAPTER 6

INFUSING TECHNOLOGY DAILY IN THE CLASSROOM

In this chapter we will discuss and explore:

- *How dialog on current events provides an opportunity to explore history in context*
- *How to use technology to create a problem-based curriculum*
- *The Internet as a powerful tool for conducting research, and online field trips*
- *Examples of how technology can replace traditional methods in Science and Mathematics*

Thoughtful dialog on current events provides an opportunity to explore history in context. Many schools now offer newspaper subscriptions in the classroom. Some, such as the New York Times, offer educational web sites which reflect and expand on the news. Scarcely a day goes by without some headline event worthy of deep class discussion. The beauty of engaging students in conversations on current events is that they see the reason for exploring history. Mark Twain reportedly once said, "History may not repeat itself, but it sure rhymes a lot."

While world politics and global turmoil are always a topic for discussion, even lesser events merit exploration. For example, the recent decision by the recording industry to launch a flurry of lawsuits against the parents and grandparents of young people who are using the home computer to download MP3 files of recorded music is a topic of great interest to many students.

This topic is a great one for class discussion because it is relates to the lives of today's students, many of whom are familiar with Napster (http://www.napster.com), Limewire (http://www.limewire.com), Kazaa (http://www.kazaa.com), and other file sharing programs. The topic offers a variety of conversations ranging from ethics, to the ability of the recording industry to respond to the desire of individuals to acquire songs, not albums. Also the topic of how Apple Computers is trying to solve the above mentioned through their iTunes (http://www.apple.com/itunes) and iTunes store. Apple has gone so far as to offer free downloads in a popular food chain, with the purchase of a meal.

A past approach would be to just open the topic for conversation based purely on a scan of the morning news. This approach however is less likely to have long-term value than one which focuses on background research as a pre-requisite for classroom discussion. In fact, you can have it both ways by starting a class with a quick overview of opinions from students on the topic being explored (file sharing), followed by their in-depth study of the topic, and a follow-up discussion. In this follow-up discussion (held a day or two later), have the students note if their research reinforced their original thoughts, or caused them to re-evaluate their positions. This meta-cognitive task helps students understand the power of informed dialog as opposed to knee-jerk reactions. It makes them more thoughtful, better informed, and far more likely to develop lifelong skills in information assessment. And, note that the goal is not to have everyone hold the same opinion, but instead to be able to document and support whatever position they have taken on the topic.

Once you move beyond the knee-jerk phase, the role of technology in exploring current events can be tremendous. First, a quick online trip to any of the daily newspapers and weekly news magazines can yield the latest articles on the pending lawsuits. Students who want to create their own reports on the subject can "clip" graphs, images, or text from these online documents (being sure to cite all their references). There is now a subscription service (Zinio at www.zinio.com) that lets you download complete magazines to be read, searched, and archived on your own computer or tablet PC. Newspaper such as the New York Times through a subscription service sends the headlines to your e-mail account every day, and grants access to the full paper any time wanted. In addition to online versions of print journals, web-play news sources are also great to work with (www.news.com from CNET, for example).

A historical view of the topic of file sharing (or anything else for that matter) can be found using Grokker (www.groxis.com) to build a contextual map of the web on the topic. Some of the sites revealed through this Grokker map can highlight the technologies behind file sharing, sources of sharing software, appraisals of damage to the recording industry, and even rants against the way the recording industry treats the artists who record for them. This level of research can, in less than an hour, provide far greater breadth and depth than a day spent purely in a paper-based library.

During this phase of research, the student will gather plenty of data and turn some of it into information. The student still needs a greater understanding to deliver classroom conversation based on their knowledge or understanding. How does one move from data to understanding, especially in the context of classroom discussions of current events?

Part of the answer can be explained as this, it is one thing to know that something happened, but altogether something else to know why it happened. The shift from "what" knowledge to "why" knowledge can be facilitated through the use of visual concept mapping, like the software application program Inspiration (www.inspiration.com). With Inspiration a student builds a graphical map that starts with the event under discussion. Next, one layer down, the student explores the multiple causes for this event by asking "why did this event occur?" The process gets repeated as deeply as the student wants to go, with the goal of building understanding each step of the way. An example might be the starting event as the recording industry lawsuits. Why did these occur? One reason is because CD sales have dropped and the industry feels this is because of file downloads. At this point there are two obvious branches going even deeper. The first explores why the CD sales dropped (maybe it is because there are no compelling CD's being produced these days), and the second is why people are downloading individual songs without paying for them.

At this point, these two branches have branches of their own. For example, why are people downloading music without paying for it? Is it because the industry has steadfastly refused to listen to the desires of customers to purchase single songs online? This could lead to a branch exploring why Apple's iTunes became an instant hit, and so on.

Technologies such as Apple's iTunes which is available to anyone with a computer can facilitate thoughtful classroom conversations on current events. By making sure that students have both the tools and strategies in place to build a basis for informed dialogs, we can help our young people become better thinkers who know how to express their thoughts with conviction and clarity.

Infusing Technology to Create a Problem-Based Curriculum

Technology can be used to create a problem-based curriculum. Project-based learning in which the curricular objectives are met through student exploration of challenging problems is one educational area where technology can be of tremendous help.

The varied roles of technology become clear when students begin working on problem-based curriculum. For example, if students are placed in teams to craft and develop projects, they need project management and documentation tools. Students must also demonstrate cooperative learning with the team mates. Group brainstorming sessions using idea- or concept-mapping technology like Inspiration can be a critical part of this process. On a simple level, students can each create their own lists of ideas and then e-mail their files to the rest of their group (critical when students share a project across school or classroom boundaries). As the projects develop, creative tools of all kinds come into play. This provides the opportunity for each individual in a group to focus on the expressive forms most natural to him or her.

I once stumbled across a lesson plan on the internet over the history of a literary super-hero. This project started with an internet search on the topic, migrate to a reading of Gil-gamesh, involving sidebar explorations into the concept of heroism, digress into a series of short student created video interviews with peers on "heroes in our lives", and quickly expand to reveal a topic so vast it could easily fill a lifetime of research. Students learned the digital media skill of digital video creation during this project.

While the informational resources of the web, physical libraries and personal contacts are incredibly large, this very vastness can be overwhelming. Contrast this scenario with the traditional textbook/lecture approach in which the information is pre-distilled to fit the time allotted. In the world of project-based learning (especially when technology is involved), the issue is not the gathering of information, but rather pruning the informational branches to reveal a tractable project that is compelling and achievable in the allotted time.

It is in this area of the project where the teacher plays a critical role. Students can find far more raw information on any topic than can be comprehended or used in a single proj-ect. Again, this is where tools like Inspiration or storyboarding their ideas come in handy. If students map out the "tree" delineating their research, they will be able to see which branches can be pruned to leave a meaningful (if more narrowly defined) topic.

In a History project on Italy, a student can design a fashion Spring Collection for 1634. In order to design these dresses, the student would need to know something about the general history of the time, especially how women were expected to dress in public. An example of what a student may find is that the Italian and Dutch women of the Northeast had much greater freedom than the Portuguese women. Also the need to explore what dyes and fabrics would have been used at the time, which means studying the history of dye chemistry and researching whether quality fabric was made in Italy at the time, or was imported from else-where. This seemingly limited project requires a tremendous amount of historical research.

While the Internet is one powerful tool for conducting research, field trips (when possi-ble) are of incredible value. Here the student becomes a researcher, and technological tools to document the research are of great value. Digital cameras, laptop computers, handheld computers, tablet PC's, sound recording equipment and various measuring tools (ranging from digital microscopes to probeware for measuring temperature, pH or other physical and chemical properties) can be of tremendous value. The critical factors here are durabil-ity and ease of use. Generally, this means using very simple equipment. Ease of use, while always important, is critical in the field. The tool should be user friendly, do its job trans-parently, and save its work automatically.

Once students are ready to create a report on their project, technology takes on a new role. Instead of being used to research a topic, technology now helps document it. In contrast to the paper-based reporting methods of the past, a variety of expressive media can be used to convey the results of this work. Teachers have a special challenge here. First, the expressive modalities need to fit the essence of the project, and, second, they need to be flexible enough to communicate the results of the work to a large audience of peers.

A project on mathematics might be filled with equations. But, without some companion graphics to illustrate these equations, the ideas behind the project might be lost. A project on the treatment of African Americans through a study of the Blues would certainly include some musical examples, but would also benefit from historical diaries, photographs, and drawings. Unless educators have learned how to assess multimedia projects, they may score some work too low and other work too highly. Rubric assessment is the assessment of choice. Rubistar (http://www.rubistar.com) is a free online source for creating rubrics.

From the student perspective, various techniques may come under the leadership of certain students. The graphic designer might be involved with image design, Web page layout and the navigational flow of multimedia. Access to the relevant software (Flash for animations, illustration software, page layout tools, etc.) is essential. This aspect of the project benefits from strong technical support, as well as an understanding of the nature of graphic design. The sound engineer would take responsibility for audio recording and editing, and work with the film person in support of any video clips used in the final project. The wordsmith would craft and edit the text, and might insure that all the elements of the final story are put together in a cohesive manner.

While this level of work appears distressing, students are generally eager to share their ideas with others, and look forward to this creative part of the project. When a single project is shared among students from different buildings or classrooms, peer-to-peer tools like Groove (http://www.groove.net/home/index.cfm) and Journal Zone (http://www.microworlds.com/jz_solutions/) most helpful.

The role of technology in project-based learning is vast, but the starting point for effective use of technology in this area requires a deep commitment from the teachers to the idea that students can gain a deep understanding of a topic through the exploration of their own ideas.

CHAPTER 7

INFUSION MADE QUICK AND EASY

In this chapter we will discuss and explore:

- *20 Quick and Easy Ways to Seamlessly Integrate Technology Daily and Weekly*

So are you getting anxious to integrate technology into your curriculum, but are intimidated by the time and tech skills necessary to plan technology activities or participate in technology projects? Here are 20 quick and easy ways in which you can seamlessly integrate technology into your daily and weekly classroom routines. Be sure to bookmark the recommended sites, so you can find them easily and use them regularly.

20 Quick and Easy Ways to Seamlessly Integrate Technology Daily and Weekly

1. **Access an online weather forecast**
   Most elementary grade teachers begin each school day with a discussion of the date and local weather. Why not take an extra minute to visit a site such as UM Weather (http://cirrus.sprl.umich.edu/wxnet/), The Weather Channel (http://www.weather.com/), or USA Today Weather (http://asp.usatoday.com/weather/weatherfront.aspx), to find out what the rest of the day might bring? If you have a few extra minutes, check out weather in other parts of the country as well.

2. **Include URLs in your monthly calendar**
   Each month, Education World (http://www.education-world.com/) provides a printable coloring calendar for classroom use. Before distributing copies of the calendar to your students, add the URLS of a few sites that will add to their understanding of the month's events -- and encourage them to visit those sites. The October calendar, for example, might offer links to sites about Christopher Columbus, daylight savings time, and Halloween. (A kid-friendly search engine

such as Yahooligans (http://yahooligans.yahoo.com/) will help you locate appropriate sites. Alternatively, students can find the sites themselves as they complete a Months of the Year Project.

3. **Access online weather forecasts in French, German, or Spanish**
Begin foreign language classes with a discussion of the day's weather. The Weather Channel (http://www.weather.com/) provides weather information for Brazil, Germany, France, and Latin America in the native language of each country.

4. **Challenge students with online mathematics problems**
Add a daily or weekly mathematics challenge to your seatwork assignments, math lessons, or extra credit activities. The Math Forum's (http://mathforum. org/), Math Problem of the Week offers word problems in five categories -- math fundamentals, pre-algebra, algebra, geometry, and pre-calculus. The AIMS Puzzle Corner (http://www.aimsedu.org/Puzzle/) Math Challenge of the Month provides a monthly math-related puzzle that is appropriate for students in upper elementary grades and middle school. Most include printable worksheets. Aunty Math's (www. dupagechildrensmuseum.org/aunty) Math Challenges for K-5 Learners offers biweekly word problems for younger students, while high school students will enjoy the news-related math problems at Math Counts (http://www.mathcounts. org/), as well as Mike's Puzzle of the Week (http://www.iwr.uni-heidelberg.de/ ~Michael.Winckler/PU/PotW.html). Most of the sites listed also include extensive archives. If you teach grades 3-8, extend your students' online math experience and encourage them to match wits with students around the world by participating in the Abacus International Math Challenge (http://www.gcschool.org/pages/ program/Abacus.html).

5. **Provide a URL in place of a quote**
Do you write a quote on the chalkboard each day, for students to reflect on and discuss? Instead of writing out the quote, provide students with the URL and have them locate the day's quote themselves. Quote of the Day (http://www. educationworld.com/a_curr/archives/quote.shtml), Quotes of the Day (http://www. quotationspage.com/qotd.html), and Quote a Day (http://www.quoteaday.com/) are all excellent sources of funny, inspirational, or thought-provoking quotes.

6. **Introduce a word of the day**
Extend students' vocabulary by including an online word of the day in opening activities, seatwork assignments, or language arts lessons. The Daily Buzzword at Word Central (http://www.wordcentral.com/) provides a word of the day and related activity appropriate for upper elementary students. Vocabulary Builder

(http://www.superkids.com/aweb/tools/words/wod.shtml), offers words and definitions for students in grades 4-6 and grades 6-9. The words and definitions at A Word a Day (http://www.wordsmith.org/words/today.html) and Word of the Day (http://www.dictionary.com/wordoftheday) are best for students in middle and high school. In addition, students in grades K-8 can safely extend their online experience by submitting phony definitions to Fake Out (http://www.eduplace.com/fakeout).

7. Keep them spelling

Spelling is not a subject that should die in elementary school. Prove it to your middle and high school students by adding spelling to language arts lessons or extra credit assignments. Each week, Carolyn's Corner (http://spellingbee.com/cctoc.shtml) offers a new list of "Paideia Words of the Week;" from the study booklet for the Scripps Howard National Spelling Bee. Invite your students to compete with the nation's best spellers!

8. Make history real

For many kids, history is only a subject in a book; one that is unrelated to real people, real events, or today's news. Personalize history lessons for those students by beginning each history lesson with a quick visit to Today in History (http://www.usatoday.com/life/lhistory.htm) or This Day in History (http://www.historychannel.com/today).

9. Utilize online work sheets

Are you worn out from trying to come up with new and creative seatwork assignments day after day after day? Make life easier on yourself by including a few online worksheets. Each week, Education World provides an original printable Scavenger Hunt (http://www.educationworld.com/a_lesson/archives/hunt.shtml) and a Writing Bug (http://www.educationworld.com/a_lesson/writing_bug/archives/writing_bug.shtml) creative writing activity. In addition, Teach-nology (http://worksheets.teach-nology.com/) offers lots of work sheets in a variety of curriculum areas. Or, add to the variety of your seatwork assignments by having students complete a weekly WebQuest (http://www.educationworld.com/a_tech/archives/webquest.shtml).

10. Offer online SAT practice

College-bound high school students always can benefit from additional PSAT and SAT practice. Super Kids provides a PSAT and SAT Vocabulary Builder (http://www.superkids.com/aweb/tools/words/sat), in the form of a word of the day.

11. Beef up your history lessons

Primary source materials add interest to any history lessons, e.g. reading Thomas Jefferson's notes on the U.S. Constitution provides insights into U.S. history that a mere reading of the Constitution cannot. When planning U.S. history lessons, visit the Library of Congress's American Memory Collections (http://lcweb2.loc.gov/) search engine to locate primary source material for whatever topic you are tackling. Encourage students to include primary source materials in their history papers as well.

12. Provide online reading comprehension practice

Add a fun reading comprehension activity to your students' language arts curriculum. Each month, The Comenius Group provides a new Fluency Through Fables (http://www.er.uqam.ca/nobel/r21270/NOVA_SCOTIA/comenius_fables.htm) lesson. Designed for students of English as a second language, the activity is appropriate for English speaking students in elementary and middle school as well. The lesson includes a brief fable and four categories of related activities: vocabulary matching exercises, vocabulary completion exercises, multiple choice comprehension exercises, and written discussion exercises.

13. Incorporate online news sources into discussions of current events

Do not limit students' current events contributions to print newspapers; encourage them to search online media as well. CNN (http://www.cnn.com/) and MSNBC (http://www.msnbc.com/news/default.asp?0ct=-34o) are excellent places to start looking for national and international news. Or check out Online Newspapers (http://www.onlinenewspapers.com/) to find your local newspaper online. The Internet Public Library (http://www.ipl.org/div/news) also provides links to local news sources by country and, for the United States, by state.

14. Make the news a learning tool

Help students better understand current events and connect today's news to their own lives by encouraging them to further explore the issues of the day. The Why Files (http://whyfiles.org/), for example, uses news and current events as the basis for science, health, and technology lessons. What caused the tornado that devastated the Midwest or the hurricane that hit Florida? How does war affect those living in battle zones? What vote-counting technique is most accurate? The Why Files will explain it all. How Stuff Works (http://www.howstuffworks.com/index.htm) also is an extensive site with information on a vast number of topics. Today's students, for example, might want to learn How Stinger Missiles Work (http://www.howstuffworks.com/stinger.htm), How Stem Cells Work (http://

science.howstuffworks.com/stem-cell.htm), or How Hybrid Cars Work (http://auto.howstuffworks.com/hybrid-car.htm).

15. Spice up your grammar lessons

Explore Daily Grammar's Lesson Archive (http://www.dailygrammar.com/archive.shtml) to find a new grammar lesson every day. The site features nearly 450 lessons on topics ranging from adjectives and apostrophes to prepositional phrases and verbs!

16. Make science a daily event

With the current emphasis on reading and math in schools, getting in a daily -- or even weekly -- science lesson can be difficult. If you're having trouble finding time for a more formal science lesson, take a minute to discuss NASA's Astronomy Picture of the Day (http://antwrp.gsfc.nasa.gov/apod/astropix.html) or Goddard Space Center's Earth Science Picture of the Day (http://epod.usra.edu/), both of which include a brief explanation of the day's photo. You might also briefly discuss a scientist or a scientific event from Today in Science History (http://todayinsci.tripod.com/) or explore a Science Question of the Week (http://www.gsfc.nasa.gov/science.html).

17. Sign up for a science experiment of the week

If you have the time for the science lesson, but not enough time to research and find a steady supply of really engaging science experiments, sign up for a science Experiment of the Week (http://www.krampf.com/news.html). Each week, a new science experiment will be e-mailed to you.

18. Make geography a daily event

For most kids, geography has something to do with maps -- and maps are boring! Extend students' geography awareness by challenging them to answer the five daily questions posed at GeoBee Challenge (http://www.nationalgeographic.com/geobee). The questions are taken from the National Geographic Geography Bee. Maybe your students will get good enough to compete in this year's event! Looking for a quicker lesson? Find the distance between any two cities in the world at How Far Is It? (http://www.indo.com/distance) By the way, National Geographic's Map Machine (http://plasma.nationalgeographic.com/mapmachine) can even make maps fun!

19. Keep them guessing!

It is Friday afternoon and most students have their eyes on the clock and their minds on a weekend of freedom. If you have access to enough computers so that students can work individually or in small groups, try to keep the learning going with some stimulating online games. Each week, Houghton Mifflin poses new, primarily math-related Brain Teasers (http://www.eduplace.com/math/brain/index. html) at three different grade levels: 3–4, 5–6, and 7–8. Solving the problems at Mystery Net (http://www.mysterynet.com/) generally demands more logic than Math. That site's features include Get-a-Clue, a daily mystery appropriate for younger students; See-n-Solve, a weekly mystery featuring USA TV's Detective Monk; and Solve-it! a monthly mystery in which students read a mystery and then solve the crime. The latter two activities are best for older students. Or, simply reward students for a week of hard work by allowing them a few minutes to play some of the online Logic Games at Super Kids (http://www.superkids.com/aweb/tools/logic). Games include Battleship, checkers, tic-tac-toe, Breakout, and more.

20. Send them away with a smile

Finally, end a successful week with Education World's Joke of the Day! (http://www.educationworld.com/a_curr/archives/joke.shtml)

CHAPTER 8

Infusing With the Web

In this chapter, we will discuss and explore:

- *Teaching and learning using the Web*
- *Online search skills*
- *Internet-based activity examples*
- *Examples of searches on various topics for all grade levels*

Online research not only infuses technology, but also aids in building critical thinking skills. One challenge of the Internet (and the Web in particular) is that information is almost too easy to find. What I mean by this is that a search on just about any domain of inquiry results in thousands of responses, some of which are probably quite useful. Faced with 23,574 responses to a search topic, a student researcher quickly encounters an overwhelming amount of hits. The student looks at the first page of search results, chooses one or two references that appear to be relevant, and then uses these few sites as the foundation for the topic that started.

A guided search helps in the learning process when requiring students to search the web. A guided search can be delivered in different formats. One source could be a handout giving the students web address which you have pre-approved. Another option could be a teacher created homepage with hyperlinks of similar web addresses as above. Another option that many schools are using is web search engines such as www.ala.org which is designed for education.

When searching the web students should focus on these three areas: finding information or data, determining its relevance, and determining its accuracy. These skills are as relevant offline as on, and are critical for students to have as we move away from textbook-supported, "teaching as telling" instruction.

How do you teach your students the best way to search the Internet? How do you help them determine if the Internet is even the place they should be searching? What can students do ahead of time to make their online searching more productive? What is the difference between a search engine and a directory? How are they similar/different? When should they start with a search engine? When should they start with a directory? How about a meta-search tool? What about the information in the "invisible Web"? What is the appropriate age for students to begin true Internet searching? What can teachers do to help? What about searching for pictures and MP3s? Who was George Boole and how did he play a role in searching on the Internet over one hundred years after his death?

Online searching is a skill that will be needed to survive in our information-rich society. With the information rapidly outpacing any one person's ability to keep up with it, we need to teach our students how to find what they need when they need it. Each of the search engines has differing features, but with a few simple rules under their belts, students can be comfortable using any of them when looking for information.

This discussion will center on strategies for helping students learn to think about and implement their search plan, and offer some ideas, tips and tricks (as well as resources) to support the teaching of these skills. Some of the major search engines and directories will be discussed (including Google (http://www.google.com), AltaVista (http://www.altavista.com), HotBot (http://www.hotbot.com, Vivisimo (www.vivisimo.com) and Yahoo (http://www.yahoo.com) as well as an open discussion of which ones are the favorites of the group and why.

The differences between search engines and directories will be explained as well as strategies for helping students narrow down their search before ever going online. The best ways of creating search strings and how to limit or broaden the number of items after the initial query will be covered in the discussion. The concept of relevancy rankings of the search results and related searches will be discussed too.

A bit of the discussion will cover fair use and the ability to find (and use) images and sound recordings, in addition to text, and the ethical treatment of that information by teaching proper bibliographic citation formats.

Searching is one of those skills that needs to be taught, just as library media specialists used to teach students how to use the card catalog (and now teach how to use the online catalog) to locate resources. Databases of information, previously offered on local computers and local networks, are now offered on the Web, and students need to be taught the process skills needed to use them effectively.

The simple fact is that we cannot expect students to develop these skills on their own, no matter how comfortable they are with the Internet. The very technology that provides us with tools to retrieve excessive amounts of data on virtually any topic can also overwhelm us in content—just as it can move us closer to our resesarch goals, it can also move us away from them. Faced with a staggering number of potential "hits," it is easy to see why many students simply invoke the incremental law of ignorance and stop after finding one or two seemingly relevant results.

For the solution, we as educators first need to teach basic research skills to all our students. They will not develop them on their own. Second, we need to constantly look for tools that can help bring context to our searches.

The topic of data visualization is gaining increased attention as the Web continues to explode in size. One company who has contributed significantly to this effort is Groxis (http://www.groxis.com), creators of Grokker, a tool that brings context to Web searches. Grokker is not a search engine. Instead it uses existing search engines to conduct a search on any topic you wish. As the search proceeds, results are placed on a map consisting of a large circle representing the search topic. This circle contains smaller circles named after categories or subcategories into which identified sites are automatically placed. Furthermore, maps can be saved and explored offline (important in schools where bandwidth is an issue). When the user clicks on a site icon, a "details" view provides a summary of the content of the site. Once online again, double-clicking on the site opens it in the browser of your choice.

Today the majority of America's teens with Internet access at home can check out "school-taught" information from the leisure of their own bedrooms. Along with everything else on their plates, today's educators also need to teach students how to evaluate and organize the vast quantities of information they find on the Web.

It is common to see students start out a search on some topic in a fairly organized manner, and then quickly move to the domain of rapid mouse-clicks, zipping from site to site in the elusive hope that the needed information will spontaneously appear. Unfortunately, this almost never happens. Furthermore, while some search engines are better for some topics than others, there is no one search tool that captures all the pertinent sites without gathering lots of irrelevant sites at the same time. The sheer quantity of sites returned for any search staggers the imagination. The most unknowable topic can result in a search list of over a thousand sites, and it is common to get twenty thousand or more responses to a fairly well-crafted query on a popular topic. Librarians have worked hard for generations to develop skills to navigate vast informational spaces.

The organization of information is challenged by both the vast quantity of information available, and the rapid growth of the Web. It is no wonder that many students opt for a few quick references to build their case, rather than perform a careful analysis of the quality of various information services.

As educators, we can do a lot to help. First, we should show students those sites we know to be valuable. In some cases these are easy to find. NASA (http://www.nasa.gov)

provides a good starting point for astronomy and space science. NOAA (http://www.noaa. gov) provides a great place to explore weather. The Library of Congress (http://www.loc. gov), National Archives (http://www.archives.gov), and Smithsonian Institution (http:// www.si.edu) provides wonderful resources on American history. All of these sites are ad-free, and filled with well-documented material worthy of any student's attention. In fact, the U.S. Department of Education provides a clearinghouse of sites with wonderful educational content. It is called the FREE site and is located at http://www.ed.gov/free. This site is updated frequently, and provides links to well-supported resources on virtually any academic topic likely to be covered in the K-12 domain. In terms of finding information, a combination of sites such as FREE and searches through engines like Google are likely to capture a lot of relevant information. What remains to determine is the accuracy of what was found.

The skills of finding, organizing, and evaluating information from the Internet and any other source, for that matter, are essential for any of us living in these chaotic times. In today's global environment, these skills are considered to be as essential as literacy and numeracy.

There are other sites on the Internet that easily lend themselves to classroom integration. A favorite of mine, Refdesk.com (http://www.refdesk.com), has a Site of the Day section containing a wealth of useful and interesting Web sites. An archive also is available. Other useful sections of the site include a Thought of the Day, Word of the Day, and Current Events. All those sections provide a wealth of research and discussion opportunities.

Refdesk also has links to newspapers, listed by state and country. Foreign language classes can access online news articles in the language studied, dictionary and thesaurus links also are easily accessible. Translation links are available, too -- all in one place, on one page. If a student or teacher needs a starting page to find resources, I definitely recommend this site.

The Internet is loaded with activities for all types of classes. You can integrate internet-based activities into an astronomy class, biology class, and or integrated science class. Activities might include current readings on topics in the field, or activities that students can do. You can give each student an e-mail account and post articles to your Web site. Students can respond individually, and then you can post their responses and have students respond to one another's postings.

Internet-based activity examples for all grade levels

- Science teacher can have students use the Internet to learn about planets, hurricanes, earthquakes. Locate appropriate sites and then create a Web page for students to use. This is called guided research. You can display the Internet on a big screen in the one computer classroom. Students can answer questions. Find a teacher to buddy up with. As time goes by, you will become more confident and comfortable with the technology (and the technology will become more reliable too).

- High school history, students study Civil War battles. The teacher can assign groups different battles, the students can research their assigned battles, collect pictures, and then give a guided tour of the battlefield, telling what happened there.

- Internet scavenger hunts are another way to integrate technology into almost any topic or subject area. Have older students create online scavenger hunts for younger students. It improves your older students' research and typing skills, and provides lower grade teachers with extra activities for their students.

- Puzzlemaker (http://www.puzzlemaker.com) can be used by teachers and students alike to develop crossword puzzles, word searches, mazes, cryptograms, and more based on curriculum vocabulary and concepts.

- Brainbooster (http://www.brainbooster.com) offers many activities that can be used to help students develop higher level thinking skills.

- ePals (http://www.epals.com) allows students to contact class or individual partners, work on writing skills, exchange weather information, compare communities, and make new friends around the world via e-mail.

- Blogging is similar to an online diary; it provides a quick and easy way for teachers and students to share work, opinions, ideas, and information. Blogging can be used with 5- and 6-year-olds, such as those at BSA Infant School; with high school students, like the literature students at New Jersey's Hunterdon Central Regional High School; and with elementary age students, such as those at Portland, Oregon's Buckman Arts Magnet Elementary School. For more information about blogging, visit the Educational Bloggers Network (http://www. ebn.weblogger.com).

- Check the daily weather for the weather in states or countries students are studying in social studies; add a math connection by using a graphing program to chart temperatures, precipitation, or storms, and then compare the results to weather in your area.

- Take virtual field trips to places connected to people or places students are learning about; for example, Thomas Jefferson's Monticello, the Great Wall of China, Alaska, or Appomattox.

- The Library of Congress (http://www.loc.gov) has wonderful collections of music (both sound files and sheet music) that can help your music department contribute to a study American History.

INTERNET RESEARCH

ENGLISH/LANGUAGE ARTS

TITLE: Online Literature / English Resources
SUBJECT: English/Language Arts
UNIT: Internet

OVERVIEW: Students will evaluate online Literature / English resources using the website list provided and/or by adding additional websites they find. For each category, students will evaluate one website.

1. Online magazines and newspapers
2. References
3. Online help
4. Encyclopedias
5. Search engines
6. National information websites

PREREQUISITE KNOWLEDGE: Ability to navigate the web and use a word processor.

TEACHER PREP TIME: minimal
Preview websites listed in Resources and overview of evaluating web resources.

ESTIMATED CLASSROOM TIME: 1 week

DELIVERABLES: Students will evaluate and summarize Literature / English web resources.

EVALUATION / GRADING: Students will be evaluated using a checklist.

Variations on a Theme

Running short on time? Have students work in teams of six, each member evaluating one category resource.

Want to take this another step? Have students create a website listing their recommended and evaluated sites. Include annotation, and post on school website (with permission).

Only one computer in the classroom? Allow students to research in teams. Have student's research web resources and prepare summaries in groups.

Teacher Tips:
- Encourage students to recommend and search for their own recommended resources.
- Spend a class reviewing the criteria for evaluating websites.
- Choose one site and have the class evaluate it using the criteria provided. Add additional criteria if desired.
- Collect all final evaluations and summarize the results (or have students compile the summary).
- Distribute a paper or electronic copy to the class for reference.
- Share the resource list with other teachers, students and classes.

MISSION: You will research and evaluate online Literature / English resources.
- Where can you find a dictionary or thesaurus online?
- Where can you collect research?
- Where can you access an electronic encyclopedia or newspaper?
- You will look at Internet resources in the following categories: online magazines and newspapers, references, online help, encyclopedias, search engines, national information websites, etc.

RESOURCES: A computer with Internet access and word processor is needed. These websites will help you answer the questions provided in *Steps*. Feel free to search the Internet for other related sites or include your favorite online Literature / English resource.

Literature / English Resources on the Web

Newspapers and Magazines Online
- The New York Times: On the Web
  http://www.nytimes.com/
  (Free subscription required)
- National Post (Canadian)
  http://www.nationalpost.com/home/
- Newslink (American sources)
  http://newslink.org/
- Guardian Unlimited (British News)
  http://www.guardian.co.uk/
- Time - American and World News
  http://www.time.com/time/
- Macleans - Canadian and World News
  http://www.macleans.ca/

References
- Dictionary
  http://www.dictionary.com
- Thesaurus
  http://www.thesaurus.com
- APA - American Psychological Association
  http://www.apastyle.org/elecref.html
- Citation Styles
  http://www.bedfordstmartins.com/online/citex.html

Online Help
- InfoPlease
  http://www.infoplease.com/
- Ask Jeeves
  http://www.askjeeves.com
- About.com Homework Help
  http://about.com/homework/
  (links to abundant resources)

Encyclopedias
- Encyclopedia.com
  http://www.encyclopedia.com
- Encyclopedia Smithsonian
  http://www.si.edu/resource/faq/start.htm
- TechEncyclopedia
  http://www.techweb.com/encyclopedia/

Search Engines
- Google
  http://www.google.com
- Excite
  http://www.excite.com
- Lycos
  http://www.lycos.com
- Yahoo
  http://www.yahoo.com

National Information Websites
- BBC - British Mega Information Website
  http://www.bbc.co.uk/

- CNN (North America, Europe or Asia)
  http://www.cnn.com/
- CBC - Canadian On-Line Information
  http://www.cbc.ca/

STEPS:

1. Begin by visiting the websites listed in *Resources,* find additional websites or add your favorite related websites.
2. **Choose one website for each of the following categories:**
   - online magazines and newspapers
   - references
   - online help
   - encyclopedias
   - search engines
   - national news websites
3. Create a spreadsheet/ table to help arrange your websites.

PRODUCT: You will now prepare a review for each of the Literature / English resource websites you chose in *Steps*

1. Answer the following questions for each website reviewed (6 in total).
2. The following checklist / questions will help you with your evaluation. Include answers to these questions for each site evaluated. Teacher Technology Skills Improvement Write your website evaluations in a word processor.
3. Answer the following questions in your evaluation.
   - Is it clear who is responsible for the contents on the page?
   - Is there a last updated date on the page?
   - Is the website easy to navigate (e.g. tabs and menus)?
   - Do images add to the understanding of website content?
   - Is interactivity available?
   - Is the site helpful? Why or why not?
   - Is there any advertising on the page? (Was it distracting or inappropriate?)
4. Your suggestions, and those of your classmates, will be collected to provide an overview of Internet resources.
5. This list of online English resources can be used throughout the year, and shared with other classes.
6. Write your reviews in a word processor.

EVALUATION: The following checklist will be used to mark your website evaluations.

Checklist (out of /80)
Online Literature / English Resources Summary
/5   Introduction
/60   Evaluation of Resources
/10   Summary / Conclusion
/5   Final Product

ENGLISH / LANGUAGE ARTS

TITLE: Online Research and Credibility
SUBJECT: English/Language Arts
UNIT: Internet

DESCRIPTION: The biggest obstacle in doing research online is the credibility of sources. In this learning resource, students will learn that it is their responsibility to check the credibility of every website they use for research purposes. This learning resource will explain the importance of verifying the credibility of a website, and provide students with important strategies for dealing with suspicious websites.

After completing this learning resource, you will be equipped with the tools to conduct accurate research online.

OBJECTIVES:
Students will:
* Learn strategies for determining the credibility of websites
* Learn what information to analyze on a website when checking credibility

PREREQUISITE KNOWLEDGE: Ability to navigate the Internet and keyboarding skills.

TEACHER PREP TIME: Approximately 30 minutes
Preview links in *Resources* and watch the corresponding video.

EVALUATION / GRADING:
Assessment will be based on the creation of an informative pamphlet and the evaluation of five websites.

GENERAL INFORMATION: Unfortunately anyone can produce a website expressing their personal beliefs whether they are reliable sources or not. This is why it is your responsibility to check the credibility of every website you use for research purposes. This learning resource will not only explain the importance of verifying the credibility of a website, but it will also provide you with important strategies for dealing with suspicious websites. After completing this learning resource, you will be equipped with the tools to conduct accurate research online.

RESOURCES: Use the following web links to complete the tasks in The *Assessment* section and for future reference.

- http://www.media-awareness.ca/english/resources/special_initiatives/wa_resources/wa_shared/tipsheets/quick_tips_authenticating.cfm
  Media Awareness Network - Authenticating Information Online

- http://www.media-awareness.ca/english/resources/special_initiatives/wa_resources/wa_shared/tipsheets/deconstructing_webpages.cfm
  Media Awareness Network – Deconstructing Web Pages

- http://www.media-awareness.ca/english/resources/special_initiatives/wa_resources/wa_shared/tipsheets/5Ws_of_cyberspace.cfm
  Media Awareness Network - 5 W's of Checking Online Credibility

ASSESSMENT: Complete tasks below and submit your answers when finished. You may wish to use some of the resources found on the previous page. Using the websites in *Resources* and a word processor application, develop an informative pamphlet educating first time Internet users on checking the credibility of a website. Follow the directions below and attach your work when complete:

1. Choose a topic to research on the Internet (i.e. Diabetes).
2. Choose four websites addressing the topic you choose.
3. Check the credibility of each of the four websites.
4. Write a paragraph evaluating the credibility of each website.

Keep in mind the following questions:

- Does the site address the specific topic you have chosen?
- What is the purpose of the site?
- Who is responsible for the site?
- Does it provide you with more information than you can find using an encyclopedia?
- Is the source of the site authoritative or does it provides you with questionable information for research purposes?
- Are you able to determine if your website is a credible source?

INTEGRATED UNIT

TITLE: Search Engines and Their Uses
SUBJECT: All
UNIT: Internet

DESCRIPTION: Students will explore Internet search engines. Topics include: how search engines work and various types / brands of search engines. Understanding will be demonstrated in *Assessment* through applied questions/answers.

OBJECTIVES:

- learn how search engines work
- experiment with different search engines
- learn how to efficiently search for information using the Internet

PREREQUISITE KNOWLEDGE:
Ability to navigate the Internet and keyboarding skills.

TEACHER PREP TIME: Approximately 30 minutes

EVALUATION / GRADING:
Questions in *Steps* /26

RESOURCES:

- http://www.yahoo.com
  Yahoo – Search Engine
- http://www.google.com
  Google – Search Engine
- http://www.askjeeves.com
  Ask Jeeves - Search Engine

STEPS:

1. Look at the following websites and take notes on each search engine.
2. Collect helpful tips and instructions on how to search the Internet.
   - Review of Google
     http://www.searchengineshowdown.com/features/google/review.html
   - What's different about Google?
     http://www.lib.berkeley.edu/TeachingLib/Guides/Internet/Google.html

- Review of Yahoo
  http://searchengineshowdown.com/dir/yahoo/review.html
- Guide on AskJeeves
  http://www.submitcorner.com/Guide/SE/askjeeves.shtml
- Information on Ask Jeeves
  http://static.wc.ask.com/docs/about/policy.html
- How Stuff Works - How Search Engines Work
  http://www.howstuffworks.com/search-engine.html

ASSESSMENT:

1. In your own words, describe how Internet search engines work. Describe unique characteristics of each search engine discussed. (Yahoo, Google and AskJeeves)

2. What new information did you learn about Internet search engines?

3. Using Yahoo, Google and AskJeeves, type your name into the search field. What results were shown?

4. What is your favorite search engine? Why?

CHAPTER 9

INFUSING WITH POWERPOINT

In this chapter we will discuss and explore:
- *How Power Point can make a powerful impression for students and teachers*
- *How to assess Power Point Projects*
- *Case Study: Biography on an Influential Writer*
- *Case Study: Book Reviews Using Power Point*
- *Case Study: Language Arts Debate Over Censorship*
- *Case Study: Trigonometry Project with Power Point*
- *Case Study: Biography of an Influential Writer*

PowerPoint is another technology tool that is exceptionally easy to use in the class room. PowerPoint is a high-powered software tool used for presenting information in a dynamic slide show format. Text, charts, graphs, sound effects and video are just some of the elements PowerPoint can incorporate into your presentations with ease. Whether it is a classroom lesson, a parents' group meeting, a teachers' seminar or an unattended kiosk at the Science Fair, PowerPoint shows you how to make a powerful impression on your audience.

If a teacher has experience, presentation skills also can be emphasized. Besides standard presentations, such as slide shows, projects may be presented in an interactive way, using a game show format, for example, "Millionaire Muslim Style," using a popular game show format to present facts about the Muslim religion. This is a creative and informative way that everyone can learn information.

Have students use PowerPoint to accompany oral reports on curricular topics. Perhaps the best integrated project I witnessed was 8th graders looking at World War II posters on the Internet. Students analyzed the posters and related them to the history of that time. I modeled this using one poster, and then students picked two or three posters to focus on and used the Internet to research their posters. A couple of students assisted me (or did I assist them?) putting the posters into PowerPoint. In a Social Studies class, groups of students who had focused on a particular poster discussed their thoughts. Then, each group presented its findings to the class, projecting the PowerPoint images up on the screen. The result was a lively and thoughtful discussion between the reporting groups and the rest of the class.

One of my favorite online tutorial sites for young audiences is the Power Point in the Classroom website. (http://www.actden.com/pp/) This website demonstrates how to create a presentation from the beginning to the end. Prepare your students for creating a multimedia presentation by having them go to this website for this computer aided instruction.

Today in History is a fun lesson where students research an event that happened on a particular day in history and then create a 10–15 slide presentation about it. They find graphics online or create their own. Most students incorporate sound effects in their presentations as well. One of the best ones was about the St. Valentine's Day massacre with Al Capone.

Power Point can also be used during creative writing classes. For example, in a Visual Poetry activity, students can read a favorite poem and create a PowerPoint presentation depicting a visual interpretation of the images in the poem. In addition, students could also write and illustrate children's stories.

For older students, they can create resume-style presentations pictures of them working at their job sites included.

In speech class, students can create slide shows to accompany their oral presentations. PowerPoint is not just for students. It works well in the classroom in a number of ways.

- Present information or instruction to an entire class.
- Create graphically enhanced information and instructions for the learning centers.
- Create tutorials, reviews, or quizzes for individual students.
- Display student work and curriculum materials or accompany teacher presentations at parent open houses or technology fairs.

You can set PowerPoint presentations to run automatically during such events, providing a slide show of classroom activities and events as parents tour your classroom or school. Encourage them to start with short presentations that contain only a few slides. Remind them to keep the text and graphic images simple. A plan never hurts either. Project-Based Learning with multimedia provides a workable outline for planning and completing multimedia projects. Advise students to follow the guidelines below:

- Plan the projects. Identify goals and content; determine overall project length and progress checkpoints; determine project activities.

- Prepare the information. Complete research and/or activity components.
- Plan presentations. Create storyboards, which are detailed plans of the text, graphics, and order of each slide.
- Create presentations.
- Present completed projects, review experiences, and discuss project highlights or trouble spots.

Assessing Power Point Projects

For an evaluation tool to use for evaluating the writing content, technical content, technical organization, and communication skills used in student-created PowerPoint projects, try:

- http://www.romecsd.org/Rocks/PowerPoint_Rubric/powerpoint_rubric.html,
- http://www.uwstout.edu/soe/profdev/pptrubric.html, or
- http://www.artteacherconnection.com/pages/powerpointrubric.htm.

Excel is another easily adaptable application. Charts and graphs are a natural with Excel. This application can be used to tally results for any kind of question. Elementary students can enter results, create graphs, and compare and contrast their results.

POWER POINT LESSONS AND ACTIVITES

ENGLISH / LANGUAGE ARTS

TITLE: Biography of an Influential Writer
SUBJECT: English Language Arts
UNIT: PowerPoint
GRADE: 6–8

DESCRIPTION: For this activity, students will work with a partner, choose an author to study and produce a PowerPoint slide show. The finished product will be presented to the rest of the class.

OVERVIEW: Students will use Internet sites and library resources that contain information about a favorite author to help prepare a biography created in PowerPoint.

PREREQUISITE KNOWLEDGE: Ability to navigate the Internet and use a word processor. Previous experience with PowerPoint or other presentation software tools would be helpful.

TEACHER PREP TIME: minimal

DELIVERABLES: Students will create a multimedia presentation using PowerPoint to present findings and demonstrate applied understanding.

Teacher Tips: Invite a local author to the class to discuss their writing style or have students write a letter to their favorite author.

EVALUATION / GRADING: Students will be evaluated using a PowerPoint Presentation Rubric.
Running short on time? Limit the number of slides students must prepare.
Want to take this another step? Have students form groups and video tape a short skit from a book written by a favorite author.

MISSION:
- A biography is simply the story of a person's life.
- Biographies analyze and interpret the events in a person's life. They try to find connections, explain the meaning of unexpected actions or mysteries, and make arguments about the significance of the person's accomplishments or life activities.
- Biographies may be about famous, or infamous, people. A biography of an ordinary person can tell us a lot about a particular time and place.

- They are often about historical figures, but they can also be about people still living.
- For this project, you will use Internet sites and library resources that contain information about a favorite author.
- Begin by using a word processing program to create a document about the writer you are researching.
- Later you can Copy and Paste the information into a PowerPoint slide show for presentation to the class.

RESOURCES:

- A computer with Internet access and PowerPoint.

These websites will help you answer questions provided in *Steps* and prepare your project. This list is a starting place; feel free to search the Internet for other related information.

Websites

- Biography Maker
  http://www.bham.wednet.edu/bio/biomaker.htm
- Biography
  http://www.biography.com/
- Biography Sites
  http://amillionlives.com/
- Dictionary.com
  http://dictionary.reference.com/

PowerPoint Resources

- Act Den
  http://www.actden.com/pp/
- Education World
  http://www.education-world.com/a_tech/tutorials/ew_ppt.htm
- Using Microsoft PowerPoint
  http://www.ga.k12.pa.us/curtech/powerwk.htm#anchor374026

STEPS:

To write your biography:

1. Select a writer you are interested in.
2. Find out the basic facts of the person's life. Use links in *Resources* to collect information.
3. Think about what else you would like to know about the person, and what parts of the life you want to write most about. Some information you might want to think about include:

- What makes this person special or interesting?
- What kind of effect did he or she have on the world? Other people?
- What are the adjectives you would most use to describe the person?
- What examples from their life illustrate those qualities?
- What events shaped or changed this person's life?
- Did he or she overcome obstacles? Take risks? Get lucky?
- What type of books did this author write (Fiction, non-fiction)?

4. Do additional research at your library to find information that helps you answer these questions and tell an interesting story.

Note: Biographers use primary and secondary sources: Primary sources include letters, diaries, or newspaper accounts. Secondary sources include other biographies, reference books, or histories that provide information about the subject of the biography. When you find images or sounds you like, check the Web page for a copyright notice. Reference information. Last Name, First Name of Author (if known). "Title of work/article/ page." *Title of Complete Document* (if applicable). Date last modified. URL (date visited).

PRODUCT: You have three quarters of the work done, your research and an outline, all you have to do now is to tell the story using PowerPoint.

1. To get started, first open a new PowerPoint presentation and choose a template. Include facts, quotes, examples, images, sound clips, videos, and animations that you think are important aspects of the topic.
2. To copy text from your word processing document, highlight the information using your mouse and then use the Edit - Copy command on the menu bar. Paste what you highlighted into a PowerPoint slide, text box.
3. Search for images that are copyright free. Save copyright free images you like by downloading and pasting images onto your PowerPoint slide.
4. Once you have collected your information, go over it carefully so that you can give clear and thoughtful reasons why you found the things you collected especially important.

TIP: Organize your slides in a creative manner, use images and sounds to enhance your viewer's experience.Note: Do not include anything that owners do not approve.
See *Resources* for information, tools and assistance with using PowerPoint.

CONCLUSION:
- Share your PowerPoint presentation with the class.
- Are there any similarities or differences between the authors?
- Are you intrigued by a new author and wish to read their book(s)?

EVALUATION:

Performance Element	Needs improvement Criterion	Satisfactory Criterion	Exemplary Criterion
1. Research and Note taking	1 The content is vague and does not create a strong sense of purpose.	3 The content is written with a logical progression of ideas and supporting information.	5 The content is written clearly and concisely with a logical progression of ideas and supporting information.
2. Text Elements	1 Overall readability is difficult with lengthy paragraphs, too many different fonts, dark or busy background, overuse of bold or lack of appropriate indentations of text.	3 Sometimes the fonts are easy-to-read, but in a few places the use of fonts, italics, bold, long paragraphs, color or busy background detracts and does not enhance readability.	5 The fonts are easy-to-read and point size varies appropriately for headings and text. Use of italics, bold, and indentations enhances readability.
3. Layout	1 The layout is cluttered, confusing, and does not use spacing, headings and subheadings to enhance the readability.	3 The layout shows some structure, but appears cluttered and busy or distracting with large gaps of white space or uses a distracting background.	5 The layout is aesthetically pleasing and contributes to the overall message with appropriate use of headings and subheadings and white space.
4. Writing Mechanics	1 Spelling, punctuation, and grammar errors distract or impair readability. (3 or more errors)	3 The text is clearly written with little or no editing required for grammar, punctuation, and spelling.	5 The text is written with no errors in grammar, capitalization, punctuation, and spelling.
5. Graphics, Sound and/or Animation	1 Some of the graphics, sounds, and/or animations seem unrelated to the topic/theme and do not enhance the overall concepts.	3 The graphics, sound/and or animation visually depict material and assist the audience in understanding the flow of information or content.	5 The graphics, sound and/or animation assist in presenting an overall theme and make visual connections that enhance understanding of concept

NOTES:

ENGLISH / LANGUAGE ARTS

TITLE: Book Review
SUBJECT: English Language Arts
UNIT: PowerPoint
GRADE: 9–10

DESCRIPTION: For this activity, students are professional book reviewers. They will work with a partner, choose a novel to review and produce a PowerPoint slide show. The finished product will be presented to the rest of the class.

OVERVIEW: Students will prepare a book review in the form of a PowerPoint presentation.

PREREQUISITE KNOWLEDGE: Ability to navigate the Internet and use a word processor. Previous experience with PowerPoint or other presentation software tools would be helpful.

TEACHER PREP TIME: minimal Review the websites in *Resources*. Review Power-Point.

DELIVERABLES: Students will create a multimedia presentation using PowerPoint to present findings and demonstrate applied understanding.

EVALUATION / GRADING: Students will be evaluated using a PowerPoint Presentation Rubric.

Teacher Tips: Invite a local writer to the class to discuss writing style.

MISSION: Have you ever read a book, seen a movie, or eaten somewhere because it had won an award? What did you think? Did it measure up?

Reviewers have lots of power, they can convince people to read, watch, and eat what they say is good and to stay away from what they say is not so good. The reviewers that offer lots of reasons for their opinions are usually the most respected. It is not unusual for people to be disappointed by award winning books, movies or restaurants.

For this activity, you are going to be a professional book reviewer. You will work with a partner, choose a novel to review and produce a PowerPoint slideshow presenting your review to the rest of the class.

RESOURCES:
- A computer with Internet access and PowerPoint.

These websites will help you answer questions provided in *Steps* and to prepare your project. This list is a starting place; feel free to search the Internet for other related information.

Websites
- Kids Read
    http://www.kidsreads.com/reviews/index.asp
- ePals
    http://www.epals.ca/projects/book_club/
- Dictionary.com
    http://dictionary.reference.com/

PowerPoint resources
- Act Den
    http://www.actden.com/pp/
- Education World
    http://www.education-world.com/a_tech/tutorials/ew_ppt.htm
- Microsoft PowerPoint Resource
    http://www.ga.k12.pa.us/curtech/powerwk.htm#anchor374026

STEPS:
1. Each group will choose a book to read.
2. Partners will use a calendar to plan the reading schedule for their novel and meeting times to discuss the novel (i.e. after each chapter or every second chapter).
3. Partner reflection logs will be completed after each group discussion and turned in to the teacher.
    - What are some words that need to be discussed?
    - Who are the main characters?
    - Any confusing parts or surprises?
    - Did the author use any exceptional words or phrases in the novel?
    - How realistic is the dialogue?
    - What do you think is going to happen next?
4. Explore WebPages that have book reviews to use as an example. If you struggle with any words feel free to use an online dictionary or one in your classroom.
5. After you and your partner have read the book and analyzed it, you will develop a PowerPoint presentation for your class demonstrating your findings. Reference information. Last Name, First Name of Author (if known). "Title of work/article/page." *Title of Complete Document* (if applicable). Date last modified. URL (date visited).

PRODUCT:

Next you will create a PowerPoint slideshow that contains opinions, information, and perspectives that you've gained.

1. Begin your PowerPoint slideshow with a slide stating who you are and the title of the book you read.
2. Give background information about your novel. Look back at your Reflection Logs for help.

    Be sure to answer the following questions:
    *   What kind of book is this? How do you know?
    *   Who would like this book?
    *   Do you and your partner like or dislike this book? Why?
    *   What have you learned about the author?
    *   What do other people think of the book?
3. Each person should give at least two good reasons supporting their opinion. Make sure to be specific in both the information and the reasoning.
4. Have each person on the team proofread and edit the slides.

You will be evaluated on content, mechanics, shared workload, completing all requirements, and your oral presentation. Be sure to review your rubric often.

TIP: Organize your slides in a creative manner, use images and sounds to enhance your viewer's experience.

Note: Do not include anything that owners do not approve. When you find images or sounds you like, check the Web page for a copyright notice. Sometimes people do not want their work copied. A good practice is looking for an e-mail link on the page and then using it to ask permission.

CONCLUSION: Time to present the Book Review PowerPoint Presentation to the class.

Together you will present the book that you read and your individual thoughts on the book. Each group member will contribute to the presentation.

*   Be sure to include your different opinions.
*   Use effective oral communication skills.
*   Did you end up agreeing that the book was great? As you heard other PowerPoint presentations, are you interested in reading other books?

Did you hear a review about a book that you completely agreed or disagreed with? Remember these experiences when you read reviews about books, movies, etc. You may or may not agree with your peers.

EVALUATION:

Performance Element	Needs improvement Criterion		Satisfactory Criterion		Exemplary Criterion	
1. Research and Note taking	1	The content is vague and does not create a strong sense of purpose. Includes some facts.	3	The content is written with a logical progression of ideas and supporting information. Includes facts.	5	The content is written clearly and concisely with a logical progression of ideas and supporting information. Information is accurate with lots of facts.
2. Text Elements	1	Overall readability is difficult with lengthy paragraphs, too many different fonts, dark or busy background, overuse of bold or lack of appropriate indentations of text.	3	Sometimes the fonts are easy-to-read, but in a few places the use of fonts, italics, bold, long paragraphs, color or busy background detracts and does not enhance readability.	5	The fonts are easy-to-read and point size varies appropriately for headings and text. Use of italics, bold, and indentations enhances readability. The background and colors enhance the readability of text.
3. Layout	1	The layout is cluttered, confusing, and does not use spacing, headings and subheadings to enhance the readability.	3	The layout shows some structure, but appears cluttered and busy or distracting with large gaps of white space or uses a distracting background.	5	The layout is aesthetically pleasing and contributes to the overall message with appropriate use of headings and subheadings and white space.
4. Writing Mechanics	1	Spelling, punctuation, and grammar errors distract or impair readability. (3 or more errors)	3	The text is clearly written with little or no editing required for grammar, punctuation, and spelling.	5	The text is written with no errors in grammar, capitalization, punctuation, and spelling.
5. Oral Presentation	1	Presenters were not prepared.	3	Presenters were somewhat prepared.	5	Presenters were prepared.

NOTES:

LANGUAGE ARTS/DEBATE

TITLE: Censorship
GRADES: 11-12
SUBJECT: Language Arts/Debate
UNIT: PowerPoint

OVERVIEW: Students will research censorship using the Internet. Findings will be reviewed and person opinion will be conveyed through a PowerPoint presentation.

PREREQUISITE KNOWLEDGE: Ability to navigate the Internet and use a word processor. Previous experience with PowerPoint or other presentation software tools would be helpful.

TEACHER PREP TIME: minimal

DELIVERABLES: Students will create a multimedia presentation using PowerPoint to present findings and demonstrate applied understanding.

EVALUATION / GRADING: Students will be evaluated using a PowerPoint Presentation Rubric.

Running short on time? Have students work in pairs to collect, research and summarize findings.

Only one computer in the classroom? Have students research in small groups and prepare final reports in teams.

Teacher Tips:
- Invite media representatives to the class to speak about censorship.
- Host a class debate.
- Host an evening showcase where students can present their work to parents, students and members of the community.

MISSION:
- What is Censorship? More importantly, how do you feel about censorship?
- How do you feel about literature, media and art being censored?
- Do you watch MTV and listen to the radio? Do you surf the net?
- Do you read books like "Catcher in the Rye"? Music, the Internet and books are all subject to this heated issue. Who makes the decisions as to what you can, or cannot listen to or read?

You will explore censorship in more detail – then be prepared to express and back up your opinion. Let's get started.

RESOURCES:

- A computer with Internet access, word processor, and presentation software (PowerPoint).

These websites will help you conduct your research. This list is a starting place. Feel free to search the Internet for other related information.

- The Catcher in the Rye – Censorship
  http://www.curriculumunits.com/catcherweb/censorship/censorshipindex.htm
- The Letters of Thomas Jefferson: 1743-1826 – The Censorship of Books
  http://odur.let.rug.nl/~usa/P/tj3/writings/brf/jefl229.htm
- Banned Books Online
  http://onlinebooks.library.upenn.edu/banned-books.html
- American Library Association (tones of information here)
  http://www.ala.org/Content/NavigationMenu/Our_Association/Offices/
  Intellectual_Freedom3/Banned_Books_Week/Banned_Books_Week.htm
- Loyola University Chicago Libraries
  http://www.luc.edu/libraries/banned/
- Censorship of Music
  http://www.cohums.ohio-state.edu/english/People/Hogsette.1/g1music.htm
- A Brief History of Banned Music in the United States
  http://ericnuzum.com/banned/
- Censorship in Music
  http://courses.lib.odu.edu/engl/jdavis/tcgmusic.html

- Internet Censorship
  http://www.epic.org/free_speech/censorship/
- National Coalition Against Censorship
  http://www.ncac.org/
- The Trials of Liberty
  http://www.indexonline.org/
- Banned Books and Censorship
  http://www.booksatoz.com/censorship/banned.htm

STEPS:

1. First, we need to collect some evidence, do some research.
2. Create a definition, in your own words, as to the meaning of censorship to you.
3. Collect supporting evidence such as laws, legislation, organizations, historical events, trends, and recent events surrounding this issue.
4. Collect your research in a word processor. Remember to cite the sources of your information.
5. Remember when you have a heated topic such as this, you need to be aware of **BIAS** in what you are reading. Writers can be quite subjective and persuasive. Use your personal judgment when reading sources. Just because it is in print (or online) does not mean it is law, truthful or fact! Your opinion and insight count a lot here. Dictionary.com defines **BIAS** as - A preference or an inclination, especially one that inhibits impartial judgment, an unfair act or policy stemming from prejudice.

PRODUCT:

1. You will create a PowerPoint presentation to present your findings.
2. You may wish to create a PowerPoint storyboard first, which will outline what your presentation will cover.
3. Include a proper title screen, credits and references at the end, as well as multimedia throughout (pictures, images, sounds etc.)
4. Please include proper references and sources for your research.
   Last Name, First Name of Author (if known). "Title of work/article/page." *Title of Complete Document* (if applicable). Date last modified. URL (date visited).
5. Include YOUR definition and summary of censorship.
6. Include some history about the issue.
7. Summarize with your opinion on censorship.

CONCLUSION:

- Share your presentation with other students in your class.
- Your teacher will then facilitate a class debate on this heated and exciting topic.

EVALUATION:

Performance Element		Needs improvement Criterion		Satisfactory Criterion		Exemplary Criterion
1. Research	1	Limited research, from limited sources	3	Well researched, from various sources	5	Thorough research from varied sources presenting different points of view
2. Storyboard / planning	1	Limited planning evident	3	Planning evident	5	Thorough planning evident
3. Content	1	Lacks detail	3	Good detail	5	Extensive detail
4. Multimedia	1	Few or no multimedia elements are included	3	Multimedia elements are included	5	Multimedia elements are included, well selected and integrated into presentation
5. Personal Opinion	1	Opinion is weakly stated without supporting evidence	3	Opinion is stated with evidence	5	Opinion is well articulated and supported with appropriate evidence

NOTES:

MATHEMATICS/TRIGONOMETRY

TITLE: Trigonometry
SUBJECT: Mathematics/Trigonometry
UNIT: Power Point
GRADE(S):   11-12

DESCRIPTION: Using the Internet, students will explore basic principals of trigonometry. Once the topic has been demystified through research and understanding, findings will be presenting in a multimedia presentation. How trig is used in daily life will be discussed.

PREREQUISITE KNOWLEDGE: Ability to navigate the Internet and use a word processor. Previous experience with PowerPoint or other presentation software tools would be helpful.

TEACHER PREP TIME: minimal

DELIVERABLES: Students will create a multimedia presentation using PowerPoint to present findings and demonstrate applied understanding.

EVALUATION / GRADING: Students will be evaluated using a PowerPoint Presentation Rubric.

Running short on time?
Have students work in pairs to collect research and summarize findings.

Only one computer in the classroom?
Have students research in small groups and prepare final reports in teams.

Teacher Tips: Facilitate the sharing of student projects with you class and with other classes to demystify trig and demonstrate its daily uses.

MISSION:
  * What is trigonometry?
  * Why do I need to learn it?
  * How is it used in everyday life?

According to dictionary.com, trigonometry is "The branch of mathematics that deals with the relationships between the sides and the angles of triangles and the calculations based on them, particularly the trigonometric functions." What does that mean? Let's find out what trig is all about.

RESOURCES: A computer with Internet access, word processor, and presentation software (PowerPoint).These websites will help you conduct your research. This list is a starting place; feel free to search the Internet for other related information.

- Ask Dr. Math
  http://mathforum.org/library/drmath/sets/high_trigonometry.html
- Dave's Short Trig Course
  http://aleph0.clarku.edu/~djoyce/java/trig/
- Frequently asked questions about Trigonometry
  http://catcode.com/trig/index.html
- Interactive Trigonometry
  http://www.ies.co.jp/math/java/trig/index.html
- Applications of Trigonometry
  http://trackstar.hprtec.org/main/track_frames.php3?track_id=54273&nocache=19
  65976621
- The Math Forum
  http://mathforum.org/library/topics/trig/
- Trigonometry
  http://www.sosmath.com/trig/trig.html
- Graphing Trig Function
  http://school.discovery.com/homeworkhelp/webmath/plotmany.html
- Trigonometry and Right Angles
  http://id.mind.net/~zona/mmts/trigonometryRealms/introduction/rightTriangle/
  trigRightTriangle.html
- Trig Function Topics
  http://www.math.com/tables/algebra/functions/trig/index.htm

STEPS: Use the links in *Resources*, and others that you find to explore the meaning of trig as well as real life application.

1. Collect your research in a word processor
2. Answer the following questions while collecting your research:
3. What is trigonometry? (use your own words)
4. What are some main functions, terms and elements of trig? (Include definition and pictures to explain you)?
5. How is trig used in daily life?

Remember to reference the source of your information. Last Name, First Name of Author (if known). "Title of work/article/page." *Title of Complete Document* (if applicable). Date last modified. URL (date visited).

PRODUCT:

You will create a PowerPoint presentation to present your findings.

1. You may wish to create a PowerPoint storyboard first, which will outline what your presentation will cover.
2. Include a proper title screen, credits and references at the end, as well as multimedia throughout (pictures, images, sounds etc.).
3. Include the information you researched in *Steps*.

Be sure to include your personal opinion as to why it is important to learn about trigonometry.

CONCLUSION: How is trigonometry used in daily life? Share your presentation with other students in your class.

EVALUATION:

Performance Element	Needs improvement Criterion	Satisfactory Criterion	Exemplary Criterion
1. Research	1 Limited research, from limited sources	3 Well researched, from various sources	5 Thorough research from varied sources presenting different points of view
2. Storyboard / planning	1 Limited planning evident	3 Planning evident	5 Thorough planning evident
3. Content	1 Lacks detail	3 Good detail	5 Extensive detail
4. Multimedia	1 Few or no multimedia elements are included	3 Multimedia elements are included	5 Multimedia elements are included, well selected and integrated into presentation
5. Personal Opinion	1 Opinion is weakly stated without supporting evidence	3 Opinion is stated with evidence	5 Opinion is well articulated and supported with appropriate evidence

NOTES:

MATHEMATICS/ALGEBRA

TITLE: Polynomials
SUBJECT: Mathematics/Algebra
GRADE: 9-10
UNIT: Power Point

DESCRIPTION: Students will create a multimedia presentation demonstrating understanding of adding, subtracting, multiplying, dividing and factoring polynomials.

PREREQUISITE KNOWLEDGE: Ability to navigate the Internet and use a word processor. Previous experience with PowerPoint or other presentation software tools would be helpful.

TEACHER PREP TIME: minimal

DELIVERABLES: Students will create a multimedia presentation using PowerPoint to present findings and demonstrate applied understanding.

EVALUATION / GRADING: Students will be evaluated using a PowerPoint Presentation Rubric.

Running short on time?
Have students work in pairs to collect research and summarize findings.

Only one computer in the classroom?
Have students research in small groups and prepare final reports in teams.

Teacher Tips: Students could be given a leadership role to introduce polynomials to other classes using their dynamic presentations!

MISSION: What are Polynomials?
According to dictionary.com, a **polynomial** is:
"An algebraic expression consisting of one or more summed terms, each term consisting of a constant multiplier and one or more variables raised to integral powers".

For example, $x^2 - 5x + 6$ and $2p^3q + y$ are polynomials.
Sound confusing? Let's do some research and figure this out!

RESOURCES:

A computer with Internet access, word processor, and presentation software (PowerPoint). These websites will help you conduct your research. This list is a starting place; feel free to search the Internet for other related information.

- BrainPop - Polynomials (you will need shockwave to view)
  http://www.brainpop.com/math/algebra/polynomials/index.weml
- Ask Dr. Math
  http://mathforum.org/library/drmath/scts/high_polynomials.html
- EdHelper.com (dozens of polynomial worksheets)
  http://www.edhelper.com/polynomials.htm
- Polynomials
  http://www.purplemath.com/modules/polydefs.htm
- Polynomials – Definitions
  http://www.purplemath.com/modules/polydefs.htm
- Polynomials (from Discovery)
  http://school.discovery.com/homeworkhelp/webmath/polynomials.html
- Factoring Polynomials
  http://learning.mgccc.cc.ms.us/math/algebra/facadvice.html
- Factoring Polynomials
  http://www.vcsun.org/~bsamii/schedule/factoring/factoring.html

STEPS:

1. What is a polynomial?
2. How do you add polynomials?
3. How do you subtract polynomials?
4. How do you multiply polynomials?
5. How do you divide polynomials?
6. How do you factor polynomials?
7. Include steps, descriptions and examples.

PRODUCT:

Using the research collected in *Steps* as your content, you are going to create a PowerPoint slide show to show your findings.

1. Be sure to take advantage of the multimedia elements to help clarify the properties and functions of polynomials (e.g. sound animation).
2. Be sure to include examples and instructions for adding, subtracting, multiplying, dividing and factoring polynomials.
3. You may wish to create a PowerPoint storyboard first, which will outline what your presentation will cover.
4. Include a proper title screen, credits and references at the end, as well as multimedia throughout (pictures, images, sounds etc.).

Last Name, First Name of Author (if known). "Title of work/article/page." *Title of Complete Document* (if applicable). Date last modified. URL (date visited).

CONCLUSION: Now polynomials are not near as confusing! Share your presentation with other students in your class.

EVALUATION:

	Needs improvement	Satisfactory	Exemplary
Performance Element	Criterion	Criterion	Criterion
1. Research	1 Limited research, from limited sources	3 Well researched, from various sources	5 Thorough research from varied sources presenting different points of view
2. Storyboard / planning	1 Limited planning evident	3 Planning evident	5 Thorough planning evident
3. Content	1 Lacks detail	3 Good detail	5 Extensive detail
4. Multimedia	1 Few or no multimedia elements are included	3 Multimedia elements are included	5 Multimedia elements are included, well selected and integrated into presentation
5. Personal Opinion	1 Opinion is weakly stated without supporting evidence	3 Opinion is stated with evidence	5 Opinion is well articulated and supported with appropriate evidence

NOTES:

SCIENCE

TITLE:	Soil – What's the Dirt?
SUBJECT:	Science
UNIT:	Power Point
GRADE:	9–10

DESCRIPTION: What kind of soil would best support the development of a new farming community? In partners, students will gather facts about soil and design an original presentation using PowerPoint. Presentation should demonstrate a soil profile by creating a slide show to illustrate the order in which soil is formed and the properties of each soil layer.

PREREQUISITE KNOWLEDGE: Ability to navigate the Internet and use a word processor. Previous experience with PowerPoint or other presentation software tools would be helpful.

TEACHER PREP TIME: minimal

DELIVERABLES: Students will create a multimedia presentation using PowerPoint to present findings and demonstrate applied understanding.

EVALUATION / GRADING: Students will be evaluated using a PowerPoint Presentation Rubric.

Running short on time?
Limit the number of slides students are to prepare.

MISSION: What kind of soil would best support the development of a new farming community? As partners, you will gather facts about soil collect your findings and design an original presentation using PowerPoint. Your PowerPoint presentation should represent a soil profile illustrating the order in which soil is formed and the properties of each soil layer.

RESOURCES:
- A computer with Internet access and PowerPoint.

These websites will help you answer questions provided in *Steps* and to prepare your project. This list is a starting place. Feel free to search the Internet for other related information.

Websites
- http://school.discovery.com/schooladventures/soil/
  Discovery

- http://ltpwww.gsfc.nasa.gov/globe/
  Soil Science Education

PowerPoint resources
- http://www.actden.com/pp/
  Act Den
- http://www.ga.k12.pa.us/curtech/powerwk.htm#anchor374026
  PowerPoint

Extra Activity
- http://www.urbanext.uiuc.edu/gpe/case2/c2brief.html

STEPS: Record answers to the following questions while researching soil properties using the links in *Resources.*

1. What is the difference between soil and dirt?
2. What materials make up soil?
3. What are the basic types of soil and how are they alike and different?
4. How many layers make up the soil and how are they alike and different?
5. Why are some soils more suited for growing and building on than others?
6. Using the information you have collected about soil, draw three colourful pictures showing what kind of soil would best support the development of a new farming community.

Last Name, First Name of Author (if known). "Title of work/article/page." *Title of Complete Document* (if applicable). Date last modified. URL (date visited).

PRODUCT: With a partner, you will recreate a soil profile replica you studied in *Steps* using PowerPoint.

1. Review your notes from *Steps* to help arrange your information.
2. Use separate slides to depict the various levels of soil. Label each level: ground level, topsoil, subsoil, weathered parent material and bedrock.
3. Include background information for each soil profile.
4. Present your data in an informative and interesting manner.
5. Plan how your PowerPoint presentation will look.
   For example, choose the slide formats (background, layout etc.), transitions, and animations. Try to keep slides consistent.

Note: Remember to cite the sources (bibliography) you used in gathering your information and include graphics to help make your presentation more visually appealing.
Soil profile: The horizontal layers (horizons) in the soil from the surface to the bedrock.

CONCLUSION: What kind of soil do you and your partner recommend to support the development of a new farming community?

- Use the information you have recorded in your PowerPoint presentation to support your findings.
- Your presentation should last no more than four minutes.
- Analyze soil properties in your school yard and predict soil quality.

EVALUATION:

		Needs improvement		Satisfactory		Exemplary
		Criterion		Criterion		Criterion
1. Research and Note taking	1	The content is vague.	3	The content is written with a logical progression of ideas and supporting information.	5	The content is written clearly and detailed.
2. Text Elements	1	Overall readability is difficult with lengthy paragraphs, too many different fonts, dark or busy background, overuse of bold or lack of appropriate indentations of text.	3	Sometimes the fonts are easy-to-read, but in a few places the use of fonts, italics, bold, long paragraphs, color or busy background detracts and does not enhance readability.	5	The fonts are easy-to-read and point size varies appropriately for headings and text. Use of italics, bold, and indentations enhances readability.
3. Soil Profile Slides	1	The soil profile slides are cluttered, confusing, and does not use spacing, headings and subheadings to enhance the readability.	3	The soil profile slides show some structure, but appear cluttered and busy or distracting with large gaps of white space or use a distracting background.	5	The soil profile slides are aesthetically pleasing and contribute to the overall message with appropriate use of headings and subheadings and white space.
4. Writing Mechanics	1	Spelling, punctuation, and grammar errors distract or impair readability. (3 or more errors)	3	The text is clearly written with little or no editing required for grammar, punctuation, and spelling.	5	The text is written with no errors in grammar, capitalization, punctuation, and spelling.
5. Graphics, Sound and/or Animation		Some of the graphics, sounds, and/or animations seem unrelated to the topic/ theme and do not enhance the overall concepts.		The graphics, sound/ and or animation assist the audience in understanding the flow of information or content.		The graphics, sound and/or animation assist in presenting an overall theme and make visual connections that enhance understanding of concept, ideas and relationships.

NOTES:

SCIENCE

TITLE:	Light and Sound Waves
SUBJECT:	Science
GRADE(S):	9-10
UNIT:	Power Point

DESCRIPTION: Students will research, compare and contrast light and sound waves, using the Internet.

PREREQUISITE KNOWLEDGE: Ability to navigate the Internet and use a word processor. Previous experience with PowerPoint or other presentation software tools would be helpful.

TEACHER PREP TIME: minimal

DELIVERABLES: Students will create a multimedia presentation using PowerPoint to present findings and demonstrate applied understanding.

EVALUATION / GRADING: Students will be evaluated using a PowerPoint Presentation Rubric.

Running short on time?
Have students work in groups to collect research and summarize findings.
Each pair could work on either light OR sound, and then join another pair to assemble a final product.

Want to take this another step?
Have students create animated examples using Flash or other animation software.

Only one computer in the classroom?
Have students research in small groups and prepare final reports in teams.

EXTENSION IDEA: Working in small groups – have students research careers that would require an understanding and use of light and/or sound waves.

MISSION: You are a lead researcher at the International Science and Technology Institute (ISTI). Working with your trusted colleague, your next project focus is on waves. Not the type you surf, but light and sound waves. In pairs, one person will assume the role of prestigious Professor L. Ite and the other the distinguished Dr. S. Hound. Professor L. Ite will be preparing a presentation on the characteristics of **Light Waves**, while Dr. S. Hound will be preparing complimentary information demonstrating **Sound Waves**. You are presenting to the academic counsel and International guests in 4 weeks! There is much to be done. Let's get started.

RESOURCES:
- a computer with Internet access
- word processor
- presentation software (PowerPoint)

These websites will help you conduct your research. This list is a starting place. Feel free to search the Internet for other related information.

Waves
- The Nature of a Wave
  http://www.physicsclassroom.com/Class/waves/U10L1a.html
- Waves, Sound and Light
  http://www.physicsclassroom.com/mmedia/waves/wavesTOC.html
- Parts of a Wave
  http://id.mind.net/~zona/mstm/physics/waves/partsOfAWave/waveParts.htm
- Brain Pop – Waves (needs shockwave)
  http://www.brainpop.com/science/light/waves/index.weml?&tried_cookie=true
- The Characteristics of Light and Sound Waves
  http://home.cord.edu/faculty/manning/physics215/studentpages/angieevanson.html

Sound
- The Phenomenon of Sound Waves
  http://school.discovery.com/lessonplans/programs/soundwaves/
- Activity – Longitudinal Wave (needs shockwave)
  http://www.explorescience.com/activities/Activity_page.cfm?ActivityID=50
- Characteristics of Sound Waves
  http://www.infoplease.com/ce6/sci/A0861183.html

Light
- Light and Optics
  http://acept.la.asu.edu/PiN/mod/light/pattLightOptics.html
- How do we know light behaves as a wave?
  http://www.physicsclassroom.com/Class/light/u12l1a.html
- How Stuff Works – Light
  http://science.howstuffworks.com/light.htm

STEPS: After you have chosen your role (Light or Sound), it is time to begin your research. For this project, your research will be found using the Internet. Include the answers to the following questions in your research.

1. Describe the following characteristics of "waves" in relation to your topic: wavelength, frequency, period, amplitude.

2. Discuss and support with (original) images reflection and refraction.
3. What is the Doppler Effect?
4. Explain the concept "diffraction of waves".

You will draw an example wave. Include labels for the following elements of your wave:
- Wavelength
- Amplitude
- Crest (or compression)
- Trough (or rarefaction)

(You can choose to use a paint program on your computer, or draw the picture on paper and than scan it into your presentation). You may choose to include pictures to demonstrate most or all of your research findings. A picture is worth 1,000 words!

Remember to reference the source of your information.
Last Name, First Name of Author (if known). "Title of work/article/page." Title of Complete Document (if applicable). Date last modified. URL (date visited).

PRODUCT:
Working with your partner, combine your research and material to create an integrated PowerPoint presentation about waves.
1. Include facts, figures, images, animation, sound or whatever media will help demonstrate the similarities and differences between sound and light waves.
2. Your final product should clearly describe, using basic, scientific language the principals and elements of light and sound waves.
3. Include pictures. Include at least one transverse wave and one longitudinal wave. (label the important elements)

CONCLUSION: Share your presentation with other pairs in your class.

EVALUATION:

Performance Element	Needs improvement Criterion	Satisfactory Criterion	Exemplary Criterion
1. Research	1 Limited research, from limited sources	3 Well researched, from various sources	5 Thorough research from varied sources presenting different points of view
2. Storyboard / planning	1 Limited planning evident	3 Planning evident	5 Thorough planning evident
3. Content	1 Lacks detail	3 Good detail	5 Extensive detail
4. Multimedia	1 Few or no multimedia elements are included	3 Multimedia elements are included	5 Multimedia elements are included, well selected and integrated into presentation
5. Personal Opinion	1 Opinion is weakly stated without supporting evidence	3 Opinion is stated with evidence	5 Opinion is well articulated and supported with appropriate evidence

NOTES:

SCIENCE

TITLE:	Using the Periodic Table
SUBJECT:	Science
GRADE:	11-12
UNIT:	Power Point

OVERVIEW: Students will explore the history, evolution, value and use of the Periodic Table.

PREREQUISITE KNOWLEDGE: Ability to navigate the Internet and use a word processor. Previous experience with PowerPoint or other presentation software tools would be helpful.

TEACHER PREP TIME: minimal

DELIVERABLES: Students will create a multimedia presentation using PowerPoint to present findings and demonstrate applied understanding.

EVALUATION / GRADING: Students will be evaluated using a PowerPoint Presentation Rubric.

Running short on time?

Have students work in pairs to collect research and summarize findings.

Only one computer in the classroom?

Have students research in small groups and prepare final reports in teams.

Teacher Tips: Students can share their presentations with other science classes working with the Periodic Table.

MISSION:

- What is the Periodic Table?
- Where did it come from?
- How do you use it?
- Let's find out!

RESOURCES: A computer with Internet access, word processor, and presentation software (PowerPoint). These websites will help you conduct your research. This list is a starting place; feel free to search the Internet for other related information.

- What was Dmitri Mendeleev?
  http://www.chemistry.co.nz/mendeleev.htm

- A Quick look at the History of the Periodic Table
  http://periodictable.com/pages/AAE_History.html
- Periodic Table.com
  http://periodictable.com/pages/AAE_PerTbl.html
- 2 Dimensional Periodic Table
  http://periodictable.com/pages/AAE_Flatprint.html
- 3 Dimensional Periodic Table
  http://periodictable.com/pages/1rotate.html
- The Development of the Periodic Table
  http://www.chemsoc.org/viselements/pages/history_iii.html
- Web Elements
  http://www.webelements.com/
- Chemical Elements.com
  http://chemicalelements.com/
- Periodic Table of Elements
  http://environmentalchemistry.com/yogi/periodic/
- Period Table.com for Students
  http://periodictable.com/pages/AAE__studentHOME.html

STEPS: Using the Internet, you will research the Periodic Table.

1. Collect your research in a word processor. Remember to copy and paste the URL into your research document for easy access later, and to cite the source of your information.
2. Answer the following questions (as a starting place for your research).
   - What is the Periodic Table?
   - How are elements grouped?
   - Where did it come from?
   - How has it changed over time?
   - How do you use it?
3. Include pictures to help explain and demonstrate your findings.

PRODUCT:

1. Create a PowerPoint presentation to demonstrate your findings.
2. Include a brief history and development of the Periodic Table, as well as instructions for use.
3. Include real-world application (e.g. how it would be used in a specific job).
4. Include a proper title screen, credits and references at the end as well as multimedia throughout (pictures, images, sounds etc.)

5. You may wish also to create a PowerPoint storyboard first, which will outline what your presentation will cover.

CONCLUSION:
- Share your presentation with other students in the class.
- Name 3 careers where you would use the Periodic Table.

EVALUATION:

Performance Element	Needs improvement Criterion		Satisfactory Criterion		Exemplary Criterion	
1. Research	1	Limited research, from limited sources	3	Well researched, from various sources	5	Thorough research from varied sources presenting different points of view
2. Storyboard / planning	1	Limited planning evident	3	Planning evident	5	Thorough planning evident
3. Content	1	Lacks detail	3	Good detail	5	Extensive detail
4. Multimedia	1	Few or no multimedia elements are included	3	Multimedia elements are included	5	Multimedia elements are included, well selected and integrated into presentation
5. Personal Opinion	1	Opinion is weakly stated without supporting evidence	3	Opinion is stated with evidence	5	Opinion is well articulated and supported with appropriate evidence

NOTES:

SOCIAL STUDIES / GEOGRAPHY

TITLE:	Interactive Map of South America
SUBJECT:	Social Studies / Geography
UNIT:	Power Point
GRADE(S):	6-8

PREREQUISITE KNOWLEDGE: Ability to navigate the Internet, use a word processor. Previous experience with PowerPoint or other presentation software tools would be helpful.

TEACHER PREP TIME: minimal

DELIVERABLES: Students will create a multimedia presentation using PowerPoint to present findings and demonstrate applied understanding.

EVALUATION / GRADING: Students will be evaluated using a PowerPoint Presentation Rubric.

Running short on time?

Have students work in pairs to collect research and summarize findings.

Only one computer in the classroom?

Have students research in small groups and prepare final reports in teams.

Teacher Tips: Contact a local South America cultural group and arrange for a speaker to come to your class. (You may also be able to locate an appropriate speaker among the students or parents of your school).

MISSION: What do you know about South America? Where is it? How large is it? How many people live there? What is the geography like? What are the politics like? Using the Internet, you will explore the geography of South America. You will create an interactive map of South America which includes your findings and research. Let's get started!

RESOURCES: A computer with Internet access, word processor and presentation software (PowerPoint). These websites will help you conduct your research. This list is a starting place. Feel free to search the Internet for other related information.

- Mr. Dowling's Electronic Passport - South America
  http://www.mrdowling.com/712southamerica.html
- Adventures in South America
  http://www.fluid7.demon.co.uk/adventures/home.htm

- South America
  http://www.politicalresources.net/s_amer.htm
- South America - Map
  http://go.hrw.com/atlas/norm_htm/samerica.htm
- South America - Maps and Facts
  http://www.geocities.com/SiliconValley/6059/sa.html
- Wonder Club
  http://www.wonderclub.com/Atlas/sa__3823.htm
- Fact Monster
  http://www.factmonster.com/atlas/southamerica.html

STEPS: Use a word processor to collect your research.

1. Download images and maps (save the source of this information to reference in your project).
2. Select your favorite map.
3. Choose a few countries, areas or regions of the map that you wish to learn more about. (minimum 3)

Remember to document the sources of your information.

Last Name, First Name of Author (if known). "Title of work/article/page." *Title of Complete Document* (if applicable). Date last modified. URL (date visited).

For each area researched look for information on the geographical structure, weather, culture, people and politics.

PRODUCT:

1. You will need to create a PowerPoint storyboard first, which will outline what your presentation will cover. It will also help you plan the navigation within your project.
2. You will use a map of Africa for your "Table of Contents". Using action buttons within the map, users can jump to information about that area.(*for help with action buttons and navigation in PowerPoint, see below*)
3. Include a proper title screen, credits and references at the end, as well as multimedia throughout (pictures, images, sounds etc.)
4. Include an overview of South America at the beginning of your presentation.
5. Your map (or index page) will link to your in depth research.
6. Include a summary in your presentation.Tips on how to make action buttons and hyperlinks in PowerPoint are available at:
   - Using Action Buttons to Create Interactive PowerPoint Shows http://www.soita.esu.k12.oh.us/Resources/tips/mspp.html

- PowerPoint 2000 Tutorial – Hyperlinks
  http://gethelp.library.upenn.edu/workshops/biomed/ppt/hyperlinks.html
- Creating Action Buttons
  http://www.washburn.edu/cas/history/stucker/PPTactionbuttons.html

CONCLUSION: Share your presentation with other students in your class.

EVALUATION:

	Needs improvement	Satisfactory	Exemplary
Performance Element	Criterion	Criterion	Criterion
1. Research	1 Limited research, from limited sources	3 Well researched, from various sources	5 Thorough research from varied sources presenting different points of view
2. Storyboard / planning	1 Limited planning evident	3 Planning evident	5 Thorough planning evident
3. Content	1 Lacks detail	3 Good detail	5 Extensive detail
4. Multimedia	1 Few or no multimedia elements are included	3 Multimedia elements are included	5 Multimedia elements are included, well selected and integrated into presentation
5. Personal Opinion	1 Opinion is weakly stated without supporting evidence	3 Opinion is stated with evidence	5 Opinion is well articulated and supported with appropriate evidence

NOTES:

SOCIAL STUDIES / GEOGRAPHY

TITLE: European Influences
SUBJECT: Social Studies / Geography
GRADE(S):   6–8
UNIT: Power Point

OVERVIEW: In groups, students will uncover and assess Europe's overall impact on North American societies past and present, specifically in relation to government, religion, art, literature, celebrations and cuisine.

PREREQUISITE KNOWLEDGE: Ability to navigate the Internet and use a word processor. Previous experience with PowerPoint or other presentation software tools would be helpful.

TEACHER PREP TIME: minimal

DELIVERABLES: Students will create a multimedia presentation using PowerPoint to present findings and demonstrate applied understanding.

EVALUATION / GRADING: Students will be evaluated using a PowerPoint Presentation Rubric.
Running short on time?
Limit the number of slides students are to prepare.

MISSION: Christianity, the Statue of Liberty, cursive writing and last but not least, pizza is all fine examples of how Europe has influenced North America. Europe has had a tremendous influence on North America. It is interesting to see the diversity of cultures in the different regions of North America and how different European lifestyles have had such an impact on our lifestyle.

In groups, you will uncover and assess Europe's overall impact on North American societies past and present, specifically in relation to government, religion, art, literature, celebrations and cuisine.

RESOURCES: A computer with Internet access and PowerPoint. These websites will help you answer questions provided in *Steps* and to prepare your project. This list is a starting place; feel free to search the Internet for other related information.

- European History
  http://www.multcolib.org/homework/eurohist.html

PowerPoint Resources

- Act Den
  http://www.actden.com/pp/
- Education World
  http://www.education-world.com/a_tech/tutorials/ew_ppt.htm
- PowerPoint Resource
  http://www.ga.k12.pa.us/curtech/powerwk.htm#anchor374026

STEPS:

1. Form teams of six.
2. Each team member must choose a topic to research in detail: government, religion, art, literature, celebrations and cuisine.
3. Collect information using the Internet or library resources concerning how Europeans influenced North America in reference to your topic chosen in Step 2.
4. Each member of the team will be responsible for contributing four PowerPoint slides to the team PowerPoint presentation.

Reminder: Only include images or sounds that you have permission to use. When you find images or sounds you like, check the Web page for a copyright notice. Sometimes people do not want their work copied. A good practice is looking for an e-mail link on the page and then using it to ask permission.

Last Name, First Name of Author (if known). "Title of work/article/page." *Title of Complete Document* (if applicable). Date last modified. URL (date visited).

PRODUCT:

1. Organize your slides in a creative manner.
2. Include images and sounds to enhance your viewer's experience.
3. Include a proper title screen, credits and references at the end as well as multimedia throughout (pictures, images, sounds etc.)

CONCLUSION: Share your PowerPoint presentation with the class.

EVALUATION:

	Needs improvement	Satisfactory	Exemplary
Performance Element	Criterion	Criterion	Criterion
1. Research and Note taking	1 The content is vague.	3 The content is written with a logical progression of ideas and supporting information.	5 The content is written clearly and concisely with a logical progression of ideas and supporting information.
2. Storyboard / planning	1 Limited planning evident	3 Planning evident	5 Thorough planning evident
3. Layout	1 The layout is cluttered, confusing, and does not use spacing, headings and subheadings to enhance the readability.	3 The layout shows some structure, but appears cluttered and busy or distracting with large gaps of white space or uses a distracting background.	5 The layout is aesthetically pleasing and contributes to the overall message with appropriate use of headings and subheadings and white space.
4. Writing Mechanics	1 Spelling, punctuation, and grammar errors distract or impair readability. (3 or more errors)	3 The text is clearly written with little or no editing required for grammar, punctuation, and spelling.	5 The text is written with no errors in grammar, capitalization, punctuation, and spelling.
5. Graphics, Sound and/or Animation	1 Some of the graphics, sounds, and/or animations seem unrelated to the topic/theme and do not enhance the overall concepts.	3 The graphics sound/ and or animation visually depicts material and assists the audience in understanding the flow of information or content.	5 The graphics, sound and/or animation assist in presenting an overall theme and make visual connections that enhance understanding of concept, ideas and relationships.

NOTES:

SOCIAL STUDIES / HISTORY

TITLE: Venus Transit Social Studies

SUBJECT: Social Studies / History

GRADE: 6–8

UNIT: Power Point

DESCRIPTION: Students will research the Venus Transit and create a PowerPoint presentation.

PREREQUISITE KNOWLEDGE: Ability to navigate the Internet and use a word processor. Previous experience with PowerPoint or other presentation software tools would be helpful.

TEACHER PREP TIME: minimal

DELIVERABLES: Students will create a multimedia presentation using PowerPoint to present findings and demonstrate applied understanding.

EVALUATION / GRADING: Students will be evaluated using a PowerPoint Presentation Rubric

MISSION: December 6th, 1882 was the last **transit** of the planet **Venus** across the Sun. There have been only six such occurrences since Galileo first trained his telescope on **Venus** in 1610. On the 8th of June 2004, our generation has the honor of witnessing a rare, phenomenal sight. After almost 120 years, Venus will arrive in all its glory, and cross the path between the Earth and the Sun. No one alive has so far seen such an event. What is the Transit of Venus? Why is this important? How does it affect me? How should I prepare? What was happening around the time of the Transit of Venus viewings (1639, 1761, 1769, 1874, 1882)?

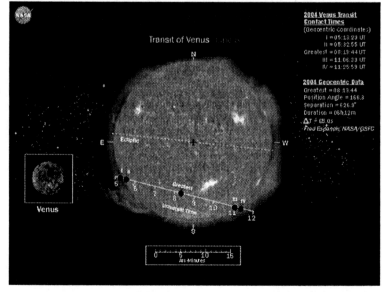

Your job will be to answer these questions and produce a multimedia timeline, using PowerPoint, dedicated to its celebration and informing people around the world about the Transit of Venus. Your PowerPoint presentation will describe Venus, the Transit of Venus and outline the historical events that occurred during past Transits of Venus.

RESOURCES: These web sites will help you collect the information you will need to learn more about the **Venus Transit 2004**.

- Sun-Earth Connection Education Forum
  Archived **Web Cast** from March 19
  http://planetquest1.jpl.nasa.gov/venus_transit.cfm
- Venus
  http://www.jsd.k12.ak.us/ab/el/planets/venus.html
- Nasa – Ask the Space Scientist http://image.gsfc.nasa.gov/poetry/venus/
  TransitFAQs.html
- Venus Transit 2004
  http://www.vt-2004.org/Kids/
- Venus Transit – Sun Earth Day
  http://sunearth.gsfc.nasa.gov/sunearthday/2004/vt_edu2004_venus_back_his.htm
- Transit of Venus – FAQ
  http://www.transitofvenus.org/faq.htm
- Hyperhistory
  http://www.hyperhistory.com/online_n2/History_n2/a.html

STEPS: Now it is time to learn about this rare occurrence that has affected our global history. Use the web sites in *Resources* to research the Venus, the Transit of Venus and historical events over the centuries.

Write down answers to the following questions:

1. Describe the planet Venus (who Venus was named after, the temperature on Venus, the distance from the Sun, color, the speed at which it travels, size etc.).
   Maximum score of 10 points.
2. Describe the Venus Transit (what is the Venus Transit, what does it look like, why is it important, how does it affect you, how should I prepare, why do transits happen, who are Kepler and Halley, who viewed the first transit?).
   Maximum score of 10 points.
3. Write one page on the major events that took place when the Venus Transit was viewed in the past (1639, 1761, 1769, 1874 and 1882).
   Maximum score of 20 points.

Are you stumped for what to research? Here are some ideas.

- What was life like way back then?
- What exploration took place during these years?
- What countries were fighting?
- Were any scientific inventions invented during these years?

PRODUCT: Timelines give a picture of the movement of peoples and cultures through time and place.

1. Use PowerPoint to create a timeline and organize your information collected in *Steps.*
2. Include the following information on separate PowerPoint slides:
    - 1 slide = a Venus Transit title page
    - 1 slide = a description of the planet Venus
    - 1 slide = a short description of the Venus Transit
    - 1 slide = a short description of one major event in **1639**
    - 1 slide = a short description of one major event in **1761**
    - 1 slide = a short description of one major event in **1769**
    - 1 slide = a short description of one major event in **1874**
    - 1 slide = a short description of one major event in **1882**
    - 1 slide = a short description of important events in **2004**
    - 1 slide = a short description of what you think life will be like in **2012**…the next expected transit
    - 1 slide = a personal reflection on the Transit of Venus
3. *Optional:* create more slides highlighting other interesting points about the Transit Venus.
4. Remember to reference all of your research.

CONCLUSION: If you are lucky enough to witness the planet Venus passing in front of the Sun, realize that you are sharing this experience with many people around the world, and people throughout history. If you are not fortunate enough to see the transit from your location, try logging onto the Internet to be a part of the fun. Use your PowerPoint presentation to educate friends and family about this amazing phenomenon. If you miss it this time, remember to tune in again in 2012.

EVALUATION:

Research Questions in *Steps* **Maximum score of 40 points.**

Final Project ~ PowerPoint Presentation Rubric **Maximum score of 24 points.**

Final Project Rubric

Criteria	Level 1 0 points	Level 2 2 points	Level 3 4 points	Level 4 6 points
Content Slides are complete with relevant information	Information incomplete	Information somewhat complete	Information complete	Information complete and thorough
References properly cited	References are not cited	References are cited but incorrect or incomplete	References are cited	References are cited, correct and compete
PowerPoint Skills (fonts and colors are easy-to-read, point size varies appropriately, use of italics, bold, and indentations enhances readability)	PowerPoint skills does not demonstrate understanding	PowerPoint Skills demonstrates some understanding	PowerPoint Skills demonstrate understanding	PowerPoint Skills clearly demonstrates understanding
PowerPoint is technically creative and grade appropriate	PowerPoint is not creative or grade appropriate	PowerPoint is somewhat creative and grade appropriate	PowerPoint is creative and grade appropriate	PowerPoint is creative and exceeds grade expectation

Additional Project Comments and Feedback:

Total Project: **Maximum score of 64 points.**

SOCIAL STUDIES / WORLD HISTORY

TITLE: Emerging Civilizations
SUBJECT: Social Studies / World History
GRADE(S):   9–10
UNIT: Power Point

DESCRIPTION: For this mission, students will complete an independent study on one ancient civilization. Their findings will be reported creatively using PowerPoint.

PREREQUISITE KNOWLEDGE: Ability to navigate the Internet and use a word processor. Previous experience with PowerPoint or other presentation software tools would be helpful.

TEACHER PREP TIME: minimal

DELIVERABLES: Students will create a multimedia presentation using PowerPoint to present findings and demonstrate applied understanding.

EVALUATION / GRADING: Students will be evaluated using a PowerPoint Presentation Rubric.

MISSION: After thousands of years of hunting and gathering, *nomads* took a revolutionary step in history by deciding to settle in an area and not migrate further. This gave way to the emergence of villages, towns, and finally, cities. These cities were created from a complex society that shared a similar cultural identity that included a language, art, government, and religious beliefs. These civilizations would not have been possible without the cooperation of all its inhabitants. For this mission, you will complete an independent study on one ancient civilization. Your findings will be reported creatively using PowerPoint.

Nomad: A member of a group of people who have no fixed home and move according to the seasons from place to place in search of food, water, and grazing land. www.dictionary. com

RESOURCES: A computer with Internet access and PowerPoint. These websites will help you answer questions provided in *Steps* and to prepare your project. This list is a starting place. Feel free to search the Internet for other related information.

Websites

- http://www.rom.on.ca/egypt/case/
  ROM - Egyptian Civilization
- http://www.civilization.ca/civil/egypt/egypte.html
  Museum of Civilization
- http://www.bbc.co.uk/schools/romans/
  BBC - Romans
- http://www.uvm.edu/~classics/webresources/life/index.html
  Romans
- http://www.historyforkids.org/learn/greeks/index.htm
  Greek History

PowerPoint Resources

- http://www.actden.com/pp/
  Act Den
- http://www.ga.k12.pa.us/curtech/powerwk.htm#anchor371026
  PowerPoint Help

STEPS:

1. Choose a topic to focus your independent study: Identify the roots of Greek civilization and recognize its achievements from the Minoan era through the Hellenistic period. OR
2. Describe the developments and achievements of Roman civilization and analyze the significance of the fall of Rome. OR Assess the distinctive achievements of Egyptian civilization. OR
3. Describe the rise and achievements of African civilizations, including but not limited to Axum, Ghana, Kush, Mali, Nubia, and Songhai.
4. Research your topic using the Internet and books from the library.
5. Collect graphics and maps that support your research.
   Reference information. Last Name, First Name of Author (if known). "Title of work/article/page." *Title of Complete Document* (if applicable). Date last modified. URL (date visited).

PRODUCT:

1. Use the information that you have gathered in *Steps* to create a PowerPoint presentation illustrating your findings. Present your data in an informative and interesting manner.
2. Include a proper title screen, credits and references at the end as well as multimedia throughout (pictures, images, sounds etc.). Keep slides consistent.

Note: Remember to site the sources (bibliography) you used in gathering your information.

CONCLUSION: Share your PowerPoint presentation with the class. What are similarities and differences between the early civilizations? How have ancient civilizations influenced society today?

EVALUATION:

Performance Element	Needs improvement Criterion	Satisfactory Criterion	Exemplary Criterion
1. Research and Note taking	1 The content is vague.	3 The content is written with a logical progression of ideas and supporting information.	5 The content is written clearly and concisely with a logical progression of ideas and supporting information.
2. Storyboard / planning	1 Limited planning evident	3 Planning evident	5 Thorough planning evident
3. Layout	1 The layout is cluttered, confusing, and does not use spacing, headings and subheadings to enhance the readability.	3 The layout shows some structure, but appears cluttered and busy or distracting with large gaps of white space or uses a distracting background.	5 The layout is aesthetically pleasing and contributes to the overall message with appropriate use of headings and subheadings and white space.
4. Writing Mechanics	1 Spelling, punctuation, and grammar errors distract or impair readability. (3 or more errors)	3 The text is clearly written with little or no editing required for grammar, punctuation, and spelling.	5 The text is written with no errors in grammar, capitalization, punctuation, and spelling.
5. Graphics, Sound and/or Animation	1 Some of the graphics, sounds, and/or animations seem unrelated to the topic/theme and do not enhance the overall concepts.	3 The graphics sound/ and or animation visually depicts material and assists the audience in understanding the flow of information or content.	5 The graphics, sound and/or animation assist in presenting an overall theme and make visual connections that enhance understanding of concept, ideas and relationships.

NOTES:

SOCIAL STUDIES / GEOGRAPHY

TITLE: Interactive Local Map
SUBJECT: Social Studies / Geography
GRADE: 11–12
UNIT: Power Point

DESCRIPTION: Students will research maps, and using multimedia software creates an interactive local map.

PREREQUISITE KNOWLEDGE: Ability to navigate the Internet and use a word processor. Previous experience with PowerPoint or other presentation software tools would be helpful.

TEACHER PREP TIME: minimal

DELIVERABLES: Students will create a multimedia presentation using PowerPoint to present findings and demonstrate applied understanding.

EVALUATION / GRADING: Students will be evaluated using a PowerPoint Presentation Rubric.

Running short on time?
Have students work in pairs to collect research and summarize findings.

Only one computer in the classroom?
Have students research in small groups and prepare final reports in teams.

MISSION: You are going to investigate your state, region or province. How large is it? How many people live there? What is the geography like? What do you know about the region's exports, politics or transportation?

Using the Internet, you will explore the geography of your state, region, or province. You will create an interactive map which includes your findings and research. Let's get started!

RESOURCES:
- computer with Internet access
- word processor
- presentation software (PowerPoint)

These websites will help you conduct your research. This list is a starting place. Feel free to search the Internet for other related information. You will need to search for information specific to your topic. Here are a few places to help you get started.

- Map Quest
  http://www.mapquest.com
- Yahoo Maps
  http://maps.yahoo.com/
- Maps.com
  http://www.maps.com
- Maps on US (US only)
  http://www.mapsonus.com/
- TopoZone (topographical maps)
  http://www.topozone.com/
- MSN Maps
  http://maps.msn.com/(ouwccw555at3r3npvdqmia55)/map.aspx

STEPS: Use a word processor to collect your research.

1. Download images and maps (save the source of this information to reference in your project).
2. Select a favorite map for your area of research.
3. Choose a few areas or regions of the map that you wish to learn more about. (minimum 3)
4. Search the Internet, using the links in *Resources*, or others that you find, to find out more information about your selected areas.

Remember to document the sources of your information.
Last Name, First Name of Author (if known). "Title of work/article/page." *Title of Complete Document* (if applicable). Date last modified. URL (date visited).

For each area researched look for information on the geographical structure, people and any other interesting information that you find. You may also choose to include information about employment, exports, transportation, tourism or politics.

PRODUCT:

1. You will need to create a PowerPoint storyboard first, which will outline what your presentation will cover. It will also help you plan the navigation within your project. You will use a map of your state, region or province for your "Table of Contents". Using action buttons within the map, users can jump to information about that area. *(for help with action buttons and navigation in PowerPoint, see below)*
2. Include a proper title screen, credits and references at the end, as well as

multimedia throughout (pictures, images, sounds etc.)

Last Name, First Name of Author (if known). "Title of work/article/page." *Title of Complete Document* (if applicable). Date last modified. URL (date visited).

3. Include an overview of your state, region or province at the beginning of your presentation.

4. Your map (index page) will link to your in depth research.

5. Include a summary in your presentation.

Tips on how to make action buttons and hyperlinks in PowerPoint are available here…

- Using Action Buttons to Create Interactive PowerPoint Shows
  http://www.soita.esu.k12.oh.us/Resources/tips/mspp.html

- PowerPoint 2000 Tutorial - Hyperlinks
  http://gethelp.library.upenn.edu/workshops/biomed/ppt/hyperlinks.html

- Creating Action Buttons
  http://www.washburn.edu/cas/history/stucker/PPTactionbuttons.html

CONCLUSION: Share your presentation with other students in your class.

EVALUATION:

Performance Element	Needs improvement Criterion		Satisfactory Criterion		Exemplary Criterion	
1. Research	1	Limited research, from limited sources	3	Well researched, from various sources	5	Thorough research from varied sources presenting different points of view
2. Storyboard / planning	1	Limited planning evident	3	Planning evident	5	Thorough planning evident
3. Content	1	Lacks detail	3	Good detail	5	Extensive detail
4. Multimedia	1	Few or no multimedia elements are included	3	Multimedia elements are included	5	Multimedia elements are included, well selected and integrated into presentation
5. Personal Opinion	1	Opinion is weakly stated without supporting evidence	3	Opinion is stated with evidence	5	Opinion is well articulated and supported with appropriate evidence

NOTES:

ART EDUCATION

TITLE:	Mozart
SUBJECT:	Arts / Visual Arts
GRADE:	9–10
UNIT:	Power Point

DESCRIPTION: Students will research Mozart using the Internet and create a multimedia presentation to present findings.

PREREQUISITE KNOWLEDGE: Ability to navigate the Internet and use a word processor. Previous experience with PowerPoint or other presentation software tools would be helpful.

TEACHER PREP TIME: minimal

Review the websites in *Resources*.

DELIVERABLES: Students will create a multimedia presentation using PowerPoint to present findings and demonstrate applied understanding.

EVALUATION / GRADING: Students will be evaluated using a PowerPoint Presentation Rubric.

Running short on time?

Have students work in pairs to collect research and summarize findings.

Only one computer in the classroom?

Have students research and prepare final reports in teams.

Extension idea - Have students research world, political, societal and cultural events of Mozart's time. What influence may his surroundings have had on this artist? When possible, play Mozart pieces while students are working on this project.

MISSION:

"People make a mistake who think that my art has come easily to me. Nobody has devoted so much time and thought to composition as I. There is not a famous master whose music I have not studied over and over." – W. A. Mozart

- Who was Mozart?
- Where did he live?
- What type of music did he create?
- How do you feel about this music?
- What is your favorite Mozart piece?

Let's find our more about Mozart using the Internet!

RESOURCES:
- computer with Internet access
- word processor
- presentation software (PowerPoint)

These websites will help you conduct your research. This list is a starting place. Feel free to search the Internet for other related information.

- The Mozart Project
  http://www.mozartproject.org/biography/index.html
- Hero History – Wolfgang Amadeus Mozart
  http://www.imahero.com/../../herohistory/wolfgang_herohistory.htm
- Composers – Wolfgang Amadeus Mozart
  http://www.essentialsofmusic.com/composer/mozart.html
- Wolfgang Amadeus Mozart
  http://www.incwell.com/Biographies/Mozart.html
- OpenMozart.net
  http://www.openmozart.net/
- Wolfgang Amadeus Mozart – Symphonies
  http://w3.rz-berlin.mpg.de/cmp/mozart_symphonies.html
- Wolfgang Amadeus Mozart - Piano Concerti
  http://w3.rz-berlin.mpg.de/cmp/mozart_piano_concerti.html
- Wolfgang Amadeus Mozart - Violin Concerti
  http://w3.rz-berlin.mpg.de/cmp/mozart_violin_concerti.html
- Wolfgang Amadeus Mozart
  http://www.mhric.org/mozart/index2.html
- Mozart's Work – Midi Files
  http://www.mhric.org/mozart/mozmid.html
- Wolfgang Amadeus Mozart
  http://www.classical.net/music/comp.lst/mozartwa.html

STEPS: Using the links provided in *Resources*, and others that you find, you will research the life and works of Mozart. Here are some questions to help get you started.

1. What is Mozart's full name?
2. Where was he born?
3. When did he write his first piece?
4. What "type" of music did he write?
5. Research a brief timeline of his life and works.
6. When and how did he die?
7. What is your favorite Mozart piece? Why?
8. Collect your research in a word processor.

Remember to document the source of you research.

Last Name, First Name of Author (if known). "Title of work/article/page." *Title of Complete Document* (if applicable). Date last modified. URL (date visited).

PRODUCT:

1. You may wish to create a PowerPoint storyboard first, which will outline what your presentation will cover.
2. Include a proper title screen, credits and references at the end, as well as multimedia throughout (pictures, images, sounds etc.)
3. You may want to view this skill video before you begin creating your presentation.
4. Include the information you researched in *Steps*.
5. Include pictures and music – just be sure to reference the source of this media.
6. Include an audio clip (if possible) of your favorite piece, and explain why you like it.

EVALUATION:

Performance Element	Needs improvement Criterion	Satisfactory Criterion	Exemplary Criterion
1. Research	1 Limited research, from limited sources	3 Well researched, from various sources	5 Thorough research from varied sources presenting different points of view
2. Storyboard / planning	1 Limited planning evident	3 Planning evident	5 Thorough planning evident
3. Content	1 Lacks detail	3 Good detail	5 Extensive detail
4. Multimedia	1 Few or no multimedia elements are included	3 Multimedia elements are included	5 Multimedia elements are included, well selected and integrated into presentation
5. Personal Opinion	1 Opinion is weakly stated without supporting evidence	3 Opinion is stated with evidence	5 Opinion is well articulated and supported with appropriate evidence

NOTES:

ART EDUCATION

TITLE:	Artist's Critique
SUBJECT:	The Arts / Visual Arts
GRADE:	9–10
UNIT:	Power Point
DESCRIPTION:	Using PowerPoint, students will critique three pieces of art.

PREREQUISITE KNOWLEDGE: Ability to navigate the Internet and use a word processor. Previous experience with PowerPoint or other presentation software tools would be helpful.

TEACHER PREP TIME: minimal

Review the websites in *Resources*. Review PowerPoint.

DELIVERABLES: Students will create a multimedia presentation using PowerPoint to present findings and demonstrate applied understanding.

EVALUATION / GRADING: Students will be evaluated using a PowerPoint Presentation Rubric.

Variations on a Theme

Running short on time?

Limit the number of slides students must prepare.

Want to take this another step?

Have students reproduce art work using a draw program.

More Information

Teacher Tips: Invite a local artist to the class to discuss their art work.

MISSION: You have just been hired by an art company to provide art critiques. You received a call from your boss to attend the new opening at the Museum of Art to prepare your first three critiques (analyze & evaluate) comparing the artists' work. Using PowerPoint, students will critique three pieces of art.

RESOURCES:
- computer with Internet access
- PowerPoint

These websites will help you answer questions provided in *Steps* and to prepare your project. Feel free to search the Internet for other related information.

Helpful Websites
- Art Terms
  http://etc.sccoe.org/i98/tier2/Tier2info/elements.html
- Dictionary
  http://dictionary.reference.com/

PowerPoint Resources
- Act Den
  http://www.actden.com/pp/
- Education World
  http://www.education-world.com/a_tech/tutorials/ew_ppt.htm
- Microsoft PowerPoint Resource
  http://www.ga.k12.pa.us/curtech/powerwk.htm#anchor374026

STEPS:

1. Choose three paintings from below and prepare PowerPoint slides critiquing each painting.
   - http://www.abcgallery.com/P/picasso/picasso258.html
     Pablo Picasso 'Girl Before Mirror'
   - http://sunsite.icm.edu.pl/cjackson/magritte/p-magritte8.htm
     Rene Magritte's ~ 'The Human Condition'
   - http://imagecache2.allposters.com/images/OWP/N2155L.jpg
     Henri Matisse ~ 'Red Interior'
   - http://www.masterpiece-repro.com/cezanne_tulipsinavase.html
     Paul Cezanne ~ 'Tulips in a Vase'
   - http://www.butterbrot.de/haring/khyz10.jpg
     Keith Haring ~ 1987
   - http://www.art.com/asp/sp.asp?PD=10009253&RFID=538897
     Georgia O'Keefe's ~ 'Autumn Leaves'

2. In your slideshow, visually compare and contrast the paintings, indicate which art techniques the artist has used, which artistic movement the work most closely relates, and your personal feelings and reactions toward the work.

Tip 1: It is imperative that you critique the work in detail and use vocabulary that is specific to the visual art world. Use the glossary of visual terminology and the principles and elements of art that are linked to from the *Resources* section.

When you find images you like, check the Web page for a copyright notice. A good practice is looking for an e-mail link on the page and then using it to ask permission.

Last Name, First Name of Author (if known). "Title of work/article/page." *Title of Complete Document* (if applicable). Date last modified. URL (date visited).

Tip 2: Search the web for other artist's critiques, take notice of what they comment on.

PRODUCT:

1. Organize your three critiques in a creative manner using PowerPoint.
2. Include a proper title screen, credits and references at the end, as well as multimedia throughout (pictures, images, sounds etc.)
3. Use images and sounds to enhance your viewer's experience.
4. You may wish also to create a PowerPoint storyboard first, which will outline what your presentation will cover.

See *Resources* for more information, tools and assistance with using PowerPoint.

CONCLUSION: Share your PowerPoint presentation with the class. Are you intrigued by a new artist? Tell your classmates about them. Why are they interesting to you?

EVALUATION:

Performance Element		Criterion		Criterion		Criterion
1. Research and Note taking	1	The critique is vague.	3	The critique is written with a logical progression of ideas and supporting information.	5	The critique is written clearly with supporting information.
2. Text Elements	1	Overall readability is difficult with lengthy paragraphs, too many different fonts, dark or busy background, overuse of bold or lack of appropriate indentations of text.	3	Sometimes the fonts are easy-to-read, but in a few places the use of fonts, italics, bold, long paragraphs, color or busy background detracts and does not enhance readability.	5	The fonts are easy-to-read and point size varies appropriately for headings and text. Use of italics, bold, and indentations enhances readability. Text is appropriate in length.
3. Layout	1	The layout is cluttered, confusing, and does not use spacing, headings and subheadings to enhance the readability.	3	The layout shows some structure, but appears cluttered and busy or distracting with large gaps of white space or uses a distracting background.	5	The layout is aesthetically pleasing and contributes to the overall message with appropriate use of headings and subheadings and white space.
4. Writing Mechanics	1	Spelling, punctuation, and grammar errors distract or impair readability. (3 or more errors)	3	The text is clearly written with little or no editing required for grammar, punctuation, and spelling.	5	The text is written with no errors in grammar, capitalization, punctuation, and spelling.

NOTES:

ART / ART EDUCATION

TITLE: Musical Theatre
SUBJECT: The Arts/Music
GRADE: 6–8
UNIT: Power Point

DESCRIPTION: The focus of this activity is Musical Theatre. Groups of three will select a musical, research it, and present a musical number from it. You will research the people behind the production; and write a review discussing sets, costumes, and logo selection. Your presentation will include a PowerPoint presentation and performance.

PREREQUISITE KNOWLEDGE: Ability to navigate the Internet and use a word processor. Previous experience with PowerPoint or other presentation software tools would be helpful.

TEACHER PREP TIME: minimal
Review the websites in *Resources*. Review PowerPoint.

DELIVERABLES: Students will create a multimedia presentation using PowerPoint to present findings and demonstrate applied understanding.

EVALUATION / GRADING: Students will be evaluated using a PowerPoint Presentation Rubric.
Running short on time?
Limit the number of slides students are to prepare.

TEACHER TIP:
- Watch a musical production that is available on tape as a class.
- Have a group discussion on their perspective of the show.

MISSION: The focus of this activity is Musical Theatre. Groups of three will select a musical, research it, and present a musical number from it. You will research the people behind the production; and write a review discussing sets, costumes, and logo selection. Your presentation will include a PowerPoint presentation and performance.

RESOURCES: A computer with Internet access and PowerPoint.
These websites will help you answer questions provided in *Steps* and to prepare your project. This list is a starting place. Feel free to search the Internet for other related information.

Websites

Information on Musicals

- http://musicals.net/

PowerPoint resources

- http://www.actden.com/pp/
- http://www.education-world.com/a_tech/tutorials/ew_ppt.htm
- http://www.ga.k12.pa.us/curtech/powerwk.htm#anchor374026

STEPS:

1. Choose a musical that is of interest to your group and is available on video.
2. Research to ensure there is enough information available and musical accompaniment sources.

   Some suggested musicals include:

   - Annie Get Your Gun
   - Guys and Dolls
   - Hairspray
   - Hello Dolly
   - Beauty and the Beast
   - Hunchback of Notre Dame
   - Mamma Mia
   - Miss Saigon
   - Titanic
   - Unsinkable Molly Brown
   - West Side Story

3. Watch the musical production on video.

   - While watching the performance take note of emotions and thoughts stirred up while watching the performance and record information concerning backdrops, characters, costumes and sets.

4. Critique the musical production. What did you like or dislike about the story, the set, actors, music etc..

5. When you find images or sounds you like, check the Web page for a copyright notice.

   Reference material. Last Name, First Name of Author (if known). "Title of work/article/page." *Title of Complete Document* (if applicable). Date last modified. URL (date visited).

PRODUCT: Next you will create a professional and well-organized PowerPoint presentation regarding the group's musical choice.

Information to include in your PowerPoint presentation:

1. An introduction to your presentation (include 'Musical Theatre' and then the title of your production).
2. When and where this musical was originally produced, when did the production open and close and what were the total number of performances.
3. The source for this musical. Names of important people who brought this production to the stage (the director, choreographer, producers and designers.
4. Names of four of the lead actors / actresses.
5. Any awards this musical received.
6. A four sentence synopsis of Act 1.
7. A four sentence synopsis of Act 2.
8. Summarize orally one professional review of this production. Is this review legitimate? Be sure to include who the reviewer is and where the review appeared.

TIP: Organize your slides in a creative manner, use images and sounds to enhance your viewer's experience.

Note: Do not include anything that owners do not approve.

CONCLUSION: Share your presentation and review with the class.
Select a short musical number for your group to present to the class.
Once presentations are complete compare musicals.

EVALUATION:

The following checklist will be used for grading the answers.

__/5 Is the group's information clearly and concisely presented?

__/5 Is the group's information accurate?

__/5 Are drawings, illustrations, charts and photographs clear and used appropriately for the subject?

__/5 Does the project reflect their understanding of musical theatre?

__/5 Did they follow all instructions provided in class about how to prepare?

____ /25 Maximum score of 25 points.

NOTES:

CHAPTER 10

INFUSING WITH EXCEL

In this chapter we will discuss and explore:
- *The benefits of using Excel*
- *Excel lessons and activities examples for all grade levels*
- *Case Study: Making an Interactive Crossword Puzzle with Excel*
- *Case Study: Create a Timeline in Microsoft Excel*
- *Case Study: Spell to Excel*

Seen by many as the industry standard for data analysis, including graphing and producing tables, Microsoft's Excel is a wonderful application that can be used to achieve student learning outcomes. As educators start to understand the usefulness of such applications, we predict that a great number of staff will not only ask for training and support on these types of applications, but demand it.

The transparent yet underlying fact is that mathematicians are begging for us to realize that simple data collection is not a viable life skill without the ability to analyze the data. Applications like Excel which help quickly organize and create graphical representations of data for easier analysis is becoming a dominant force not only in the educational arena, but in the corporate world.

It is no wonder why many educators from all levels are fast learning that applications like Excel not only need to be introduced in a students' K-12 program, but it need to be introduced early and revisited often to reinforce the skills associated with such applications. Yet many educators seem to be intimated by the level of understanding and competence required to effectively use applications like Excel in their teaching. In fact, many of our staff developers are often told by the educators who they work with, "If I do not understand it, do you think that my students will?" While this statement is no doubt true, we encourage teachers to think of using technology, in this case applications like Excel, as they would any other tool in teaching. As with anything, it takes time to learn a new skill.

The Benefits of using Excel

Using Excel can enhance understanding of content within a graphic presentation of the information; it provides a visual representation of data that makes it easier to analyze. Excel reduces the difficulty of plotting data and allows students a means for interpreting the data.

You can also reverse the traditional process of analyzing data by giving students a completed chart and see if they can reconstruct the underlying worksheet. This goes a long way toward helping them understand the relationship between the data and the chart.

Excel can easily convert any chart or data set into a web page, making it very easy to share information among groups. Many universities are using this model for data sharing between students who are not even on the same continent.

Excel's ability to dynamically generate charts and graphs in seconds makes it easy to quickly demonstrate relationships between numbers.

As a teaching tool, students can see how different types of graphs and charts can be used to represent the same series of data. As one teacher stated, "For years it took me three to five days to teach kids the use a pie chart, bar graph, and/or a line graph to accurately represent information. Now with Excel, it makes it so much easier because the kids are far more motivated to use the application to manipulate data and to chart any information."

One of the best things is that you can compare data between any two or more variables. Using storage devices (disks), you can store data and use it to conduct a comparative analysis of any information that you have collected over time. For example, you can compare data collected by a group of collaborating teachers within one school, one county, or around the world.

The natural graph structure of Excel can be used by students to create game boards or patterns. Calendars or timelines also are easily created with Excel. Older students can create interactive lessons or activities. The database capabilities of Excel allow easy sorting and classifying of information.

Spreadsheets, such as those created in Excel, also can be used in sociology and psychology to chart different observations.

Students can use the Internet to study weather in another country over a period of time, then use Excel to record and compare the weather in that country to their own.

EXCEL LESSONS AND ACTIVITES

LANGUAGE ARTS

TITLE: Making an Interactive Crossword Puzzle with Excel

SUBJECT: Language Arts

GRADE: All

UNIT: Excel

	A	B	C	D	E
1					
2		e	g	g	s
3		a			o
4		s			f
5		y	m	c	a

OBJECTIVE: To make a crossword puzzle that will tell your students if they type the right letters or not. We will start with four small words which form a square.

STEPS:
- Open Excel and type the letters above in the same places you see them.
- Click on the letter A in gray (column heading), leave your mouse button depressed and drag over to column heading F.
- Put your cursor on the line between any two column headings, click and drag until Excel informs you that you have a column width of 7.00 (54 pixels).
- Click on the number 1 in gray (row heading), leave your mouse button depressed and drag down to row 6.
- Put your cursor on the line between any two row headings, click and drag until Excel informs you that you have a column height of 37.50 (50 pixels).
- Click on the letter E in cell B2, leave your mouse button depressed and drag to the letter "a" in cell E5. All letters should now be highlighted.
- From the **Format** menu select **Cells**, then select the **Alignment** tab
- Select Center alignment from both the Horizontal and Vertical blocks.
- Click on the **Font** tab, and select 24 in the size box.
- Click on the **Border** tab. Select Outside and then also select "Inside". Click **OK**.
- The next step will be to color all of the squares without letters in them.
- Click in cell A1 (on your Excel worksheet, not on the picture above), depress the Ctrl key and leave it depressed until you have clicked on all squares that do not have letters in them. If you click and drag you must release the mouse button at the end of a line (but do not release the Ctrl key).
- Now click and drag another line of cells, until all are highlighted. (Note: The last cell selected will be outlined in black, but not filled with the highlight color. It **is** selected)
- Release the Ctrl key (but do not click on the worksheet), and click on the Fill Color button on the Formatting toolbar.

Two steps to go! Next you will add comments at the starting letter of each word, to serve as a clue to the word.

- First, the letter e. This one will require a clue for across and a clue for down. Put them in the same comment with an empty line between the two clues.
- Right-click the letter e (in cell B2) and select Insert Comment. Highlight anything that is already in the comment box and type the clues.
- Continue until you have clues written for each word.
- Final Step! This step is what makes the puzzle interactive. If a student types the wrong letter in a box, the letter will turn red when the student hits the **Enter** key. This process is called setting conditional formatting.
- Click on the letter e in cell B2.
- From the **Format** menu, select **Conditional Formatting.**
- In the Condition 1 window, change the middle box to "equal to" and in the long box to the right type the letter e.
- Select the **Format** button and select a color you wish to use for correct letters. Some people use green (for Go), but I think blue shows up better.
- Click **OK.**
- With the **Conditional Formatting** window still open, click the button labeled **Add >>.**
- In the Condition 2 section, select "not equal to", type the letter e in the box to the right and select the Format button to select the color Red for incorrect letters.
- Click **OK.** The letter e turns blue.
- With the letter e still selected, find the Format Painter button on the Standard toolbar. It looks like a paint brush.
- Double-click the paint brush.
- One at a time, click on each of the other eleven letters. ["Trust me; there is method to my madness."]
- Each of the other letters should now be red, because they have been formatted incorrectly. Right? [Psst! The answer is "Right!"]
- Select the letter g in cell C2
- From the **Format** menu, select **Conditional Formatting**. See what pops up? See the Method in my Madness?
- All that you have to change in the Conditional Formatting window is the letter. Be sure to change only the letter. Leave the quotation marks. Also, make sure you change both letters.
- Repeat this process until all twelve letters in your puzzle are blue.
- Delete the letters. The Comment and formatting instructions will still be in each cell.
- Save your work.

If you want to avoid having a student changes your work accidentally, save your puzzle as a template.

INTEGRATED SUBJECTS

TITLE:	Create a Timeline in Microsoft Excel
SUBJECT:	Language arts/math/social studies/science
GRADE:	2 and up
UNIT:	Excel
OBJECTIVE:	Use a spreadsheet to create a timeline.

DESCRIPTION: Students create a timeline. They designate periods of time by utilizing fill colors to fill in groups of cells. Text can even be entered sideways to mark the events being represented. If students are feeling creative, they can enter text inside a drawing such as a rectangle or add pictures to jazz up the timeline. Younger students might just use pictures to represent events on their timeline.

A timeline can represent information from many different curriculum areas such as science, social studies, math, and language arts. Timelines often look at changes over time in areas such as transportation, technology, space travel, and so on. Timelines also work well when representing people's lives (a student, a character from a story, or a famous person) and events throughout history.

Sample timelines:

Sample 1: Technology Timeline
This timeline features rotated text within cells, borders around the cells, and cell fill colors.

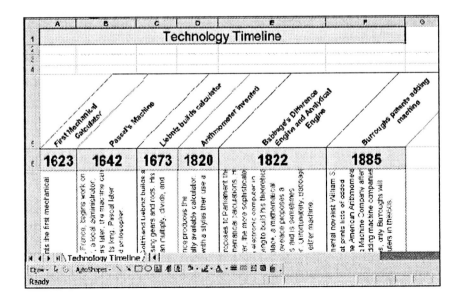

Sample 2: A Day in the Life of...

This timeline features rotated text within cells, cell fill colors, and clip art to enhance the appearance. Also, lines attach an event with its time.

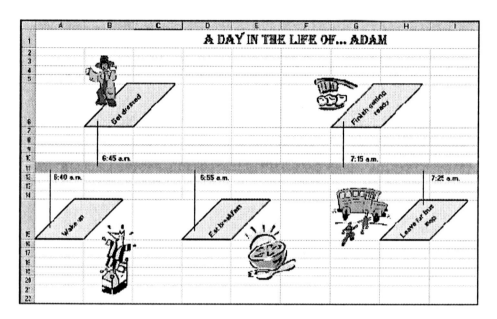

Two variations on these timelines:

Sample 3:

This timeline uses drawings (rectangles) with text typed inside.

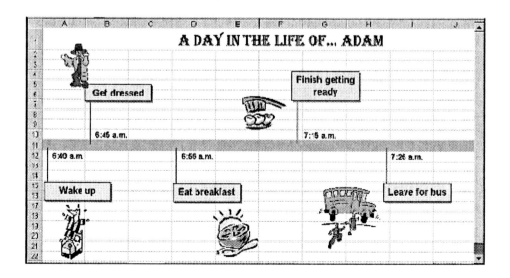

Sample 4:

This timeline uses drawings (rectangles) with text typed inside.

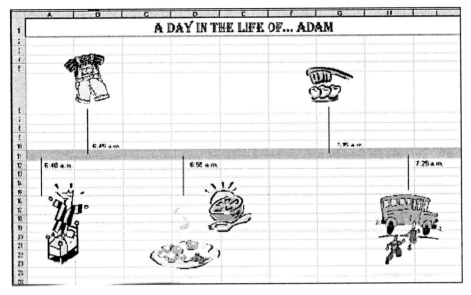

How to:

1. First plan your timeline. Do any necessary research and then sketch out the timeline on paper.
2. Start Microsoft Excel, and make sure a new, blank spreadsheet is open.
3. Type a title across the top of the spreadsheet, and format the text as you like.
4. Skip several rows, and then type the first date or time of your timeline. You might want to wait to format all the dates or times at once.
5. Next, type a short description above or below the date or time cell, whichever works best for your timeline.
6. To format the description so it is turned sideways, select Cells from the Format menu. Click the Alignment tab (see picture below). Select the Orientation for the text by clicking on the picture sample or by typing a number in the Degrees box. Change the Text alignment (horizontal or vertical), and then click OK.
7. Diagram to the right.

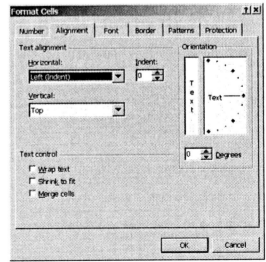

8. Tip: You might want to format a group of cells (for example, all cells that should be rotated) at the same time.

9. First select the group of cells, choose Cells from the Format menu, apply the formatting you want, and then click OK. All selected cells will now be formatted the same. Just type your text in those cells and press ENTER. They will be rotated automatically because you preformatted them.

10. Finish typing the text for your timeline and format the cells as needed (font, size, color, and so on). If you want to add a box around a cell or group of cells, click the Borders button on the toolbar.

11. You can change the width of your columns as necessary. Position the mouse pointer on the lines separating any two column headings (between the column letters), and then drag the line right or left to change the column's width.

12. Fill in cells with color. First, select the cells you want to color. Then, click the Fill Color button (paint bucket) on the Drawing toolbar. (If the Drawing toolbar is not visible, click View, Toolbars, and then Drawing.)

13. If you would like to add pictures to your timeline, select them from the clip art selection or another source (such as the Internet, a picture CD, a scanner, or a digital camera). Resize and move them as needed.

14. Do not forget to save your timeline frequently

15. Tip: To add text inside a drawing, such as a rectangle, first draw the shape. Click the Rectangle or Oval button on the Drawing toolbar, and use the mouse to draw the shape where you want it.

16. Next, right-click (click with the right mouse button) inside the shape, and select Add Text from the shortcut menu. Type your text, and then format it. Resize and move the shape as needed. If you'd like, fill the shape with a color by using the Fill Color button. Just be careful not to make the fill color too dark if the font is a dark color, too.

17. Be sure to draw a line from the shape to the timeline to connect the event with the date or time.

LANGUAGE ARTS

TITLE:	Spell to Excel
SUBJECT:	Language Arts
UNIT:	Excel

STEPS: Getting Started

Setting Default Font

1. Go to Tools and click Options.
2. Click the General Tab.
3. Where it says Standard Font, select Arial. Make the font size 14. Click OK.

Entering Data

Enter data using keyboard. Use tab, arrow keys, mouse or enter to travel between cells. Tab moves you to the right. Enter moves you down. Remember: The active cell is highlighted showing a double box.

- In A1 type: Spelling Word
- In B1 type: ABC Order
- In C1 type: ZYX Order
- In D1 type: Antonym
- In E1 type: Synonym.
- In F1 type: Number of Letters
- In G1 type: Extra

Press Enter to go to row 2.

- In A2 type: girl
- In A3 type: light
- In A4 type: small
- In A5 type: down
- In A6 type: mother
- In A7 type: cold
- In A8 type: short
- In A9 type: brother
- In A10 type: laugh
- In A11 type: city

To Replace or Edit Data

1. Move the mouse over the cell containing the data that you want to change and then click the left mouse button once to replace the contents of the cell.

2. Begin typing in the new data to replace contents. To edit the contents of the cell, click the left mouse button twice to get the flashing insertion point.
3. Use the arrow keys or on your keyboard to move the insertion point to where you want to add or remove characters.
4. Use the delete key to remove the characters to the right of the insertion point.
5. Use the backspace key to remove characters to the left of the insertion point. When you are finished making changes to the data, press enter.

II. Formatting Your Chart - The Basics

1. To highlight one cell, just click that cell.
2. To highlight a row, hold the left mouse click and drag across the part of the row to change.
3. To highlight a column, hold the left mouse and drag down the part of the column you would like to change.
4. To highlight the entire chart, left click cell A1 and then scroll and hold the shift key and left click cell G11.
5. To highlight individual cells, hold the shift key as you left click each cell.

III. Formatting Columns and Rows

Changing the Column Width

1. Double click the line between column A and column B to automatically size the column.
2. Change column B width next. Click on the B. The whole column is highlighted.
3. Right click with the mouse. A menu will appear.
4. Select Column Width with one click.
5. The column width window will appear.
6. Type in 12 to change width and click OK.
7. Column B is now 12 characters wide.

Change Column C with the Mouse

1. Click on column C. The whole column is highlighted.
2. Move the mouse + over the to the right edge of the column heading until it changes to a +
3. Press down and hold with the left button as you drag the edge of the column to a new position.
4. Try releasing mouse at 12.00 to see if text fits.
5. The width of A, B and C are now adjusted.
6. Adjust the remaining columns with the exception of G and F.

Changing Row Height

1. Click on cell 1(the gray cell).
2. Right click mouse.
3. Choose Row Height with one click.
4. Type in the number 55 and click OK.
5. You can also change row height by using the mouse and dragging the arrow key just as you did with the column widths.

Let's change all the remaining rows to a different height.

1. Highlight cells 2 through 11 by dragging the mouse.
2. This time go to Format on the menu bar.
3. Click Row and then Height.
4. Change number to 25 and clock OK.
5. All the remaining rows will now be the same height.

IV. Formatting Cells

Changing Font

1. Highlight cells A1 to G1.
2. Using the font box, scroll and select Comic Sans.
3. Select font size, scroll and select 20.
4. Your font should now be changed. Do not change column widths at this time.

Changing Font Color

1. Select color before you type by clicking font color icon on toolbar.
2. Click color and type.
3. You can highlight text after it is typed.
4. Right click mouse to get format menu.
5. Click format cells. Click font tab.
6. Click font color to select color.

Changing Alignment

1. With A1 to G1 highlighted, right click the mouse to get the format menu.
2. Highlight and click Format Cells. There will be six tabs at the top of this format window.
3. Click the alignment tab. Then select the following:
   In the horizontal column select general in the vertical column select center then click to place a check in the wrap text box. Click OK.
4. All text should now fit with the exception of the last column. Adjust accordingly.
5. The alignment icons on the tool bar may also be used to align text.

Adding Borders

1. Highlight your entire text by clicking cell A1, scroll to G11 and shift/click.
2. The entire spreadsheet should be highlighted.
3. Go to the menu bar at the top and pull down the format menu.
4. Highlight and click cells to see the six tab notebook.
5. Click on borders. Click the heavy style line in styles menu.
6. Next click each space under the border menu format lines.
7. You can also use the border icon on the toolbar menu.

Formatting Cells with Color and Patterns

1. Highlight cells A2 to A11.
2. Right click to get format menu and click format cells.
3. Click Patterns tab. Choose a color or go to patterns and select a pattern.
4. Click OK after pattern selection.
5. To select only color, you can choose the cell color icon on the toolbar menu.

Protection

1. Highlight the entire chart by dragging the mouse or using the key. You can also select the select all button.
2. Go to tools on the menu toolbar. Select protection.
3. Click protect sheet to protect.
4. To unprotect the sheet go through the same process.
5. Click the save button to save progress

V. Inserting, Deleting and Clearing Rows and Columns

Rows (Insert and Clear)

1. Highlight cell 4 in the first column.
2. Right click to get the format menu.
3. Select and click Insert. You can also go to the menu bar and click Insert then row.
4. In the Insert menu click add a row to insert the row. Type in the word night.
5. Highlight the word night. Right click to get menu.
6. Click clear to remove name.
7. Click the undo button to replace the text.

Columns (Delete)

1. Highlight the G column with the word Extra.
2. Right click to get menu and select delete. When the menu appears click delete.
3. The column will disappear.

VI. Moving Data

Dragging with the Mouse
1. Highlight the cells you wish to move.
2. Move the mouse to the border of the cells that are selected until it changes from a + to a pointer.
3. Press and hold the left mouse button and drag the cells where you want them and then release to place.
4. Click undo on the toolbar to move the cell back to its original position.

Using Cut and Paste to Move Data
1. Highlight cells that you want to move to a new location.
2. Move the mouse pointer over the cut icon and click left mouse button.
3. Select the cell where you want to place the data. This cell will become the top left cell of the new location.
4. Move the mouse to the paste icon and click with the left mouse button. The data now appears in the new location.
5. Click undo to undo the move. Double click the active cell with the marching dotted lines to undo the cut feature.

Copying Data
1. Highlight cells A2 to A12 to copy.
2. Click copy icon with left mouse button.
3. Select cell B2 to the place for the list of words in that row and left click the paste icon.
4. The list will be copied at the insertion point.
5. Double click to undo the copy feature.
6. Copy the words into column F. Change the font style in column F.
7. Highlight the spelling words in column B. Move the mouse to the bottom right corner of the selection until it becomes a +. Hold the left mouse button to drag and copy the text.

VII. Spellchecker and Ascending and Descending

Spellchecker
1. Highlight A1 to spell check worksheet from the beginning.
2. Select parts to spell check by highlighting.
3. Make changes of spelling in the spelling dialog box.

Ascending and Descending

1. Highlight the cells in the ABC column.
2. Click ascending icon on toolbar for words alphabetized.
3. Click ascending icon for numbers from least to greatest.
4. Click descending for numbers from greatest to least.

VIII. Page Setup

Page Setup

1. Click the magnifying icon.
2. Click the Setup box and the tab labeled Page.
3. Click Landscape to change the layout for this chart.
4. Click Margins tab.
5. Click the two bottom boxes, center horizontally and center vertically, to center chart.
6. Click OK.

Header and Footers

1. Click header and footer tab.
2. Click Custom Header.
3. Type Spell to Excel in the center box.
4. Format font by highlighting and clicking the A. Change font and font size to 26 point. Click OK.
5. Click Custom Footer.
6. Type your name in the center box and press enter. Click the calendar button to add date.
7. Highlight your name and the date. Change the font style and size to 20 point. Click OK.
8. Click Sheet. Notice the gridlines option. Click OK and then Close.

Margins

1. Click Margins tab.
2. Practice dragging the lines with the mouse to change the margins.

Zoom

1. Click Zoom to enlarge your worksheet.
2. Click Zoom again to see the entire worksheet.

Next and Previous

1. If your worksheet is more than two pages you can use the next button to go to the next page of your worksheet.

2. To go back to the previous page, click the previous button to return.

IX. AutoSum Function

1. Type the number of letters in each word in the E column.
2. Highlight the entire row. Click the Center alignment button on the toolbar.
3. Click the AutoSum function button. The sum or total number of letters appears in cell E13.
4. Add a border around the bottom row.

X. Save and Print

Print

1. Go to file on menu toolbar.
2. Pull down menu and click print.
3. Check setup and click OK.

Save

1. Go to file on menu toolbar and click Save.
2. Highlight entire chart. Go to edit on the menu bar. Click Clear to delete contents.

Save the template by doing a Save As and renaming. (Ex: SpellExcel)

CHAPTER 11

INFUSING WITH WORD PROCESSING

In this chapter we will discuss and explore:
- *How word processing helps in organizing and communicating*
- *Word lessons and activities examples for all grade levels*
- *Case Study: The Great Bean Race*
- *Case Study: Literature E-Circles*
- *Case Study: Creating a Personal Narrative in MS Word*
- *Case Study: Creating Poetry Notebook in MS Word*

Facilitate students' ability to use word processors (depending on age, of course) and they can do a lot with technology on their own without taking up teacher time.

Word processing is a standard application available in almost every school. A word processing program can be used for desktop publishing—students can create newsletters and magazines, advertisements and flyers, even business cards.

The drawing tools included in most word processing programs allow students to create pictures and logos, puzzles and more. Stories can be illustrated. Cookbooks can be created with imported graphics or custom illustrations. Using the HTML conversion utilities, students can create Web pages from word processing documents. Interactive documents can be made with the use of hyperlinks.

Word processing features, such as tracking and commenting, help facilitate collaborative projects. Tables are useful for collecting data and recording information. If a word processing program was the only application available, a teacher could have a technology-rich classroom with little effort.

Keyboarding instruction can be taught and then the weekly spelling list used for practice and warm-ups. This is sort of like the old 'write the words 5 times' assignment.

Students eventually become proficient with word processing for writing essays. Students can use word processing to report on a week-long commentary of their daily experience or to use columns to create a newspaper based on topics from their local newspaper. Students also can use a word processing program to record 'What I Learned This Week,' a learning journal. The student types one or two sentences throughout the week; then on Friday, the teacher prints the entire document and sends it home for parental signature.

Word processing helps in the act of organizing ideas with a view to communicate in writings to others does more than simply demonstrate what knowledge we have. It activates, reinforces, and transforms, that knowledge. Writing is a purposeful, often painstaking, process, the execution of which is perhaps the most educational cognitive activity in which we and our students can be engaged. It is a process appropriate to learners of all ages and all subject areas, right across the K-college curriculum and beyond.

Word holds so many possibilities for teachers and students. It is a very robust program that allows the users to create exciting projects. In order to use this program effectively in your classroom, it is important that you have a working knowledge of how to use the program.

WORD LESSONS AND ACTIVITIES

SCIENCE

TITLE:	Great Bean Race
GRADE:	3-5
SUBJECT:	Science
TOPICS:	Plant Growth
UNIT:	Word

Key Learning: Measurement, Comparing Variables for Growth

Time Needed: 7 weeks, 2-3 hours of class time per week

Background: From the Classroom in Arizona, United States

DESCRIPTION: The Great Bean Race is on! Compete with classrooms from other regions to see which collaborative team can grow the tallest bean plant. Controlling for certain variables (including growth time and bean seeds), seven or eight teams in each classroom design and conduct a controlled bean-plant experiment to investigate ideal conditions for growth. Students synthesize bean-plant information into a newsletter that describes the project, their group bean plan, and facts about beans.

Curriculum-Framing Questions

- **Essential Question**

  Is it possible to conquer the impossible?

- **Unit Questions**

  What are the perfect conditions for growing a bean plant?

  Why are plants important to us?

- **Content Questions**

  What are the different parts of a plant?

  What does a plant need to live?

  What are the functions of different plant structures?

  What is photosynthesis?

Instructional Procedures

Preparing for the Unit

Six to eight weeks prior to unit:

Contact two classrooms in different regions to participate in the project, preferably engaging those in regions with different climactic conditions. To locate other classes for participation in The Great Bean Race, try www.epals.com and www.kidsgardening.com.

Three weeks prior to the unit:

Germinate lima beans with varying amounts of light (12 hours, 18 hours, and 24 hours) to demonstrate how the amount of light affects plant growth. Engage students in this work; it will be a good "teaser" for the unit to come. Review and/or teach the scientific terms: inference, variable, hypothesis, processes, analyze

Getting Started

- Read the classic fairy tale *Jack and the Beanstalk* to students.
- Discuss the story and begin to talk about the realities and fantasies of the story while filling out a class T-chart to compare fact and fiction. Begin to probe students to think about how a beanstalk could grow so tall and so strong.
- Discuss the impossibilities of growing a beanstalk that big, but discuss how you might go about trying to conquer the task to make it possible. Chart students' responses and keep this chart up throughout the unit. Introduce
- Germinate one lima bean seed for each student to be used later in the challenge. Loosely fold a moistened quarter-sheet of paper towel around each seed.
- Suspend the paper towel packet inside a sealable plastic baggie using a small bit of tape. Zip the bags closed, and, using a permanent marker, write a student's name on each baggie. Tape the bags to a window that gets at least indirect natural light.

Asking Questions and Tapping Prior Knowledge

1. Pose the essential question to students; *is it possible to conquer the impossible?* Have students discuss the question in a pair-share grouping and prompt them to use examples that demonstrate their ideas. Students can think of things in their everyday lives that seem impossible and discuss ways they may be able to make it possible.
2. Bring the discussion back to the whole group and have students discuss what they talked about.
3. Chart student ideas and keep the chart up for students to refer to throughout the unit.
4. Introduce the science journal. Students use the journals to make observational drawings, write notes, and develop outlines and charts. Most importantly, students write journal responses to questions posed in class.
5. Have students write their first journal entry by reflecting on the Essential Question on their own.
6. Have students begin to develop a Know-Wonder-Learn (K-W-L) chart about plants. Prompt questioning during this process and record student responses (such as, Plants need water, but how much is too much? Too little? Plants need soil,

but how do soils differ? Plants need light, but how much? What kind of light?). Throughout the unit, come back to the K-W-L chart before and after each activity, and add new information.

Investigating and Learning About Plants

Conduct the following experiments and activities to answer the following Content and Unit Questions:

- Could humans and animals live without plants?
- What are the different parts of a plant?
- What does a plant need to live?
- What are the functions of different plant structures?
- What is photosynthesis?

Investigating Light

Referring back to the K-W-L chart, discuss the effect of light on plant growth. Use the following questions to help guide students in their learning:

1) If light is what makes a plant grow, what is the ideal amount of light to optimize growth?
2) Outdoor plants are exposed to the amount of sunlight available during the day. If they were exposed to more light, would they grow more?
3) Is indoor or outdoor light better? Are they the same?
4) Have students record their hypotheses and predictions in their journal, along with their rationale. Present to the class the plants that have been growing the past three weeks with 12, 18, and 24 hours of light. Have students record and evaluate results.

Investigating Phototropism

1) Present this simple demonstration: Place a 4-inch bean plant in a curtained box, and move a small lamp to a different side of the box every half hour.
2) Have students illustrate the plant and its position as it changes with the change of the light source in their science journals.
3) Have students share in a pair-share grouping what they discovered and the results of the investigation.
4) Encourage students to draw conclusions about light and plants.

Investigating Plant Parts and Photosynthesis

1) In small groups have students visit The Great Plant Escape web site at http://www.urbanext.uiuc.edu/gpe/gpe.html
2) Have them become detectives in Case One to learn about plant parts and photosynthesis.

3) When students have finished the case, have them write what they learned in their science journals.

4) While small groups are investigating at the Web site, have learning stations set up around the room where students can observe and investigate roots, leaves, and stems of real plants.

5) Have students draw diagrams with labels in their science journals.

6) While the groups are conducting the experiments and activities, rotate through the groups and hold conferences to assess understanding.

7) After students have visited the Web site and participated in all of the learning stations, have a class discussion about what students learned.

8) Clarify and expand on the content, and answer any questions focusing on the importance of plants as givers of oxygen and takers of carbon dioxide.

Investigating Soil Porosity and Absorption

1) Using background information, explain that soil serves plants in different ways. The soil study will evaluate the porosity and moisture-holding nature of soil. If soil absorbs too much water, there are no air pockets around the roots, and the plant "smothers." If the water drains completely, the plant will die of thirst.

2) Set out six buckets of soil (loam, clay, sand, humus, potting soil, and native soil). Students look at and feel the samples and write a journal entry predicting and supporting their reason for choosing which soil is best for both holding water AND allowing air pockets to remain around the roots.

3) Working in groups of six, students set up a funnel and filter over a plastic soda bottle for each soil sample. Place 250 ml (loosely packed) of soil in the funnel. Pour 250 ml of water (all at once) onto the sample, and record how long it takes water to begin draining from the funnel.

4) Measure the amount of water that drained through the sample. Subtract this quantity from the original 250 ml to find the amount of water held in the soil.

5) Have students record the data in the form of a chart, and continue with the remaining soil samples.

6) Have students write a comparison of their prediction and what was observed. Discuss student findings with the whole class.

Investigating Soil pH and Other Properties

1) Referring back to the K-W-L chart, ask, Are all soils equal? Use simple soil-test kits to determine the pH of the six different types of soil. Construct charts in science journals, and record the results.

2) Lead the class in a discussion of the other properties of soil they think are important. Soil is composed of organic and inorganic matter. Components

include sand, silt, clay, and humus. None is perfect in its own right, but each has properties that promote plant growth. In proper combination, these components contribute to a good soil that does the following:

- Holds the right amount of moisture
- Is porous enough for air circulation around roots
- Acts to "anchor" the rooted plant
- Has a proper pH
- Provides nutrients, including nitrogen and minerals

3) Have students list the properties of each component in their science journals to refer to when conducting their bean plant experiment. This information will help them decide which soil combination they want to use in The Great Bean Race.

Reflecting on Learning and Getting Started

1) Re-form groups. Have students share journal entries about light, water absorption, and soil. Then have the students submit a Group Plan for growing the tallest bean plant.

2) Have students predict how tall they think their plant will get. Any changes made in growing conditions during the challenge should be documented and explained using this form. Students gather materials and prepare for The Great Bean Race! (Lima bean seeds were pre-germinated, and each group should select two seeds to use in the challenge.)

The Great Bean Race Begins

1) On an agreed upon date, begin the challenge. Plant the seeds, and record daily growth and temperature in a Plant Log.

2) Take digital pictures of growth or make observational drawings, and measure (in inches and centimeters) weekly.

3) At the end of each week, have students compare plants.

4) Describe the differences and similarities between the plants and the group bean plan, and tell what might explain these in the plant log and journal. Emails sent between classes can keep students informed of how other plants are growing. Any changes to the growing conditions should be recorded on the group bean plan.

Creating Student Newsletters

1) To address and answer the Unit and Content Questions, *Could humans and animals live without plants?* and *What does a plant need to live?,* students create a group newsletter that includes the following information:

- About the Great Bean Race
- The Importance of Plants

- About Our Epals
- Our Bean Plan
- A Poem
- Facts About Lima Beans
- A Graph and Survey Results (surveys may include growth of one plant over time (line graph), comparison of growth of all plants (bar graph), or results of a survey of student's favorite beans (pie chart).

2) Show students the newsletter example and discuss the requirements.

3) Hand out the newsletter checklist and discuss the project requirements with students.

4) Once students have had an opportunity to see the checklist, model using the checklist with a sample newsletter to show them what quality work looks like and how they can use the checklist to ensure they are meeting project requirements. This newsletter will be shared with their Epal classrooms and the group's family members as a way to keep them up-to-date and informed about what is being learned in class.

5) The students will showcase some of the highlights from the unit so far and tie in the science content across the curriculum. It will be created before the race is over and after the students have learned about plants and created their Group Plan. The graphs and poetry could be created during math and language arts. Mini-lessons about citing resources, writing poems (cinquain, acrostic, free verse, and so forth), using spreadsheet programs to make charts and graphs, and inserting charts and graphs into their newsletter will need to occur along the way to ensure student understanding and success. These skills could also be taught prior to the unit as well.

6) After each newsletter is complete, have students fill out the collaborative assessment to assess their group's participation.

Analyzing Results

1) At the end of three weeks, to answer the Unit Question, *What are the perfect conditions for growing a bean plant?*, students analyze results of growth investigations. Students compare and contrast their experimental designs and subsequent results with those of the other participants.

2) Students synthesize information and develop a conclusion on the best methods for growing bean plants in their science journals.

3) Using graphing software, students create a graph comparing their final plant height with those of their Epal's and analyze the results by drawing conclusions about why the plants grew as high as they did.

Drawing Conclusions

1) Now that students have participated in the experiment and seen the conclusions firsthand, have students begin to reflect on their initial prediction and what they have learned.

2) Place students in small groups to discuss the following Essential and Unit Questions:
   - *Is it possible to conquer the impossible?*
   - *What are the perfect conditions for growing a bean plant?*
   - *Could humans and animals live without plants?*

3) Remind students to use results and examples from the bean plant experiment to support their opinions and ideas.

4) Bring the discussion back to the whole group, and chart student responses to the Essential Question next to the original responses from the beginning of the unit.

5) Ask students to reflect about what they have learned using the Essential, Unit, and Content Questions (post on chart paper or on the board) as a guide to help with their responses. In addition, each student writes a reflective paragraph on the Essential Question giving real-world examples supporting their opinion.

6) Read *Jack and the Beanstalk* again to students. Take some time to discuss the possibilities of growing a beanstalk that tall and how their own bean growing experience ties into the story.

Wrapping Up

1) Students analyze the different groups' bean plant growth data and come to a conclusion about the best growing conditions for plants in a reflective writing activity.

2) Digital pictures of the students participating in the bean plant experiment would be a great addition to the portfolio page.

3) This will go in their portfolio that showcases the year's units.
   Prerequisite Skills
   - Functional keyboard and mouse skills (typing, navigating, copying, pasting, and saving on a computer)
   - Basic knowledge of word processing software
   - Ability to measure length in inches, capacity in milliliters, and degrees in Fahrenheit

Differentiated Instruction
Resource Student
   - Enlist support from resource personnel to help the student study vocabulary and

concepts, and complete work that may take more time or revision than science-class time permits

- Allow written tasks to be completed orally, or allow the student to dictate responses
- Develop a daily "to do" schedule of tasks to help focus the student's effort during project work
- Recognize the student's strengths and put them to use when assigning group tasks
- Assign students to groups in a thoughtful manner
- Reduce assignments or allow more time as needed

Gifted Student

- Encourage the student to investigate related topics and make a report to the class
- Examples might include pollination, vegetative propagation, seed dispersal, or how plant varieties develop. If the student has special technical abilities, have the student apply them to the development of the class Web page
- If the student has special writing abilities, allow the student to take the lead on email correspondence between classes

English Language Learner

- Work with the ELL teacher to make a dictionary of terms in the first language and English language to aid vocabulary development
- Have the student dictate journal entries to the ELL teacher, and clarify science concepts (the ELL teacher may help assess student learning as well)
- During class, pair students when the language load indicates a need for this (for example, during journal writing time)
- Accept assignments written in the first language for later translation
- Enlist the help of first-language speakers in the school who have greater English proficiency to help the novice
- Shorten assignments, or allow more time as needed

ASSESSMENT PROCESSES

Science Learning Assessment: Students will write responses to prompts presented in class. These responses serve as the basis for evaluating science concept development during the course of the unit. Student responses will be evaluated using the Science Content Rubric.

Student Newsletter Assessment: Students will use the checklist to ensure they are meeting all project requirements. This can be used as a final assessment to assess student work on the newsletter. Using the collaborative rubric students will assess their group's work.

Student Objectives

Science

Students will be able to:

- Analyze variables of plant growth by completing plant lab activities
- Work like scientists to plan, conduct, analyze, and report the results of a discrete experiment
- Make sequential observational drawings of a plant to show how it changes as it grows
- Make periodic measurements and record plant height, then make a chart showing growth over time

Process and Technology Skills

Students use a science journal to:

- Document the methods of their investigation in an organized way, with a complete hypothesis, experimental design, results, and conclusion
- Write reflective responses to teacher queries throughout the course of the unit
- Draw diagrams and illustrations that show processes and effects
- Enter data in a spreadsheet, make charts that show growth over time, and interpret the meaning of the chart
- Work cooperatively in small groups

Student Publishing Objectives

Using desktop publishing software, students produce a classroom newsletter that includes:

- Lab reports that detail the planning and implementation of their Great Bean Race investigations
- Group plans
- Information learned about plants and how that information helped to develop a group plan
- Epal information, a map of each state, and an explanation of how the plants might grow differently in each state
- Poetry about plants
- "Facts at a Glance" sections that synthesize information from a variety of electronic sources (such as online encyclopedias, scientific sites on the Internet, and so forth)
- Citations
- Graphs with a captions that explain what is shown symbolically

LANGUAGE ARTS

TITLE:	Literature E-Circles
GRADE:	5–7
SUBJECT:	Language Arts
TOPICS:	Literature, Writing, Technology
UNIT:	Word

KEY LEARNINGS: Analyzing Narrative, Appreciating Reader Interpretations
TIME NEEDED: 2 weeks, 90 minutes daily
BACKGROUND: Odyssey Story from North Carolina, United States

National Education Technology Standards (NETS)

Grades 6-8 Performance Indicators:

- Apply productivity / multimedia tools and peripherals to support personal productivity, group collaboration, and learning
- Collaborate with peers, experts, and others using telecommunications and collaborative tools
- Select and use appropriate tools and technology resources to accomplish a variety of tasks and solve problems

Student Objectives

Students will be able to:

- Analyze a literary character
- Identify and describe the narrative elements of a book
- Reflect on moral issues raised in a book
- Read critically using a variety of reader-response techniques
- Identify a theme supported with specific references to a book
- Break down complex tasks into manageable pieces
- Reflect metacognitively on the use of reading strategies

DESCRIPTION: Students in different middle schools read the novel *Holes* by Louis Sachar and meet in virtual literature circles (or *e-circles*) to discuss their interpretations of the novel. Comprehension questions and a modified Socratic discussion method promote deep thinking about characterization, plot, style, author intent, and personal interpretation. Students meet face-to-face to create technology-supported projects that demonstrate their understanding and appreciation of the text. An online survey marks changes in attitudes about reading and the ethical questions the novel presents.

Curriculum-Framing Questions
- **Essential Question**
  Why should words be chosen carefully, and why do people tell you to be careful what you say?
- **Unit Questions**
  Why do people interpret books differently?
  How did the book impact you or change your outlook on life?
  How are the events and characters in the book similar to events and characters you have known or experienced?
  What can I learn about myself and others from reading this book?
- **Content Questions**
  How did the author use dialogue to depict the characters?
  How did the author play around with time to tell his story?
  What techniques did the author of *Holes* use to develop the characters, setting, and plot?

Instructional Procedures

Prior to instruction collaborate with local teachers. Arrange to read the book together, and plan your literature e-circle themes. Set up online virtual literature circles for cross-school discussions using a free bulletin board, such as Boards2Go http://www.boards2go.com or Quicktopics http://www.quicktopic.com.

Prepare bookmarks with a reading schedule on one side and reader response strategies on the other (as described in Phase I). Plan a time in which classes from the different schools can meet for group presentations and a reading celebration.

Phase I: Getting Ready to Read, 1 or 2 periods

This phase includes introducing the topic and text, assessing initial thinking, introducing online discussion, and preparing to read. Conduct a Think-Pair-Share activity. Ask students to do a quickwrite on one of the following topics, and then share what they have written with a partner:
- When have you learned something important from a story?
- Why do people read stories?
- How is reading a story different from reading other kinds of writing?

Follow up with a whole-class discussion.

Ask students if they have ever been blamed for something they did not do. Conduct a discussion about how they had responded to the accusation and what do they think now of their response. Distribute copies of Louis Sachar's *Holes*. Have the class look at the cover, and ask students to discuss what the cover art evokes in the reader and why the publisher may have chosen that imagery. Read the text on the back of the book, the note about the author, and the list of other books by Louis Sachar. Many students will remember reading the *Wayside School* series of books and will enjoy comparing the style and themes of *Holes* to the author's earlier books. Ask students if they ever use any of these strategies before starting a book and discuss why they are useful actions to take.

Have students complete a survey to assess their attitudes about reading. After students complete the survey, discuss class (but not individual) results. Ask, how do we think alike? How are we different? How can we account for our similarities and differences? Build a climate of trust and acceptance for the varying points of view and interpretations of the book that will arise as students read *Holes*.

Teach students to respond actively to the text by recording their thoughts on sticky notes as they read. Print the following list of response strategies on bookmarks:

- Personal Connections to the Text
- Reactions, Opinions, Feelings
- Questions, Inferences, Predictions
- Vivid Imagery
- Wonder Words (memorable language or moving passages)
- Evaluation (the way the book is written—what works? what does not work?)

Introduce students to the online message board you have set up, and explain processes for online discussion. Student discussions should focus on answering the following Curriculum-Framing Questions:

- Why should words be chosen carefully, and why do people tell you to be careful what you say?
- Why do people interpret books differently?
- How did the book impact you or change your outlook on life?
- How are the events and characters in the book similar to events and characters you have known or experienced?
- How did the author use dialogue to depict the characters?
- How did the author play around with time to tell his story?
- What techniques did the author of Holes use to develop the characters, setting, and plot?
- What can I learn about myself and others from reading this book?

As the unit progresses, small groups create projects related to the book. Assign students to small groups of three to five. Try to make groups diverse so students share a variety of opinions and reading experiences. Assign roles to individuals so everyone in the group contributes. Roles might include team recorder, materials manager, art director, and technology expert. Pass out response strategy/schedule bookmarks and help students record the number of pages they should read each night. (If students read during class and at home, most can finish the book in one week.)

Phase II: Reading and Reflection, 5 or 6 periods

During this phase, students engage in the following actions every day:
- Read the book
- Keep a reading response journal
- Meet in online discussion groups
- Participate in literature lessons or Socratic seminars

First Half of Each Period

Students engage in independent reading, response journal writing, and e-circle discussions. During independent reading, students write responses to the text on yellow sticky notes. After reading a scheduled number of pages, they record and expand their notes in their journal and write a response to the prompt for that day's e-circle. This entry serves as the "ticket" into the ongoing e-circle discussion. Use the independent reading-responding time to meet with individuals or small groups who need extra support. To encourage steady reading effort, record the number of pages the class has read at the end of each period. Seeing the number of pages grow on a "Class Reading Progress" chart can be motivating. Every three days, ask students to select their three best notes, write a reflection about the strategies they used, and turn them in for assessment. Have students complete their daily reading response before engaging in the e-circle. As students join an e-circle discussion, they either respond to teacher prompts or, depending on their maturity, carry on a student-driven discussion. You may want to print and post samples of online dialogue to remind students of the discussion parameters.

Second Half of Each Period

Focus on direct instruction on a literary theme, reading strategy, or technology tool that you need to teach or is dedicated to a Socratic seminar. Teach students about Socratic seminars methods and provide them with a seminar guide and grading rubric. Walk through a sample Socratic seminar question process, explaining important points. If this is a new activity, you might want to introduce the activity and conduct a mock seminar before you focus on discussing the text. Post prompts online in the e-circle space in advance, so students can begin thinking about the upcoming discussion. Focus the discussion on the following Curriculum-Framing Questions in order to promote transfer of thinking skills and reading strategies to other literature:

- Why should words be chosen carefully, and why do people tell you to be careful what you say?
- Why do people interpret books differently?
- How did the book impact you or change your outlook on life?
- How are the events and characters in the book similar to events and characters you have known or experienced?
- How did the author use dialogue to depict the characters?
- How did the author play around with time to tell his story?
- What techniques did the author of Holes use to develop the characters, setting, and plot?
- What can I learn about myself and others from reading this book?

Phase III: Creating a Project, 3 or 4 periods

Introduce the project by showing the sample presentation and sharing the project rubric, asking for input and making revisions as necessary. Guide students through a project-planning process, such as the following:

1. Select a theme from the book that is especially meaningful to you, one that you can connect to your life or the lives of your classmates.
2. Think about what you want to tell others about the theme in life and in the book.
3. Brainstorm ideas for the project. Try to think of as many ideas as you can that are unusual and meaningful.
4. Choose a format for your project (such as a multimedia presentation, dramatization, video, Web site, mock trial, newsletter, or brochure).
5. Make a plan for completing the project with deadlines and responsibilities.
6. Help each other stay focused and do high-quality work.
7. Answer one or more of the following questions and support your answer with evidence from the book, survey results, and quotes and responses from others in your e-circle:
   - Why should words be chosen carefully, and why do people tell you to be careful what you say?
   - Why do people interpret books differently?
   - How did the book impact you or change your outlook on life?
   - How are the events and characters in the book similar to events and characters you have known or experienced?

Asking students to complete the preceding checklist as they work will help keep them on track. As students are working on projects, conduct whole-class or small-group instruction on the following skills as appropriate:

- Brainstorming
- Distinguishing good ideas from bad ideas
- Developing a project plan
- Addressing interpersonal group problems (such as encouraging workers who are not doing their share, managing bossy group members, drawing out shy students, and so forth)
- Evaluating your own work
- Solving problems (such as working with technology, locating resources, and getting good help and advice)

Plan a celebration for sharing the projects with the online groups.

Phase IV: Conclusion and Reflection

Place students in new small groups to reflect on the unit. Ask them to discuss the following questions:

- What did I learn from the people in my e-circle?
- What strategies did I use to help me apply this book to my life?
- Is *Holes* a good book? Is it a great book?

Prerequisite Skills

Student should have familiarity with:

- Digital and video cameras
- Multimedia presentations
- Web page authoring

Differentiated Instruction

Resource Student

- Supply visual guides
- Break activities into manageable sections, and record tasks on a calendar
- Provide extra time to complete assignments
- Supply a copy of the book on tape or CD
- Group the student with more capable learners
- Encourage cooperation by explaining to the class that *collaboration* means working together to meet goals

Gifted Student

- Encourage the student to create supplemental assignments or extensions
- Provide technologies that offer advanced features

English Language Learner
- Provide copies of the text in the student's first language
- Show the student how to use a computer microphone to record the student reading aloud
- Provide a glossary

Assessment Processes

Give students daily class work and homework grades for maintaining their reading status. Each day, check with students to see how many pages they have read. Ask comprehension questions to gauge general understanding. Grade the e-circle participation. Give points for showing the following:
- Effective interaction about the book
- Elements of good reader-response
- Acceptable spelling, usage, and grammar
- Ask students to self-assess their use of reading strategies periodically throughout the reading of the book.

Materials and Resources

Printed Materials
- Sachar, L. (1998). *Holes.* New York: Farrar, Straus, and Giroux.
- Sachar, L., Yelnats, S., & Newman, J. (2003). *Stanley yelnats' survival guide to camp green lake.* New York: Random House Children's Books.

Supplies
- shovel
- other story-related props
- poster board
- markers
- paint
- rolls of paper

Internet Resources
- Desert USA
  www.desertusa.com
  A virtual field trip to an American desert
- *Holes* ThinkQuest
  http://library.thinkquest.org/J0113061
  A unit study based on Holes

- Louis Sachar
  www.louissachar.com
  Story synopsis and interview with the author about Holes
- Quicktopics.
  www.quicktopics.com
  A free message board for e-circle
- Boards2go
  www.boards2go.com
  Another free message board for e-circles
- Zoomerang
  www.zoomerang.com
  A free online survey tool
- Atomic Learning
  www.atomiclearning.com
  Online tutorial of many software program

DVD

- *Holes.* DVD Directed by Andrew Davis. Burbank, CA: Walt Disney Home Video, 2003.

Technology—Hardware

- Internet access to participate in the online discussions
- Computers, digital cameras, video cameras, or presentation equipment might be required to complete some projects

Technology—Software

- Online discussions for e-circles
- Internet browsers for students to participate in online discussions
- Presentation software for students who want to create multimedia presentations

ENGLISH / LANGUAGE ARTS

TITLE: Creating a Personal Narrative in MS Word
SUBJECT: English / Language Arts
UNIT: Microsoft Word

What will I learn today?
You will learn how to create a personal narrative in a word processing document.

What hardware and/or software does the techtorial apply to?
You will need a computer workstation with network/Internet access and MS Word.

Lesson Objective
This lesson will teach you how to create a personal narrative.

STEPS:
1. Open Microsoft Word

2. Save your document
    - Go to FILE, SAVE AS
    - Where it says *File Name* give the document a name – Something you can remember that pertains to the actual lesson you are creating. For example, personal narrative.
    - Where it says *Save in:* Click on down arrow and locate your student folder
    - Click Save

3. Create a Header and Footer
    - Go to View Header/Footer
    - Type your first and last name
    - Press the Tab key on your keyboard (this will move your cursor to the middle of the page)
    - Type the header title: Personal Narrative
    - Press the Tab key on your keyboard (this will move your cursor to the right side of the page)
    - Enter the date by clicking the Insert Date button on the Header/Footer toolbar
    - Click Close on the toolbar

4. Type: Personal
    Narrative of *Your Name.* For example:

Personal Narrative of Bubba Smith

- Make the font size 36
- Click Center Align
- Click Bold
- Press Enter two times after your title
- Click Align right
- Turn Bold off
- Make the font size 12
- Double space your narrative by doing the following:
  Go to Format and Paragraph
  Click the drop arrow by Single and choose Double
  Click OK

5. Type your personal narrative.
   - DO NOT alter font, size, or color. You must TYPE the information first and if time allows, you may alter the format.
   - **REMEMBER:**
     Save often by going to File and Save
     Press tab at the beginning of each paragraph
     you do not have to press enter except at the end of each paragraph!

6. If time permits, insert an image that illustrates the poem.
   - Go to Insert – Picture – ClipArt
   - Find the picture you would like to insert
   - Click the picture to insert it

7. Resize the image
   - You can resize the image by dragging a corner of the image (where the black dots are)
   - **Things to Remember:**
   - ✓ SAVE periodically! You should only have to save NOT Save As!
   - ✓ PRINT only AFTER teacher approval – DO NOT HIT THE PRINT ICON!
     - o Go to FILE, Print Preview
     - o Then go to FILE, PRINT
     - o Make sure you know *where* you are printing!

LANGUAGE ARTS

TITLE: Introduction to Word Processing
SUBJECT: Computers & Internet, Language Arts
GRADE: Kindergarten–2

DESCRIPTION: Children are being introduced to the computers in the school (Macintosh and PC). They are being asked to write and recognize their name and draw a picture of themselves. They will also be asked to name certain parts of the computer.

MISSION:
After completion of the activities children will be able to:
- write their name and recognize their name
- draw a picture of themselves
- recognize pictures that have been presented to them be name and sight and match these pictures with a picture that has been hidden

SKILLS:
- Children will be able to recognize the letters of their name on the keyboard (previous practice has been given)
- Children will be able to recognize pictures and name parts of the computer.

RESOURCES:
- Computers
- Stencil with pictures and names of parts of the computer
- Outline

STEPS:
1. Children have been previously shown pictures of: the mouse, the keyboard, the CPU and the monitor. These pictures have been displayed to the children and several children are questioned.
   - Where is the mouse?
   - Where is the keyboard?
   - Where is the CPU?
   - Can we see anything on the monitor?
   - What does it look like?
2. Children are then given a stencil to match the names with the pictures.
3. When this is completed they are then asked to go to the computer and write their name and draw a picture of themselves underneath.

4. With Kindergarten it is necessary to have the computers set to the Word Processing Package and then have the students quickly changed to the Drawing section.

    The actual skill of changing to the Drawing package is too difficult at this stage.

ASSESSMENT: Have children compare each others drawings and names. Print as many as possible in the lesson time.

LANGUAGE ARTS / ENGLISH

TITLE: Creating Poetry Notebook in MS Word
SUBJECT: Language Arts / English
UNIT: Microsoft Word

MISSION: What will I learn today?
You will learn how to create a multiple-page booklet in a word processing document.
What hardware and/or software does the techtorial apply to?
You will need a computer workstation with network/Internet access and MS Word.

STEPS:

1. Open Microsoft Word

2. Save your document
   - Go to FILE, SAVE AS
   - Where it says *File Name* give the document a name – Something you can remember that pertains to the actual lesson you are creating. For example, la_poetry.
   - Where it says *Save in:* Click on down arrow and locate your home folder
   - Click Save

3. Create a Header and Footer
   - Go to View Header/Footer
   - Click *Switch between Header and Footer*

   - Type your name at the left
   - Right after your name, type P# (for period and the number)
   - Press tab to go to the center
   - Type Poetry Notebook
   - Press tab to move to the right
   - Click the Insert Date button
   - Click Close on the Header/Footer toolbar

Typing a Title for your Poem:
4. Now, type the title of your poem
   - The title needs to be centered
   - Highlight (select) the title
   - Click Center Align Button to center the title

- Click the Bold button to make the text bold
- Click right after the title to place your cursor at the end of the line
- Press enter about 2 times.
- Press CTRL and Enter to insert a page break after the title.

5. Click *Left Align* to return to regular alignment

6. Click *Bold* to turn bold off

7. Type the poem.
   - DO NOT alter font, size, or color. You must TYPE the information first and if time allows, you may alter the format.

8. Insert some clipart that illustrates the poem.
   - Go to Insert – Picture – ClipArt
   - Look on the right side of the window at the clipart area
   - Enter a word that might be something about your poem and click search
   - Scroll through the list of pictures to see which one you would like to insert
   - Once you have chosen, click the picture and it will insert into the text area
   - If you do not like the picture you inserted in your text, click it once and press delete

9. Resizing and moving the image
   - Click and drag the image and/or drag a corner to resize it

When you have completed your poem, go to a new page by inserting a page break.
REMEMBER: You can insert a break easily by pressing CTRL-Enter

10. REPEAT STEPS 8 – 15 to add three poems to your notebook. Your notebook must include one of each type of poem:
    - Cinquain
    - Haiku
    - Limerick

READING

TITLE: Concept Books
SUBJECT: Reading
GRADES: 9–12
UNIT: Word

DESCRIPTION: When Marshall McLuhan observed that "the medium is the message," he might have been talking about the kinds of books that your students will create with this project: books whose form is a direct reflection of their nonfiction subject. Whether your students create an "antiqued" journal about local history, a book on CD about the music business, or a Web-based book about the impact of the Internet on kids' lives, they will amaze you with their ability to combine research and imagination to create their own "collector's editions."

OBJECTIVES:
- To research and write a short work of nonfiction
- To "publish" this nonfiction work as a self-made book designed to fit the subject matter
- To participate in a public exhibition of one-of-a-kind nonfiction books

PREREQUISITE SKILLS:
- Ability to conduct Internet research using Microsoft Internet Explorer
- Familiarity with Microsoft Word
- Introduction to Microsoft Publisher and Microsoft FrontPage
- Basic understanding of the nonfiction form and "book arts

Time Allotted:
Four class periods, plus work outside of class

STEPS:
1. Although this project is designed to be completed by individual students, you may want your students to work on it in teams. If so, form the teams before launching the project to save time.
2. Preview the Web sites listed under Resources. Some of them provide suggestions for high-quality nonfiction books for young adult readers, in case your students need inspiration. Other Web sites focus on the book arts and making books. Save as Favorites the sites you find most useful.
3. Under Resources, you will also see two Microsoft Office XP tools for your students' use.

4. Bring your class together for a kick-off discussion about books, book arts, and publishing. Talk about unusual book formats that your students have seen; you may even want to use an overhead projector to show some examples from the Web sites listed under Resources. Also talk about new book forms, such as electronic and Internet-published books.

5. Tell your students that they are about to create their own one-of-a-kind books on nonfiction topics of their own choosing.

6. Distribute photocopies of the Student Activity pages, and begin Step A.

7. When all of your students' books (in their various forms) are complete, hold a publication party. Have each student make a brief presentation about his or her work, and then display all the books around your classroom for the rest of the school to come and see.

ACTIVITY

DESCRIPTION: A popular television comedy of the 1990s once dealt with a character's "coffee table book" about coffee tables-an amusing concept even before we learned that, with the flip of the cardboard legs, the book actually turned into miniature coffee table. With this project, you'll go one step further by creating your own brief "concept book" about a nonfiction subject you care about.

Step A

1. Discover Your Topic

2. Software: Microsoft Internet Explorer 5 or later; Microsoft Word version 2002

3. What to Do: Your first task is to figure out what your nonfiction concept book should be about.

4. Start Word, and create a new, blank document that you can use to keep track of your book ideas and possible research resources.

5. Start by getting a sense of how many options you have in nonfiction. Check out one or more of the nonfiction "best book" lists that your teacher has saved under Favorites. If any of those titles inspires a book idea of your own-or seems promising as a research source for you-note it on your list in Word.

6. Add to your book idea possibilities by listing:

7. One to three things that you like to do for fun (from snowboarding to playing chess to listening to music).

8. One to three things that you wonder about in the world (like how submarines stay underwater while cruise ships float, or how anger affects brain chemistry).

9. One to three things from history that you would like to know more about (such as what it was like in your town 100 years ago, or the role that women played in

Native American cultures).

10. While you can write an interesting book about just about anything, you will need ready research resources to get this project done in the time you have. Of all the topics on your list, choose your favorite, and then conduct several searches using Internet Explorer to find at least three easily accessible resources about it, including one book. If you can't find three research sources

11. Go to your second favorite topic, and so on.

12. Make your final selection of the topic you will focus on for your nonfiction book. Clearly designate your choice on your topic list, indicate the research resources you have identified, and hand it in to your teacher. If you have chosen the same topic as someone else in class, your teacher may ask you to alter it. Otherwise, you are ready to begin making your book!

Step B

1. Design Your Book

2. Software: Microsoft Word version 2002; Microsoft Internet Explorer 5 or later; Microsoft Publisher 2000

3. What to Do: Even before you begin writing, you will want to think through the design of your concept book.

4. Open the Book Brainstorming document that your teacher has provided. On the File menu, click Save As, and save the document with your name.

5. Scroll down to the "Medium = Message" section of the Book Brainstorming document, and use the results of your brainstorming to answer the following questions:

6. Medium: Given my topic, what medium should I choose for my book? Your basic choices are print (with as many options for shape, size, and design as you can imagine, as well as a choice of picture book rather than text-focused book); Web-based; audio book in CD or tape form; or interactive CD, with graphics and text. If you decide on a medium other than print, answer the rest of these questions with the "packaging" of your finished book in mind; you may need to skip some questions altogether.

7. Shape: Given my topic, what shape should my concept book take? (For example, you might want your book about the L.A. Lakers to be shaped like a basketball; a book about driving across country might fold out like a map. Your book could also be a simple, standard book shape.)

8. Cover: Given my topic, what should appear on the cover of my book? You may have a particular piece of artwork in mind, or a generic idea for a cover graphic, or simply type.

9. Size: Given my topic, about how big should my book be, in terms of page dimension? The simplest option here is 5½" X 8", which is standard letter-size paper folded in half horizontally. But you could opt for larger pages (as large as 11" X 17" in standard paper sizes) or much smaller.

10. Now review the "Storyboard" section of the Book Brainstorming document. The table that appears here is set up to help you plan a 16-page book (not including covers). If you have any initial thoughts about what should go on each page, add these notes to your storyboard now; otherwise, you will come back to this table after Step C. If you are planning a book in a medium other than print, you can use this table to begin planning out your screens, Web page sequences, or audiotape segments. You can change the size and shape of the cells by clicking on the table, selecting Table Properties from the Table menu, and then modifying the columns, rows, or cells.

11. Save your Book Brainstorming document. Give your teacher a printout or electronic copy if requested.

Step C

1. Develop Your Contents
2. Software: Microsoft Internet Explorer 5 or later; Microsoft Encarta Encyclopedia; Microsoft Word version 2002
3. What to Do: Now it is time to develop the "brains" of your concept book-the text and other material that go inside.
4. Use Internet Explorer and Encarta Encyclopedia to do basic research on your topic. You should also draw from print resources and interviews with experts to round out your research. Use note cards or open a new Word document to keep track of your citations and bibliography.
5. As you do your research, gather graphics and photos (with proper citations) that you might use to illustrate your book. When you get ready to write your text in Microsoft Word, keep the following points in mind:
6. You are creating a book rather than a term paper. While you must convey information accurately and credit your sources (at the end of the book), the tone of your writing should be lively.
7. Adapt your writing style and format to match the book medium you chose in Step B. If your book is Web-based, think through how much text you want to appear on each screen, and how the pages can be hyperlinked together. If you are producing an audio book, keep in mind as you write your text that the book will be read aloud. If you are creating a picture book or interactive CD, the text may play a secondary role to the graphics.

8. Use the Storyboard section of your Book Brainstorming document to plan and guide your writing.
9. Save your work often
10. Save your work often
11. When your first draft is complete, trade with a classmate. Read each other's work and offer suggestions regarding editing, additional information, or adapting to the medium.
12. Revise and proofread your text, and provide a printout or electronic copy to your teacher for review.

Step D

1. Publish!
2. Software: Microsoft Word version 2002; Microsoft Publisher 2000; Microsoft FrontPage version 2002; Microsoft Windows Media Player
3. What to Do: It is book-making time!
4. After revising the draft you created in Step C, produce the contents of your concept book in the medium that you have selected. For example:
5. For a print book, you can use Word or Publisher. Design your pages for readability and graphic interest. Experiment with fonts to achieve a look that fits your topic. Print out pages (in color or black-and-white) and prepare for binding. You can also use Word or Publisher to create the cover for your book. Print out the cover, and then mount it on cardboard or other heavy material cut in the shape you chose in Step B.
6. For a Web-based book, use FrontPage to design and organize your Web site. Import or copy and paste your text from your Word document. Import your graphics into the appropriate Images file for easy use in Web design.
7. For an audio book, record your narration on your computer or on tape. To create a CD, use Windows Media Player. Develop your CD or tape sleeve using Word or Publisher to integrate graphics and text.
8. For an interactive book, use the software of your choice. Use Word or Publisher to create your CD sleeve.
9. Before going "final" with your book in whatever medium you have chosen, ask a classmate to review for meaning and presentation. Incorporate your classmate's editing suggestions.
10. Publish, post, or burn! Take extra care with the final production of your book so that the "outside" (that is, the cover, home page, or packaging) invites your audience inside.
11. Show off your finished concept book at the publication party that your teacher has scheduled! Remember: Books come alive in the hands of an audience.

Resources

Book Arts

- "Book," article in Microsoft Encarta Encyclopedia
  http://encarta.msn.com/ (search for "Book")
- The Center for Book Arts-Exhibition Archives
  http://www.centerforbookarts.org/history/h_archives.html
- MakingBooks.com Kid's Page
  http://www.makingbooks.com/kids/index.html
- Microsoft Office XP Tools to Download for This Project

CHAPTER 12

INFUSING WITH
DIGITAL MEDIA

In this chapter we will discuss and explore:
- *Digital media in education offers various contemporary and emerging technologies*
- *Digital media students can express themselves with images, movies, music, and text*
- *Teachers across the country are using digital media to enliven lessons, meet instructional standards, and guide their students toward more productive futures*
- *Digital media lessons and activities examples for all grade levels*
- *Case Study: Digital Video Project on The Group of Seven*
- *Case Study: The Apprentice*
- *Case Study: Information Brochures*

Today's students learn in different ways than previous generations, and so require a different set of learning tools. The new technology lets students learn in the multi-sensory mode they need to process information and express themselves using the media of their time

Digital Media utilizes technology as a vehicle for developing, monitoring, and presenting instruction while keeping in mind the challenges of educating an increasingly diverse population. Digital Media in education offers various contemporary and emerging technologies such as distance education, tools, courseware, DVD, 3-D, Virtual Environments, and Artificial Intelligence and determine how these developments will shape learning environments in the future.

Digital media have led to new methods of communications that affect how we work, play and see ourselves and our environment. Through studio and seminar sessions, students will explore ways of constructing types of digital media and consider the aesthetic, technical, and social effects of this work. Through critiques of student work, readings, and discussion, we will examine the evolving formal criteria and social implications of this work.

Digital media (as opposed to analog media) usually refers to electronic media that work on digital codes. Digital media ("Formats for presenting information" according to Wiktionary:Media) like digital audio, digital video, and other digital "content" can be created, referred to and distributed via digital information processing machines. Digital media represents a profound change from previous (analog) media.

With digital media, students can express themselves with images, movies, music, and text. This technology offers a flexible set of learning tools that can help students demonstrate their individual strengths — empowering them as creators of content, rather than just consumers.

Teachers across the country are using digital media to enliven lessons, meet instructional standards, and guide their students toward more productive futures. Whether students are making visual records of science experiments, producing historical documentaries, or creating digital stories, with digital media, every subject comes to life. Digital media technology integrated into curriculum, help learners and how they learn, and the role digital media can play in the classroom. Students can create poetry photo books, scientific documentaries, original music, art portfolios, and more. With digital media, there is no limit to what they can create.

Students creating multimedia projects to be incorporated into content areas such as math, art, science, and second language learning encourage various ways of investigating and knowing. The computer is used to record data, organize observations, find information, develop models, document, write, draw, create communicate and thereby learn about other people and ourselves.

Digital media can help students focus on ways of using multimedia to support students' questions, ideas, and understanding. The following list of digital media is based on a rather technical view of the term media. Other views might lead to different lists.

- Compact Disc
- Mini-disc
- Digital video
- Digital television
- e-Book
- Video Game
- Internet
- World Wide Web
- and many Interactive Media

There are many advantages to using media in digital form, whether your intentions are to limit the media to classroom use, or to allow students to have access to the materials outside the classroom.

Pod casting in education is a new digital media. Educational pod casting is the ability to have content on the go. Pod casting allows you to listen to lectures or lessons on demand. Pod casts can deliver educational content for listening or viewing on your computer and an iPod, freeing learning from the constraints of a physical classroom.

A pod cast is audio or visual content that is automatically delivered over a network via free subscription. Once subscribed to, pod cast can be regularly distributed over the Internet or within your school's network and accessed with an iPod, laptop, or desktop computer (both Macs and PCs).

Research shows that students learn better and master basic skills in less time when they are engaged in learning. Digital projects are highly motivating for students, and since they can easily be shared, students are inclined to spend more time on task and revise their work to ensure that it is just right.

While working on digital projects, students cultivate important skills such as researching, reading, writing, and speaking. They also build higher order thinking skills, including problem solving, collaboration, and the ability to gather and analyze data.

With so many opportunities for different types of creative expression, digital media provides the perfect way to support project-based learning in the classroom. Digital media projects lend themselves to students working in groups, with roles divided based on interests and skills.

One exciting way teachers are discovering a new way to bring excitement into their classrooms and help students make meaningful connections to research topics is through documentaries. By introducing documentary filmmaking into their curriculum, they have created an environment where all students are successful and motivated to do their best work. Digital video is an easy way for you to bring documentary filmmaking into your classroom. Whether it is science, social studies, or language arts, students can become experts on a topic, creatively demonstrate their knowledge, and easily share that knowledge with others.

Documentaries give students the opportunity to be creative and express themselves using the digital tools they're most comfortable with. At the same time, they master basic skills, such as researching, reading, writing, and speaking. They also build critical skills, such as problem solving, collaboration, and the ability to gather and analyze data.

DIGITAL MEDIA LESSONS AND ACTIVITIES

ART EDUCATION

TITLE: The Group of Seven
SUBJECT: Art Education
GRADE: 9–10
UNIT: Digital Video

DESCRIPTION: In a group of seven, students will each choose one artist from the Group of Seven to research. They will explore the background of the artist and develop an understanding of the artistic styles used in that art form. Students will use a computer program to draw an original art piece using similar elements of style of that artist's work. As a group, students will prepare a short video to tie all of the research on the artists together.

PREREQUISITE KNOWLEDGE: This learning resource assumes the student has a basic knowledge of the Internet, drawing software and basic video production.

TEACHER PREP TIME: 1.5–2 hours. If you have not worked with a video camera before you may want to become comfortable.

DELIVERABLES: Students will submit their video and artwork.

EVALUATION / GRADING: Group videos will be evaluated using a checklist provided in *Evaluation.*

Running short on time?
Have students present using a photocopy of one of the artist's pictures.

Want to take this another step? Have students make artistic comparisons between the artist they have studied and one other artist (not a member of the Group of Seven).

Only one computer in the classroom? Have students who are researching the same artist pair up to use the computer.

Teacher Tips: If students are unfamiliar with using the video camera, allow them time to practice.

MISSION:

The **Group of Seven** had a passion. Their passion was to show Canadians and the world the beauty of Canada. In this mission you will sharpen your understanding of Canada's famous Group of Seven. In a group of seven, you will each choose one artist in the group, explore the background of the artist, and develop an understanding of the artistic styles used in that art form.

To demonstrate what you have learned, you will use a computer program to draw an original art piece using similar elements of style of that artist's work.

Working in a group, prepare a short video to tie all of the research together. It is up to you how the video will be presented (i.e. an interview or skit or art show). Try to be as creative as possible. Remember you want to intrigue your audience.

RESOURCES: Use the following web links to complete the learning resource.
- Tom Thompson Gallery
  http://www.tomthomson.org/groupseven/index.html
- National Gallery of Canada
  http://www.national.gallery.ca/education/school/slide_kits/group_seven/gallery/index_e.html
- National Gallery of Canada
  http://national.gallery.ca/collections/virtual_tour/gallery109.html
- Art 2 Life: Canadian Century
  http://www.art2life.ca/user_agreement.cfm
- Information on the Group of Seven
  http://www.linereeh.dk/Thesisintro.html#2
- History of the Group of seven
  http://www.groupofsevenart.com/history.html

Be sure to document the source of your Internet research.
Last Name, First Name of Author (if known). "Title of work/article/page." *Title of Complete Document* (if applicable). Date last modified. URL (date visited).

STEPS
Individual:
Write a short description of the Group of Seven.

Group:
- Have each person in your group chooses one member of the Group of Seven.
- Identify, research, and describe the artist's background, their artistic style (i.e. visual characteristics and themes found in their artwork).
- Using the links listed in Resources, find two examples of that artist's work to share with the group.
- Briefly describe the subject matter and document the title, date, location, medium of the work and anything else you find of interest.

- In your group, each member will have the opportunity to introduce the artist they have researched and showcase two pieces of their work.
- Compare the artistic styles of each artist. How are these works similar in their subject matter and in their painting style? How are the styles different? What is a similar characteristic of each style of art? How does color affect the mood in each of the painting?
- Record your research using a word processor.

PRODUCT:

1. When out enjoying the beauty Canada's outdoors has to offer, the **Group of Seven,** like many artists, would make small oil or pencil sketches of what they saw. In their studios, they would work from the sketch to develop a larger, finished composition. With permission from your teacher or on your own time, sketch a nature scene using a pencil and paper. From your sketch create a more finished, original composition using a computer program such as **Paint/ Draw** . Apply the **elements and principles of design** from the Group of Seven artist you researched in Steps.Submit your artwork to your teacher for marking.

2. **Digital Video:** As a group, prepare a **short edited video** to tie all of the research on the artists together. It is up to you how the video will be presented (i.e. an interview or skit or art show). Try to be as creative as possible. Remember you want to intrigue your audience.

TIPS: You may want to include **audio** (appropriate music that compliments video), your sketch, scanned pictures or graphics from the Internet and maps.

Please try to limit your documentary to a maximum length of ten minutes.

Be sure to save your work at regular intervals!

CONCLUSION: Host a **showcase** with your classmates presenting your video and artwork to other classes and or parents. Exhibit the sketches with the video.

EVALUATION:

Group of Seven Checklist   Maximum score of 75 points.

☐ Description of the Group of Seven

☐ Background information on chosen artist is complete

☐ Artist's artistic style is described

☐ Grammar and punctuation

☐ Artwork using similar art elements of Group of Seven artist

☐ Digital Video

Group Work

☐ Active contribution to group

NOTES:

SOCIAL STUDIES, LANGUAGE ARTS, MATH

TITLE: The Apprentice
SUBJECT: Social Studies, Language Arts, Math
GRADE: K-5
UNIT: Digital Media

OVERVIEW: A field trip to a local business helps students learn about what the business does and its role in the community. Instead of giving an oral report or writing a report about the tour, the students combine their audio, text, and photos to create a brochure and presentation that is interesting and makes use of high-level thinking skills.

DESCRIPTION:

In this project, students study a local business, such as a recycling center. During a tour of the business, students use an iPod, a voice recorder, and a digital camera to record interviews and observations and to take photos. To share their learning, some groups of students combine their digital media in a Power Point presentation about the business. Other groups use Pages to create a brochure about the business that incorporates text, photos, charts, and graphs.

STEPS:

1. During a tour of a local business, have students use an iPod and a voice recorder to record their questions and the responses as well as their observations of what they see, hear, and smell. The students should also use a digital camera to take photos during their tour.

2. Have students work in small groups to download their photos into a photo editing program and their audio recordings into an audio or music library. They should edit and title their photos and listen to and name their audio clips.

3. Have each group use Kidspiration or Inspiration software to plan their presentation or brochure.

4. Have each student group review its plan and make any needed changes. Students should then use Pages to create any text and charts or graphs they will use in their project.

5. The students should create their Power Point presentation or their Pages brochure using the templates available in the software. Have them include photos, charts or graphs, text, and audio (if using Power Point).

6. When their projects are complete, have students share them with the rest of the class.

7. Power Point presentations can be shown on the group's computer or projected on a large screen. Pages brochures can be printed for viewing.

MISSION:

After completing this project, students will be able to:

- Use technology to create a presentation demonstrating what they have learned
- Have developed critical thinking and problem-solving skills that will help them manage and use information
- Work cooperatively in small groups
- Compose a report to describe and provide information about a person, object, or situation
- Organize data in charts

TECHNOLOGY SKILLS

After completing this project, students will be able to:

- Use a digital camera to take photos
- Import photos into a photo library
- Use an digital voice recorder to interview people and to record observations
- Import audio clips into a music library.
- Use Power Point to create a presentation that includes audio, photos, and graphs or charts
- Use Pages to create a brochure that includes text, photos, and graphs or charts

Preparation and Duration

- Before beginning the project, you should make arrangements with a local business for a tour, set up transportation, and get all necessary permission forms signed.
- In addition to the trip, this project will take two to three class periods to create the presentations and brochures. One more class period will be needed for sharing the projects.

ASSESSMENT:

- Students can assess each other's presentation or brochure by applying a teacher created rubric.
- PDF versions of the Power Point presentations and the Pages brochures can be added to the students' electronic portfolios.

PREREQUISITE SKILLS:

Before beginning the project, students should have the following skills:

- Using a digital camera

- Using an iPod or a voice recorder to record audio
- Using a photo editor to import, organize, and edit photos
- Importing audio files into audio library
- Using Kidspiration or Inspiration to create a planning document
- Using Power Point to create a presentation or Pages to create a document

Facilitation Tips

A signup sheet for using Power Point or Pages is useful for allowing students to choose what application they want to use to share their learning. Use this signup sheet to determine the makeup of groups. Ideally, groups would have four to five students.

Technology Tips

- If students are using the same photos and audio, the media needs to be downloaded onto all of the computers that are being used. If the computers are on a network, you can turn on sharing so students can easily access each other's photos and audio.
- When taking digital photos, students need to have the wrist strap on and hold the camera carefully.
- Depending on the grade level and skills of the students, assistance may be needed with typing their text and other computer skills.
- At least two computers will be needed for this project. Ideally, there would be one computer for each group of students.

LANGUAGE ARTS, INFORMATION LITERACY

TITLE: Information Brochures
SUBJECT: Language Arts, Information Literacy
GRADE: Elementary
UNIT: Digital Media

DESCRIPTION: Welcome to the information age! Students are challenged to survive in a jungle of bits and bytes of data all wanting a spot in long-term memory. How can students conquer, organize, and effectively share the information that interests them? This project provides an excellent way to teach about the information genre and introduce research to students.

PROJECT OVERVIEW

This project allows each student to become an expert on an information topic of his or her choice. Students explore their topics using multiple sources and collect images to illustrate the information. They each then use Pages to create a brochure as a way to express their knowledge and share their passion with others.

STEPS:

1. Have each student choose a topic about which he or she wants to become an expert. Suggest to the students that they avoid topics that are too broad (such as animals) or too narrow (such as Australian frill lizards), as well as topics about which they are already experts. Each student should choose a different topic so limited resources in the school library can be used concurrently.

2. Students should learn more about the topic from a variety of resources, such as library books, the Internet, personal interviews, and newspaper and magazine articles. They should have at least four book sources and two sources from the Internet. Students should take notes as they read and save any images they want to use in their Photo Library.

3. Have each student use a template in Pages to create a brochure with information about the research topic. Each brochure should include:
    *   The student's name
    *   A front and back
    *   A source list so others can easily find the sources used
    *   Clip art, photos, or other images
    *   A summary of information about the topic, including key things to know and fascinating facts

4. Students should share what they have learned with others. The completed brochures can be displayed in the classroom or the school's media center or library for other students to browse. The brochures are also great conversation starters for parent conferences, open houses, and other similar events.

OUTCOMES

After completing this project, students will be able to:
- Learn and use basic research skills
- Summarize key points about a large topic area
- Visually present a summary of what they have learned in a brochure format

TECHNOLOGY SKILLS

After completing this project, students will be able to:
- Conduct research using the Internet
- Save images in an Photo Library
- Create a brochure using Pages that combines text and images

Preparation and Duration

This project can take anywhere from one week to two months. You could have students spend one hour a day for five days on this project or weave parts of the project into the students' reading and library times. All students can be in a lab working on the brochure at the same time or they can work in small chunks of time over a period of many weeks.

ASSESSMENT:

Assessment with a teacher-created rubric works best for this project. Key areas to assess are research skills and the students' ability to summarize and present information in a coherent form.

TOOLS AND RESOURCES

Macintosh computers, printer (color printer, if available), scanner (optional), Pages, Photo

PREREQUISITE SKILLS

Before beginning this project, students should have the following skills:
- Creating a Pages document using templates
- Replacing placeholder text in Pages
- Adding images from Photo to a Pages document

FACILITATION TIPS

- A Pages template allows the students to focus on the content of the brochure rather than on the "how to."

- If computer availability is limited or students do not have an assigned computer, consider storing student files on a server or portable storage device. This allows students to use any computer that is available whenever it is available.
- Daily rotation schedules on the computers can give all students the opportunity to work on their projects on a regular basis. Having students work on the project for short periods of time each day allows them to focus on small parts of their projects and track their progress on a regular basis.
- It is a good idea to require students to complete a minimum amount of research and reading before starting the brochure. This allows them to have a better idea of what information is important to share about the topic.
- Class, school, and district policies should be considered when using research, especially images, from the Internet. This is a good opportunity to teach about copyright and fair use as they relate to images.
- Research skills can be taught cooperatively with a library media specialist, who can help teach research skills, organization of a school's library collection, credibility of source material, and other relevant skills.

TECHNOLOGY TIPS
When printing each brochure, double-sided printing is useful.

- If the classroom printer does not have a duplexing feature, you can print each page separately, and then glue the pages together, back to back.

LANGUAGE ARTS

TITLE: Stories and Poems
SUBJECT: Language Arts
GRADE: 7 & 8
UNIT: Digital Media

DESCRIPTION: Students can use technology to enhance their poetry by illustrating it with images, movies, music, photos, and narration. Digital media software enriches the experience by enabling students to create professional-looking digital media collections to publish their work, allowing them to go beyond the textual aspects of writing as they incorporate their own digital media elements

PROJECT OVERVIEW:

In this project, students gather biographical stories from family members, practice oral storytelling skills, and tell their stories to an audience of peers. They then condense the themes of their stories into ten-line poems, which they showcase in a digital class portfolio using Power Point.

STEPS:

1. Have the class study the elements of storytelling and oral presentations. Model storytelling techniques for the class.
2. Have each student collect a biographical story from a family member about events from that person's life. The stories can be humorous or serious.
3. Students should prepare to tell their stories orally, without a script and without memorizing them. Student partners can rehearse and practice the techniques of eye contact, gestures, facial expressions, voice, and so on.
4. Have students tell their stories in front of the class. They should use rubrics to evaluate each other's stories.
5. Have students condense their stories into poems of ten lines that capture the stories' themes. Since each poem is limited in length, students must choose the most important elements for their poetry.
6. Ask a team of students to create a class "poem template" master slide in Power Point so that all the students' poetry pages have the same design. The template should be made available to all students. The template should have a poem border, text box for a poem, place for title, student name and grade, and placeholders for graphics and digital photos students add.
7. Have each student type his or her poem into the text box in the template. They

should add images such as digital photos, scanned photos, or images located on the Internet. The photos might be of family vacation locations, famous places, or well-known landmarks students' families have visited. Students can also add to their slides movies, narration, and sound bites or quotes from family members and friends. Students can use applications like Movie Works or iMovie to create movies of them telling their stories or reading their poetry and then add those movies to their slides. Students should use digital cameras to take photos of themselves for the introductory "cover" slide and their individual slides. Students can create audio files as they read poems aloud or describe photos or movies they import. They can also import sounds or background music internet or CDROMS that can be played automatically on each slide.

8. Students should combine their individual Power Point slides into a class collection of poetry.

9. Share the poetry collection presentation with the whole class and copy it to CDs to share with students' families.

EXTENSION: Students can use Pages to create a class publication of their poetry, which can be in the form of a brochure, newsletter, class booklet, digital portfolio, or advertisement. Students should choose a template for the type of document they are creating.

OUTCOMES:
After completing this project, students will be able to:
- Create biographical stories from true events in a family member's life
- Learn and use oral presentation and storytelling techniques
- Condense stories to ten-line poems, summarizing their themes
- Work as part of a group to complete a group digital media project

After completing this project, students will be able to:
- Work collaboratively to create a class collection of poetry using digital media
- Use Power Point to create slides with text, images, movies, and other elements
- Use applications such as iMovie, Adobe Premier, Windows Media Player, iTunes, Movie Works Deluxe, and Power Point to create a digital media poetry collection
- Use technology to design, develop, and publish their work

PREPARATION AND DURATION:
Days 1-3: You model storytelling techniques, teach terms, do practice exercises with students; students harvest stories from family members and begin to prepare an outline.

TIME ALOTMENT:

Days 4-7: Students practice oral presentation techniques with a partner; practice stories at home; tell stories in front of class; class audience grades with rubrics.

Days 8-11: Students compress theme of stories into 10-line poems; type poems in the Power Point template on computers for class collections.

Days 12-14: Students work in groups; locate Internet resources; create multimedia collections of poetry in Power Point, and combine individual slides into one class poetry collection presentation.

ASSESSMENT:

- Student audience members can use teacher-created rubrics as each student tells his or her biographical story. The rubrics can contain categories such as eye contact, voice, gestures, preparation, interpretation, audience response, and organization.
- For group work, checklists can be used to assign individual tasks and monitor progress.
- Final class projects can be assessed by you, the teacher, noting both individual and group contributions.
- Students can use rubrics to do self assessment and peer evaluation.

RESOURCES:

Internet
- http://images.google.com
- http://yahooligans.com/Around_the_World

Photos of nature scenes
- http://yahooligans.com/Sports_and_Recreation
- http://yahooligans.com/Arts_and_Entertainment/Music

Pictures of sports, hobbies, music, books, clubs, and so on
- http://digital.nypl.org/mmpco/browse.cfm?trg=folder

Images from the large collection found in the New York City Library
- http://www.50states.com/
- http://images.google.com/images?q=states&ie=ISO-8859-1&hl=en

Tools

Computer, digital video cameras (optional), digital cameras, scanner (optional), Power Point, movie editing software, photo editing software, music library software

Prerequisite Skills

Before beginning this project, students should have the following skills:

- Basic computer skills, such as accessing files, saving, and copying and pasting
- A beginning knowledge of Power Point
- Using any of the digital media applications each student will use
- Using peripherals—digital cameras, scanners, and so on
- Using the Internet to do searches

Technology Tips

- More proficient students can create the class templates, assist other students with peripherals and software, and help assemble the final collection.
- The master slide template that students create can be made available to the rest of the class on a classroom webpage or via a Mac account.

CHAPTER 13

INFUSED SOURCES FOR INFUSED TEACHING

In this chapter we will discuss and explore:
- *Tutorials and Staff Development*
- *Teacher tools and freeware sources for the classroom*
- *Learning games for students*
- *Tutorials for teachers and students*
- *Student Worksheets*
- *Educational Clip Art and Graphics*

The beauty of internet for us classroom teachers is the wealth of valuable sources available. Throughout my years of never having a big enough budget to offer my students everything I wanted in the infusion of technology, I have found many free programs and sites. Many learning templates, black line masters and rubrics are found on the World Wide Web as well. This list is a starting point. Feel free to search the Internet for other related information.

Tutorials and Staff Development
One of the major complaints of educators is "not enough time". Web tutorials can assist in developing the necessary skills needed to become tech savvy teachers and students. Tutorials can be completed in one's own time, in the classroom as well as outside of the classroom.

Adobe Training for Educators
Photoshop, Photo Elements, Illustrator, Acrobat, In Design, Go Live
- http://www.adobe.com/education/training/main.html

Technology Tutorials Found on the Web

Appleworks, Inspiration, Kidspiration, KidPix, Hyperstudio, iMovie, Photoshop, Digital Cameras

- http://www.internet4classrooms.com/on-line2.htm#kpOffice

Online Practice Modules

PowerPoint, Word, Excel, Macintosh, Windows, Webquest, Works, Inspiration, Hyperstudio.

- http://www.internet4classrooms.com/on-line.htm

Electric Teacher Power Point

New to PowerPoint? Use this easy tutorial to get you started. Also gives activities for classroom use.

- http://www.electricteacher.com/powerpoint.htm

Digital Cameras

Learn everything from the basics of using a digital camera to capturing digital video, calculating image size and more.

- http://www.shortcourses.com/)

Kidspiration/Inspiration

Download these manuals and print for your reference. These manuals provide a step-by-step guide to creating work using these programs.

- http://www.monroe.k12.fl.us/training/technology/TrainingDocs/
  Inspiration%20Tutorial.PDF

Learn 2 Type for Kids

Is a FREE Web site that helps you master the skills of touch-typing. Interactive exercises automatically adjust to your skill level. The better you get, the more challenging the exercises become. You can come and go as you please and pick up right where you left off.

- http://kids.learn2type.com/

Tapped In

Scheduled in-service programs and informal collaborative activities are held on-line by an international community of education professionals, K-12 teachers and librarians, professional development staff, teacher education faculty and students, and researchers.

- http://www.tappedin.org/

Teacher Tap

A free, professional development resource that helps educators address common technology integration questions by providing practical, online resources and activities.

- http://eduscapes.com/tap/

Thirteen/Ed Online
Free workshops that cover all types of hot topics in education today.
*   http://www.thirteen.org/edonline/concept2class/index.html

Online Classes - Learning Center
Free online courses taught by experts and offered at different levels. Courses include: Word, Excel, PageMaker, desktop publishing, Adobe Photoshop to name a few.
*   http://www.hplearningcenter.com/

PBS TeacherLine
Funded by a grant by the USDOE, this site offers several courses. You may search by grade level for an appropriate course
*   http://teacherline.pbs.org/teacherline/modules/catalog.cfm

Here are a few Freeware sources to get you started:

Intel
*   http://www.intel.com/education/teachtech/classroom/using_internet/software.htm

Education World
*   http://www.homeworkplanet.com/search/Education/K-12_Resources/Online_
    Learning_Games/Freeware_Downloads/

Free Web Pages
Filamentality: Hotlists
*   http://www.kn.pacbell.com/wired/fil/
TrackStar: Bookmarks
*   http://trackstar.4teachers.org/trackstar/index.jsp

Lesson Plans
Blue Web'n Sites
*   http://www.kn.pacbell.com/wired/bluewebn/
Core Knowledge
*   http://www.coreknowledge.org/CKproto2/resrcs/lessons/index.htm
eThemes: K-12
*   http://www.emints.org/ethemes/resources/by-grade.shtml
GEM: Lesson Plans
*   http://www.eduref.org/Virtual/Lessons/index.shtml
NYTimes: Lessons
*   http://www.nytimes.com/learning/teachers/lessons/archive.html

PBS Teacher Source
- http://www.pbs.org/teachersource/

Teachers Network
- http://teachersnetwork.org/lessonplans/index.htm

Teacher Resources

Creative Thinking
- http://www.virtualsalt.com/crebook2.htm

Curriculum Web
- http://oswego.org/cur/standards/resources.cfm

eduScapes
- http://eduscapes.com

Electric Teacher
- http://electricteacher.com/

Graphic Organizers
- http://www.eduplace.com/graphicorganizer/

Internet 4 Classrooms
- http://www.internet4classrooms.com/

New Teacher Tips
- http://www.teachnet.org/ntol/ntol_how_to.htm

Reference Desk
- http://www.eduref.org/

Rubrics Generator
- http://rubistar.4teachers.org/

Teachers' Mentor
- http://teachersmentor.com/

Teaching Tips
- http://www.nea.org/tips/library.html

Technology Tips
- http://www.essdack.org/tips/index.html

Tech Trekers
- http://www.techtrekers.com/

Algebra Tutoring

Algebra Lessons
- http://www.purplemath.com/modules/index.htm

Learning Games

U.S. Map Game
- http://www.mazeworks.com/chessprb/index.htm

States & Capitals
- http://www.mazeworks.com/chessprb/index.htm

Chess Puzzles
- http://www.mazeworks.com/chessprb/index.htm

Crossword Puzzles
- http://www.nytimes.com/learning/teachers/xwords/archive.html

Mancala / Wari
- http://www.rocketsnail.net/mancala/classic.htm

Mastermind
- http://www.javaonthebrain.com/java/mastermind/

Othello / Reversi
- http://www.artifactinteractive.com.au/arcade/reversi.html

PBS Kids Games
- http://pbskids.org/go/

Peg Puzzle
- http://www.mazeworks.com/peggy/index.htm

Language Tutorials

Spanish Language Lessons
- http://www.bbc.co.uk/languages/spanish/lj/

Italian Language Lessons
- http://www.bbc.co.uk/languages/italian/lj/

French Language Lessons
- http://www.bbc.co.uk/languages/french/lj/

German Language Lessons
- http://www.bbc.co.uk/languages/german/lj/

Language Translation
- http://www.google.com/language_tools?hl=en

Reading

Book Adventures
- http://bookadventure.org/

Poetry Archive
- http://www.poets.org/audio.php/prmViewAll/A

Math

Math Facts Game

- http://home.indy.rr.com/lrobinson/mathfacts/mathfacts.html

Math Magician

- http://www.oswego.org/ocsd-web/games/Mathmagician/cathymath.html

Math Puzzles

- http://mathforum.org/library/drmath/sets/select/

Interactive Math

- http://nlvm.usu.edu/en/nav/vlibrary.html

Multiplication Facts

- http://quizhub.com/quiz/f-multiplication.cfm

History

American Civil War

- http://the-research-center.com

Country Profiles

- http://news.bbc.co.uk/2/hi/country_profiles/default.stm

Geography Games

- http://www.lizardpoint.com/fun/geoquiz/index.html

U.S. Government

- http://bensguide.gpo.gov/index.html

World Maps

- http://www.nationalgeographic.com/xpeditions/atlas/

Science/Chemistry

Biology Chemistry

- http://pbskids.org/zoom/activities/index.html

Chemical Elements

- http://biochemhub.com/

Explore Science

- http://www.exploratorium.edu/explore/index.html

Solar System

- http://sse.jpl.nasa.gov/planets/index.cfm

The Why Files

- http://whyfiles.org/

Zoom Science

- http://pbskids.org/zoom/activities/sci/

Vocabulary

Writer's Almanac

- http://writersalmanac.publicradio.org/

Grammar Lessons

http://www.dailygrammar.com/archive.shtml

Spelling Pictures

- http://quizhub.com/quiz/f-spelling.cfm

Homophones

- http://quizhub.com/quiz/f-homophones.cfm

SAT Vocabulary

- http://quizhub.com/quiz/f-vocabulary.cfm

Literature Guides

- http://endeavor.med.nyu.edu/lit-med/lit-med-db/poems.html

Spelling Test

- http://the-research-center.com

Vocabulary Development and Builders

- http://the-research-center.com

Reference

Google: News

- http://news.google.com/

Today in History

- http://lcweb2.loc.gov/ammem/today/today.html

Colleges Search

- http://apps.collegeboard.com/search/adv_typeofschool.jsp

Nutrition Data

- http://apps.collegeboard.com/search/adv_typeofschool.jsp

Official U.S. Times

- http://www.time.gov/

U.S. Street Maps

- http://maps.google.com/

Weather Forecast

- http://weather.gov/forecasts/graphical/sectors/

Encyclopedia

- http://en.wikipedia.org/wiki/Main_Page

Word of the Day

- http://www.nytimes.com/learning/students/wordofday/index.html

Reference
- http://the-research-center.com

Weather
- http://www.nws.noaa.gov/

World Facts
- http://go.hrw.com/atlas/norm_htm/world.htm

World Maps
- http://go.hrw.com/atlas/norm_htm/world.htm

Zip Codes
- http://www.usps.gov/ncsc/lookups/lookup_ctystzip.html

Ask Jeeves
- http://www.ajkids.com/

Medical Info
- http://www.merck.com/pubs/mmanual_home/contents.htm

Nutrition Data
- http://www.nutritiondata.com/

Search: MSN
- http://search.msn.com/

Google Search
- http://www.google.com/search?safe=vss

Social Issues
- http://www.multnomah.lib.or.us/lib/homework/sochc.html

Electronic Dictionary
- http://www.answers.com/

Homework

Homework Help
- http://www.multcolib.org/homework/

Kids Click Search
- http://sunsite.berkeley.edu/KidsClick

Teacher Tools

ABC Teach

Forms (research, report, book report), awards, calendars, shape books, word searches, crossword puzzles, dot-to-dot, much more.

- http://www.abcteach.com/

AppleWorks Educator Templates

Templates for all curriculum areas in addition to lesson plan and newsletter templates.

- http://henson.austin.apple.com/ali_appleworks/templates.htm

Bookmarks Online

Store your favorite web sites online.

- http://www.backflip.com/

Certificates for Teachers

Create personalized certificates for your students.

- http://certificates4teachers.com/

Education World Tools and Templates

Awards, calendars, organizers, posters, holiday worksheets, parent-teacher communications, etc.

- http://www.educationworld.com/tools_templates/

Discovery School Teaching Tools

Features Puzzlemaker, Clip Art, and Worksheet Generator.

- http://school.discovery.com/teachingtools/teachingtools.html

Easy Test Maker

Create and print tests: True-False, Multiple Choice, Short Answer, Matching, and Fill-in-the-Blank.

- http://www.easytestmaker.com/default.aspx

Federal Resources for Educational Excellence

More than 30 Federal agencies formed a working group to make hundreds of federally supported teaching and learning resources easy to find.

- http://www.ed.gov/free/index.html

Free Educational Videos

The VPW Classroom Information Network offers a list of high-quality educational videos and teaching materials FREE to educators and youth leaders. This list is kept up-to-date and changes as new programs are added or existing programs are discontinued.

- http://www.vpw.com/educational/

Free Stuff for Educators

A must visit! Eighteen pages of "free stuff".

- http://kalama.com/~zimba/freeforteachers.htm

Freebie of the Week

Check weekly for a new freebie.

- http://www.dailyapples.com/freebies.htm

Fun Calculator

Over 75 fun calculators.

- http://www.myteachertools.com/old/calculators.htm

Hotlist Creator

Create a list of Internet sites for your students to access in the classroom as well as at home. Use the list in your lessons.

- http://wizard.hprtec.org/

iTools

A variety of search, language, research, financial and map tools.

- www.itools.com

Google Search Engine

#1 search engine on the Net (my opinion).

- www.google.com

Keyboarding Resources

Printable keyboards, frequent word list and more.

- http://jeffcoweb.jeffco.k12.co.us/isu/itech/keybo/keydx.htm

Microsoft Office Templates

Go to Education section.

- http://officeupdate.microsoft.com/templategallery/

Printable Posters

Hundreds of printable posters for your classroom.

- http://print-a-poster.p-rposters.com/

Project Poster

Put your student's work on the web. (Use initials only please when posting work).

- http://poster.hprtec.org/

Report Card Comments

Over 300 adjectives and phrases for your use in preparing report cards and progress reports.

- http://www.teachnet.com/how-to/endofyear/personalcomments061400.html

Rubrics

A rubric generator for every kind of lesson.

- http://www.tcet.unt.edu/START/instruct/general/rubrics.htm

Rubistar Rubrics
Rubric Templates.

- http://rubistar.4teachers.org/

Saving Teachers Money

Different sites featured each week. Be sure to visit the "recently featured sites" for a chance to obtain a free laptop.

- http://www.savingteachersmoney.com/

School Notes

Post class announcements, homework, etc.

- http://www.schoolnotes.com/

School Grants

Offers grant opportunities for grades PreK-12, grant writing tips and sample proposals.

- http://www.schoolgrants.org/

Sites for Teachers

Contains only links to sites that contain teacher's resource and educational material. The sites are ranked by popularity. No more surfing countless pages to find the occasional "good" site.

- http://sitesforteachers.com/

Teacher Treasures on the Internet

Another comprehensive listing of valuable links.

- http://www.kenton.k12.ky.us/tr/trsr.html

Student Worksheets

Ed Helper

Worksheets on many curriculum areas Grades 1 - 12.

- http://www.edhelper.com/

Kids Domain Printables

Numerous types of printables including curriculum and holiday.

- http://www.kidsdomain.com/grown/links/Printable_Worksheets.html

Teach-nology Worksheets

Worksheets and worksheet makers. Also, graphic organizers, rubric maker, crossword, word search, science lab form, assignment form, much more. Scroll down to bottom of page for free worksheets.

- http://www.teach-nology.com/worksheets/

Learning Page

Primary worksheets for alphabet (tracing), calendar, money, senses, time, measuring, numbers. Sign up (free) to access these pages. Click on "basics sheets".

- http://www.learningpage.com/

Super Kids Math Worksheet Creator

Create worksheets for addition, subtraction, multiplication, division, fractions, greater than/less than, rounding.

- http://www.superkids.com/aweb/tools/math/

Discovery School Worksheet Generator

Create your own worksheets or search the database for ready made items.

- http://school.discovery.com/teachingtools/worksheetgenerator/index.html

Billy Bear's Worksheet Games to Print

Worksheets in different curriculum areas, also handwriting. Primary

- http://www.billybear4kids.com/worksheets/start.html

Educational Clip Art and Graphics

About.com

- http://webclipart.about.com/library/weekly/blclpexp.htm

The Teacher's Guide

- http://www.theteachersguide.com/Edgraphicscolor.html

Awesome Clip Art for Kids

- http://www.awesomeclipartforkids.com/

Cool Clips

- http://search.coolclips.com/CoolCLIPS.asp?Type=Subject&Data=23&snort=1&level=1

School Graphics

- http://www.countryclipart.com/school.htm

Teacher Files

- http://www.teacherfiles.com/clip_art.htm

School Icons

- http://www.schoolicons.com/eng/

Visual Resources: Photos and Clip Art

- http://eduscapes.com/tap/topic20.htm

The Picture Collection

- http://digital.nypl.org/mmpco/

Pics4Learning

- http://pics.tech4learning.com/

Totally Free Pictures

- http://www.picturesfree.org/

CHAPTER 14

TIPS TO GET STARTED

In this chapter we will discuss and explore:
- *10 tips to get you started using technology*

You may be feeling a little overwhelmed by the thought and practice of technology infusion. Below are ten easy tips to infuse technology. Use the tips as a checklist in order to prepare for infusing technology into your classroom.

1. Gain Perspective! Put last year into perspective. To achieve this perspective, ask yourself these questions:
- Did I use technology?
- If I did, did the technology enhance the lessons? If not, why not?
- If I did not use technology, how can I use it this year to enhance and/or reinforce what I teach?

2. Get Organized!
- Go through old files and delete those that are useless or outdated.
- Group remaining files in folders by subject and/or topic.
- Back up important and regularly used files.
- Transfer all previous student projects to a ZIP disk.
- Check all bookmarked Internet sites, and delete those that are no longer valid or useful.
- Organize remaining bookmarks by subject or topic.

3. Take a Course!
- Take an online course to learn about teaching and learning with technology. There are tons of tutorials on the Internet on a variety of topics.
- Attend local workshops on software or hardware you might want to use.

4. Join a ListServ

- Contribute to a discussion or message board.
- Subscribe to a mailing list or newsletter, such as those offered at Surfing the Net with Kids or Education World.

5. Explore The Literature!

- Subscribe to online or print publications, such as Learning and Leading with Technology (International Society for Technology in Education), Reading Today (International Reading Association), and Instructor (Scholastic), to learn more about integrating technology into your teaching and student learning.

6. Experiment with Software!

- Explore new software programs to use with your students. Create a temporary folder and practice using the software. If what you do does not work, do not save it. If it does work, save it as a template or guide.
- Choose the best programs and decide which lessons might fit best with each. Practice teaching a sample lesson. Trying new software for the first time in front of students is the wrong time to find out it does not work.
- Design student instruction sheets for simple projects or activities using the best programs. Easy, short, step-by-step directions will allow students to use the software independently.

7. Install Timesaving Technology!

- Locate, install, and practice using technology that can make your job easier. Consider programs such as an electronic grade book to record student work, an electronic lesson planner, a word processing program to create parent letters (add clip art for interest!), and a database program to create labels and mail merge word-processed letters.

8. Create A Classroom Climate!

- Visualize the climate you want to establish and organize your classroom accordingly. Decide where to locate the learning centers, the writing center, and the computer center. (Be aware of the physical limitations of your classroom computers. Cords, for example, are only so long!)
- Set up a computer-learning center and create a launch page of curriculum-related sites for students. Provide technology-related activities for each unit of instruction you plan to teach.
- Decide how often and under what circumstances students will use technology. Post a list of rules.

9. Polish up Existing Lessons!

- Take a look at the previous year's lessons and decide which ones can use more punch or a technological boost. Many pencil and paper activities can easily be adapted to word processing. Consider using drawing programs, such as Kid Pix and Print Artist.

- Another easy way to infuse technology into the curriculum is to give students several options when creating book reports. Making slide shows, multimedia reports, and posters are other options students might choose to explore individual learning styles.

- Explore lesson plan archives to see what other teachers are doing. Visit such sites and log places in your plan book. That will help you remember to use them when you get to the lessons and avoid the search for that slip of paper that has sunk to the bottom of your book bag.

10. Explore and Try Something New!

- Locate tools that will make learning more exciting, interesting, and relevant for students. A multimedia encyclopedia adds sound and video clips to basic information and provides links to related topics. A word processing program helps students with the steps in the writing process. Quality software can be individualized to allow students to practice curriculum skills at their own ability level.

- WebQuests can help students use the Internet to work toward curriculum goals. Telecollaborative projects, such as those found at GlobalSchoolhouse.com are a wonderful way to integrate curriculum while students work with their peers around the world.

- Learn to use technology that extends the power of the computer, such as a scanner, digital camera, video camera, and projector.

APPENDIX

PRE AND POST SELF ASSESSMENT

	Absent	Aware	Confident	Proficient	Mastery
Understand the importance of the use of technology as a tool in today's classroom.	1	2	3	4	5
Understand and use the learning theories applicable to specific kinds of learners.	1	2	3	4	5
Manage software and hardware resources in ways that facilitate learning.	1	2	3	4	5
Design and use rubrics that describe what learners will be able to do as a result of technology-based projects.	1	2	3	4	5
Use the computer to design curriculum-based learning activities.	1	2	3	4	5
Use cooperative and collaborative learning strategies, with pairs, small groups, and large groups of students.	1	2	3	4	5
Identify and use management practices that facilitate students working in small groups, individually, and as a class.	1	2	3	4	5
Understand and demonstrate basic operations of a multimedia computer system—install software, multitask, open, save, print.	1	2	3	4	5

	Absent	Aware	Confident	Proficient	Mastery
Select productivity, multimedia, and curriculum software appropriate to the learning task.	1	2	3	4	5
Use peripheral devices such as scanners, digital cameras, and scan converters to enhance learning tasks.	1	2	3	4	5
Plan and implement technology-connected lessons that are correlated to the Texas Content Standards.	1	2	3	4	5
Identify and practice the ethical use of computer resources, including the internet, with students.	1	2	3	4	5
Stay abreast of technology theory and applications in the classroom by reading professional journals and discussing current issues and trends.	1	2	3	4	5
Use terminology related to computers and technology appropriately.	1	2	3	4	5
Can define the teacher's role as a facilitator of learning.	1	2	3	4	5
Can describe several ways in which from one to four or five computers can be used effectively in the classroom.	1	2	3	4	5

GLOSSARY

As with all new technologies, there's some specialized vocabulary that is helpful to know. Here are some of the current buzz words you may encounter:

Applets: Small software applications that download with a Web document, enhancing its presentation on your screen and eliminating the need for specialized viewing software to be permanently installed on your computer.

BBS (Bulletin Board System): An online forum for users to browse and exchange information; a public discussion area.

BPS (Bits per second): The speed at which information is transmitted via a modem.

Browser: Special software necessary for navigating Web pages and viewing text and graphics. Netscape and Microsoft Explorer are two widely used browsers.

Bulletin Board System (BBS): An online area which members can access at any time to post and/or read messages.

Chat: A method of online communication that allows users to communicate in "real time." Information is typed on one user's computer and immediately is displayed on the other user's computer.

Compression: A method of "shrinking" a file to be downloaded in order to reduce transmission time. Most downloadable files on the Internet are compressed and require a special utility in order to be restored to their original size after downloading.

Dial-up: To connect your computer to another computer by calling it up via a modem.

Direct Internet Access: A way of connecting a computer to the Internet without using a commercial online service such as America Online or CompuServe. Direct Internet access can be purchased through an independent local or national Internet Service Provider (ISP).

DNS (Domain Name Server): A computer that matches domain names like www. Scholastic.com to numeric addresses, making them easier to locate. A "no DNS entry" message appearing when accessing a Web site means either that the site is unable to handle more traffic at that time, or that the site name has been incorrectly entered in the browser.

Domain: Similar to a street address, servers on the Web have addresses to allow other computers to locate them electronically.

Download: To receive a file from another computer into your own computer. Scholastic Network has collections of files to download, and many Internet and Web sites do, too.

E-mail (Electronic mail): E-mail messages are sent electronically across the Internet from one computer to another. In order to send e-mail to another person, you must know his or her e-mail address.

FAQ (Frequently Asked Questions): Many sites, including Scholastic, maintain FAQ lists in their customer service areas. Answers to common questions can then be accessed at any time.

Frames: A Web page layout technique which divides the page into several smaller pages on one screen. Not all Web browsers support frames.

FTP (File Transfer Protocol): A method of transferring files from one computer to another.

GIF: One of the formats for displaying graphics on Web pages.

Home Page: The first, introductory page at a Web site, from which other pages at the site can be accessed. Also, a site on the Web where an individual, school, company, or other organization may present its own assortment of articles, graphics, and links.

HTML (Hypertext Markup Language): the coding specifications inserted into computer text that indicate how Web pages should be displayed by browsers.

http:// (Hypertext Transfer Protocol): The standard prefix for most addresses (see also URL) on the Web. A Web browser will be necessary to access the site.

Hypertext Links: Highlighted and/or underlined words or images on a Web page which link that page to other related pages or files. Navigation is accomplished by clicking a mouse on the hypertext link.

Internet: The worldwide network of computer networks that are connected to each other, providing file transfer, remote login, e-mail, news, and other services.

Internet Service Provider (ISP): Any organization that provides direct Internet access.

Java: A programming language which accommodates applets into Web page design.

JPEG: One of the formats used to display graphics on Web pages.

Links: The hypertext words or images on a Web page which lead to other related files, pages, or sites on the Web. See also Hypertext Links.

MIME (Multipurpose Internet Mail Extension): Allows the transmission of text, graphics, video, and sound across the Internet as an attachment to an e-mail message.

Modem: A device that allows a computer to connect to the Internet over conventional phone lines. Modem speeds are expressed in "bits per second" (bps). Modems with speeds lower than 14.4k bps will not be able to navigate the Web effectively.

Online: You are "online" when your computer is connected to a host computer, providing access to the Internet.

Plug-ins: Small software accessory programs that work in conjunction with a Web browser to give it added capabilities such as the ability to play sounds or video. Unlike applets, which your computer uses only when connected to a Web page that contains them, plug-ins must be installed on your computer in advance and configured to work with your browser.

Search Engine: One of several services on the Web designed to help users locate Web sites on specific subjects. The user types in a search word or phrase and is given a range of sites to choose from. Two popular search engines which can search the entire Web are Yahoo (http://www.yahoo.com) and AltaVista (http://www.altavista.com).

Server: A machine that makes services available on a network. A file server enables others to access files, while a Web server is the computer system that makes its Web pages available to others through the HTTP protocol.

T/1 or T/3 lines: High-speed network links that greatly reduce the time users wait for Web pages to download.

URL (Universal Resource Locator): The "address" of a Web page. Most URLs begin with the prefix http://, but you may also see ftp:// (file transfer protocol) in a URL.

Web Page: The common name for one page of information on the Web. Each page displays text and can incorporate graphics, sound, video, and other special effects.

World Wide Web (WWW): A collection of multimedia pages and resources that sit on the Internet and which are woven together through the use of hypertext links.

RESOURCES

- Anderson, L. W. & Krathwohl, D. R. (2001). *A taxonomy for learning, teaching, and assessing.* New York: Longman.
- Bandura, A. (1994). *Self-efficacy.* www.emory.edu/EDUCATION/mfp/BanEncy.html*
- Bloom, B.S., (Ed.). 1956. *Taxonomy of educational objectives: The classification of educational goals: Handbook I, cognitive domain.* New York: Longman.
- Bransford, J., Brown, A., & Cocking, R. (2000). How people learn: Brain, mind, experience, and school. Washington, DC: National Academy Press.
- Campbell, B. (2003). *The naturalist intelligence.* Seattle, WA: New Horizons for Learning. www.newhorizons.org/strategies/mi/campbell.htm
- Cotton, K. (1998). *Education for lifelong learning: Literature synthesis.* ED 422608. Washington, DC: OERI.
- Costa, A. L. (Ed.). (2000). *Developing minds: A resource book for teaching thinking.* Alexandria, VA: ASCD.
- Dunn, R. (1995). *Strategies for educating diverse learners.* Bloomington, IN: Phi Delta Kappa.
- Ennis, R. H. (2000). Goals for a critical thinking curriculum and its assessment. In A. L. Costa (Ed.), *Developing minds: A resource book for teaching thinking,* (pp. 44-46). Alexandria, VA: ASCD.
- ERIC (1996). *Multiple intelligences: Gardner's theory.* ED 410226. Washington, DC: OERI.
- Facione, P. A. (1998). *Critical Thinking: What It is and Why it Counts.* Santa Clara, CA: OERI. www.insightassessment.com/pdf_files/what&why98.pdf
- Facione, P. A. (1990). *Critical Thinking: A Statement of Expert Consensus for Purposes of Educational Assessment and Instruction: Executive summary.* Millbrae, CA: California Academic Press. www.insightassessment.com/pdf_files/DEXadobe.PDF
- Gardner, H. (1993). *Multiple intelligences: The theory in practice.* New York: Harper Collins.
- George Lucas Educational Foundation. (2001, November 1). *Project-based learning research.* Edutopia. www.edutopia.org
- Goodrich, H. A. (1997). Understanding rubrics. *Educational Leadership,* 54(4). http://www.middleweb.com/rubricsHG.html
- Hall, Inc. Walsh, J. A. and Sattes, B. D. (2005). *Quality questioning: Research-based practice to engage every learner.* Thousand Oaks, CA: AEL and Corwin Press.

- Intel® Teach to the Future. (2003). Project-based classroom: Bridging the gap between education and technology. Training materials for regional and master trainers. Author.
- Jarrett, D. (1997). Inquiry strategies for science and mathematics learning. Portland, OR: Northwest Regional Educational Laboratory. http://www.nwrel.org/msec/images/resources/justgood/05.97.pdf
- Lewin, Larry, Betty Jean Shoemaker (1998). *Great performances: Creating classroom-based assessment tasks,* Virginia: Association for Supervision and Curriculum Development.
- Marzano, R. J. (2000). *Designing a new taxonomy of educational objectives.* Thousand Oaks, CA: Corwin Press.
- Marzano, R. J. (1998). *A theory-based meta-analysis of research on instruction.* Aurora, CO: McREL, 1998. www.mcrel.org/PDF/Instruction/5982RR_InstructionMeta_Analysis.pdf *(PDF; 172 pages)
- Marzano, Robert J, Jay McTighe, Debra J. Pickering (1993). *Assessing student outcomes: Performance assessment using the dimensions of learning,* Virginia: Association for Supervision and Curriculum Development.
- Messina, J. J. and C. M. Messina. (2005). *Overview of critical thinking.* Tampa Bay, FL: Coping.org
- McTighe, J. (1991). *Better thinking and learning.* Baltimore, MD: Maryland State Department of Education.
- Merriam Webster's Online Dictionary, http://www.m-w.com/
- Miller, P. (2001). *Learning styles: The multimedia of the mind.* ED 451340. Classroom Assessment. *Questioning strategies.* Pinellas School District and Florida Center for Instructional Technology.
- National Research Council. (1996). *National science education standards.* Washington, DC: National Academy Press.
- Palincsar, A.S. & Brown, A. L. (1984). Reciprocal teaching of comprehension-fostering and comprehension-monitoring activities. *Cognition and Instruction, 1*(2), 117-175
- Paris, S.G., Wasik, B.A., & Turner, J.C. (1991). The development of strategic readers. In R. Barr, M. L. Kamil, P. Mosenthal, & P. D. Pearson, (Eds.), *Handbook of reading research, vol. 2,* (pp. 609-640). New York: Longman.
- Railsback, J. (2002). *Project-based instruction: Creating excitement for learning.* Portland, OR: Northwest Regional Educational Laboratory. http://www.nwrel.org/request/2002aug/index.html*
- Schoenfeld, A. (1992). Learning to think mathematically: problem solving, metacognition, and sense making in mathematics. In D. A. Grows (Ed.). *Handbook of research on mathematics teaching and learning,* (pp. 334-370). New York: Macmillan.

- SRI International. (2000, January). *Silicon valley challenge 2000: Year 4 Report*. San Jose, CA: Joint Venture, Silicon Valley Network. http://pblmm.k12.ca.us/sri/Reports.html
- Thomas, J.W. (1998). *Project-based learning: Overview*. Novato, CA: Buck Institute for Education.
- Thomas, J.W. (2000). *A review of research on project-based learning*. San Rafael, CA: Autodesk. http://www.k12reform.org/foundation/pbl/research*
- Wiggins, G. & McTighe, J. (2001). *Understanding by design*. New Jersey: Prentice-Hall, Inc.

Printed in the United States
64637LVS00007B/2

9 781934 043400